SOMEBEACHSOMEWHERE

SOMEBEACHSOMEWHERE

The HARNESS RACING LEGEND from a ONE-HORSE STABLE

MARJORIE SIMMINS

NIMBUS PUBLISHING

Nimbus Publishing Limited
3660 Strawberry Hill Street, Halifax, NS, B3K 5A9
(902) 455-4286 nimbus.ca

Printed and bound in Canada

NB1521

Design: Jenn Embree
Cover: Somebeachsomewhere's world record performance at the Red Mile in Lexington, Kentucky, September 27, 2008. (*Dave Landry*)
Editor: Angela Mombourquette

Library and Archives Canada Cataloguing in Publication

Title: Somebeachsomewhere : the harness racing legend from a
    one-horse stable / Marjorie Simmins.
Names: Simmins, Marjorie, author.
Description: Includes bibliographical references.
Identifiers: Canadiana (print) 2021009799X | Canadiana (ebook) 20210098112
ISBN 9781771089326 (softcover) | ISBN 9781771089913 (EPUB)
Subjects: LCSH: Somebeachsomewhere (Race horse), 2005-2018. | LCSH: Harness
    racehorses—Canada—Biography. | LCSH: Harness racing—Canada—History—
    21st century. | LCSH: Harness racing—United States—History—21st century.
    | LCGFT: Biographies.
Classification: LCC SF343.S66 S56 2021 | DDC 798.4/60929—dc23

Nimbus Publishing acknowledges the financial support for its publishing activities from the Government of Canada, the Canada Council for the Arts, and from the Province of Nova Scotia. We are pleased to work in partnership with the Province of Nova Scotia to develop and promote our creative industries for the benefit of all Nova Scotians.

MIX
Paper from
responsible sources
FSC
www.fsc.org   FSC® C103113

CONTENTS

Part III
HORSE OF A LIFETIME

For Don, who knew this was my story.

For all the horses I've known, who helped me to write the story.

And for "Beach," who graced every life he touched.

INTRODUCTION

Somebeachsomewhere: A Harness Racing Legend from a One-Horse Stable is a story of improbabilities and magic. Our unlikely hero is a big and bold pacing horse named Somebeachsomewhere, known to all as "Beach."

His human partner is a small-town Nova Scotia car dealer named Brent MacGrath, the leader of a group of six friends who pool their money to buy a horse—a Standardbred colt, a pacer, a harness horse, who may grow up to be competitive, or not. A really promising pacing yearling normally costs $100,000 or more. The friends have $40,000 to spend.

But through a combination of instinct, horse sense, and luck, they come away from the prestigious Lexington Selected Yearling Sale with a horse that looks as though he might be pretty good.

Pretty good? Beach turns out to be the horse of a lifetime, the Canadian horse of the century—a streaking locomotive of a stallion that smashes records and delights ever-larger crowds who hold "Beach Parties" when they know he is racing. "The Best that Ever Looked Through a Bridle," say his fans around the world. In a nutshell, he's international harness racing history on four lightning legs—and by May 2019 his full life story has not yet been written.

That was when my heart began to pump as hard as a harness racer's heart does; the moment his driver asks for his all in the homestretch.

My writer's instincts, coupled with a lifetime of experiences as a horse-woman who loves to write about horses, were about to serve me well.

Or so I hoped.

"Don," I said to my late husband, Silver Donald Cameron, on that fateful blue-skied spring day in 2019, "I don't think Beach's story has been written about in full—you know, in book form."

Don, a distinguished author and filmmaker, smiled. "Really?" he said. "Now isn't that something? Do you know someone who could write that story?"

"Yes," I said, smile as wide or wider. "I think I do."

"Then what are you doing sitting here? Time for a trip to Truro."

Truro, home to five of the six members of Schooner Stables, and to Truro Raceway, the home track of Somebeachsomewhere.

I must have looked a bit stunned.

"Now," said Don. "Get in the car and go now. This one's yours, my love. Don't lose it."

He was right.

I phoned Brent MacGrath first, and he kindly said he could see me. Then I got in our car and drove two and a half hours west from Isle Madame, Cape Breton, to the shiretown of Truro, on the mainland of Nova Scotia, and then to Pye Chevrolet on Prince Street, for my first interview with MacGrath, who is company vice-president, a Beach co-owner, and who, for Beach's entire career, has been the primary spokesman for Schooner Stables. MacGrath wasn't quite sure which sky I'd dropped out of when I first talked to him on the telephone, but by the time I showed up at his office door he'd researched me—and my husband.

"Silver Donald Cameron has the Order of Canada," Brent MacGrath said, his voice warm with admiration.

"Yes," I said, "and the Order of Nova Scotia. As a come-from-away, he's almost prouder of that."

"Proper thing," said Brent MacGrath, Maritime born and raised. "But you're the horsewoman, right? And you want to talk about Beach?"

Did I ever.

Brent MacGrath, Marjorie Simmins, and Whim Road Lady ("Lady"), owned by Pooker McCallum, Truro Raceway. (RHONDA MACGRATH)

There was so much that excited me about taking on this new book. I've ridden horses all my life. I've been a horse owner, and for longer, a horse leaser, taking care of other people's horses as though they were my own, but only for a couple of days a week, and without the full financial burden of horse ownership. I've jumped horses around hunt courses, played mock polo, ridden them for long hours over dappled forest trails, and then galloped them down long Pacific Ocean beaches. I was lucky to study dressage for one summer, and enjoyed the hunter-jumper scene for most of my early years on the West Coast of Canada.

When I came to the East Coast, and after some time out of the saddle, I returned to English riding. After a terrible accident (you can read about it in my book *Year of the Horse: A Journey of Healing and Adventure*), I came back to riding, but decided to try Western, and learned about the disciplines of Trail, Showmanship, Reining, and Western Pleasure. Given the opportunity to ride a magical steed named Winnie, I even went back in the show ring, and to my joy and surprise, collected ribbons and self-esteem.

A lifetime in and around barns—and yet, I'd never been to a Standardbred track. Nor did I know the fascinating history of the breed, and its huge racing and breeding presence around the world, for both trotters and pacers.

But I was eager to learn.

People who spend their lives around horses often talk about their "heart horses." Horses, like people, have different personalities and abilities. A horse person will have many different sorts of connections to horses over a lifetime. All are precious, or at the very least, worthy of our time and intellect, as they represent opportunities to care for a precious animal, and to learn. But heart horses—well, they are something else. They claim our hearts, usually from that first time we look into dark eyes that are filled with intelligence, or humour, or simple goodwill. When these good qualities are coupled with brilliance, at whichever area of endeavour the horse practices, their human companions can be smitten beyond calculation.

And of course the horse doesn't have to be brilliant at anything other than being a fellow creature, but if he or she is bred to perform certain tasks, loves to perform these, and is uniquely good at their job, the heart's cup can overflow.

Beach was a heart horse to his six Maritime co-owners, to his millions of fellow Canadians, and to the countless men and women, boys and girls who are involved in the wide world of harness racing as practitioners, observers, and fans. The bay bomber paced into all those hearts with ease, and took up permanent residence.

That's what horses of a lifetime do.

Through the magic of technology, Beach has sired colts and fillies around the world. He's changed the sport, changed the industry, changed the future of his breed. You will catch a glimpse of him in the foals of the foals of forever—a glimpse of the great-hearted pacer from Truro, Nova Scotia.

PART I

DREAMING ON A HORSE

Chapter 1

"MAYBE I'LL BUY A HORSE"

BRENT MACGRATH WAS OUT TO BUY A HORSE—AND THIS WAS HIS lucky day.

A full-time car salesman from Truro, Nova Scotia, and a part-time trainer of Standardbred harness horses, MacGrath had owned a few horses over the years. This time, he was looking for something special, and at a special event. It was Friday, October 4, 2006, at the prestigious Lexington Selected Yearling Sale in Lexington, Kentucky, and Brent MacGrath had just seen a horse that had stopped him in his tracks.

"My eyes were wide when I looked at Beach in his stall and saw that magnificent, tall, broad horse," he says, remembering that day—fourteen years ago now and still close to memory. "It was his overall presence and how he looked. He was strong, happy, kind, had a good eye and good colour. His conformation, how correctly he stood, it was all excellent."

"Beach," as he was more commonly known, actually had the longer racing name, Somebeachsomewhere. He was a sixteen-month-old bay colt, sired by Mach Three from Ontario, and born to Wheres The Beach, also from Ontario. He also ticked all the boxes on MacGrath's wish list.

"I wanted to have an Ontario-sired horse and to be in the Sires Stakes Program in Ontario," says MacGrath. "We're Canadian. I wanted to have a Canadian horse, and Ontario was the place to be for racing." He laughs.

"I didn't even have a catalogue with me. I wasn't looking at the breeding information, other than what it says on the card on their stall door. I might have looked in every door for thirty seconds, but if they weren't Ontario-sired, I didn't really zone in on them."

All the memories of that day are happy ones, and vivid. "When I saw Beach, the friend I was with said to me, 'How do you keep them straight in your head? I like so many of them.' And I said, 'Two ways I keep them straight: I only have three horses on my list at all times and the list is in my head.' The minute I saw Beach he went to the top of the list and of course, never came off.... When you're spending your own money, you better keep it straight!"

In fact, MacGrath was spending not just his own money, but five other people's money as well, totalling $40,000—and not a cent more, they'd all agreed. MacGrath was shopping on behalf of Schooner Stables, a syndicate of Maritimers from Truro, Nova Scotia, and Shediac, New Brunswick.

The story of how Schooner Stables came together, and how MacGrath came to be in Lexington that day, is a winding and curious tale.

"My business partner Garry Pye and I had had long-term and positive dealings with Stephen Tufts, a bank manager at the Toronto Dominion Bank," says MacGrath, who co-owns Pye Chevrolet and three other dealerships with Pye. "Garry and I had missed Stephen's retirement party, didn't know anything about it. I asked Garry if we should offer to take Stephen to the Little Brown Jug, and Garry said sure. So I called Stephen."

Founded in 1946, the Little Brown Jug (LBJ) takes place every year on the third Thursday after Labour Day, in Delaware, Ohio. The popular race is named after a pacer of the same name (1875–1899), who won nine consecutive races and, in 1975, became a United States Trotting

Association (USTA) Hall of Fame Immortal. Featuring one of the biggest races for pacers of the year, "the Jug," with its country-fair atmosphere, is a popular event.

Tufts, a long-time racing fan, knew all about the Little Brown Jug. But he had other ideas.

"So he says, 'Be a great trip, but a week or so later is Lexington week,'" says MacGrath. "Then he said, 'Could we substitute Lexington for the Little Brown Jug?'"

The world-famous Lexington Selected Yearling Sale includes four days of auction sales and a week of racing. Like any horseman, MacGrath knew about the Lexington event, but he had never attended, so the idea had some appeal.

MacGrath's answer was fateful. "I said, 'Yeah, no problem. *Maybe I'll buy a horse.*'"

Was he serious?

"I was serious, but it wasn't on the radar. I was not intending to buy a horse, but I wasn't going to go to Lexington and not have a look. We were starting to make a few dollars, so I said to Garry, 'I'll speak to the guys.'"

"The guys," at that point, included Garry Pye, Jamie Bagnell and Pam Dean from Truro, and Reg Petitpas from Shediac, New Brunswick. Bagnell, Dean, and Petitpas were long-time customers at the dealership. (Stuart Rath, Bagnell's business partner, would join a little later.)

MacGrath also asked long-time friend and horseman, Donnie Hall, if he wanted in on the buy. But for Hall, a partner on most of the previous horses that MacGrath had trained, the timing was not perfect. Hall had recently married, and he and his wife, Debbi, had purchased a home in Florida. Despite missing out on the opportunity to be a Beach co-owner, says MacGrath, "Donnie was and still is Beach's biggest fan." Hall was also the first person other than MacGrath to train Beach a mile in Truro.

MacGrath says Donnie went on to play a huge role in Beach's care and training during their unforgettable week in Lexington. But that's a ways ahead in the future. Back to the original Schooner Stables group, starting with Garry Pye.

"Before we met, Garry had never been to a horse race in his life," says MacGrath of his long-time business partner and now good friend. "I was buying $2,000 babies, Maritime-breds, and Garry was partners with me on all of them. It was something I wanted to do, and I was doing a good job for him at the dealership, and he wanted to help me with my passion. Financially, I probably couldn't have done much without him at that time. So Garry threw in $10,000 for the Kentucky venture, I had $10,000 of my own, and then I asked Pam and Rod Dean."

Next up, Reg Petitpas.

"I'd known Reg through racing for a number of years," says MacGrath, "and he'd bought some trucks from me. He had a business in New Brunswick. I called him and invited him in. He said yes."

Then MacGrath rang Jamie Bagnell.

"Jamie had been involved with horses years ago with his dad," says MacGrath. "They had a breeding operation over in Tatamagouche. So I knew he had a bit of interest, but he'd gotten busy and away from the sport." MacGrath grins. "He jumped in."

And the sixth partner?

"Stu Rath is another businessman in Truro. Jamie's business de-iced airplanes and recouped the de-icing, the glycol, re-cleaned it and did it again. The business was in a really big growth stage; Jamie wanted a partner and reached out to Stu Rath. Turned out they had business in Indiana when Lexington was on and decided to stop there on the way back. So there you have Jamie and Stu working together. After I bought Beach I said to Jamie, 'Look, if you want to invite Stu into the syndicate, I'm fine with that. He's a good guy.' That's how Stu got involved."

Six people, at $10,000 each, with $40,000 allotted to purchase the horse. Where did that extra $20,000 go?

"That was for expenses and set-up," says MacGrath. "Once you have a horse, you have to bring him home and then look after him."

But he hadn't bought him yet.

"There were a thousand horses at the sale," says MacGrath. "And I must have looked at four hundred of them." He looked at Beach twice; once in his stall, and once in the "walking ring," where, pre-sale, a half-dozen horses are walked by their grooms, allowing onlookers to make comparisons.

"Beach was a man among boys," says MacGrath, who was becoming more and more certain he wanted to buy the big colt. Losing no time, he raced to the auction arena for the 7:00 P.M. start.

Lady Luck continued to support his desire. Beach would be first up for sale that evening, and because the races were running late, there were just a few onlookers and one other bidder. (There have to be at least two bidders for any one horse before an auction can begin.)

"The races went late that day," MacGrath explains. "One of the stakes races required a race-off. It dragged the races out an extra hour. So it was just me and few others." The auctioneer began his chant, the sentences seemingly joined in a rapid-fire stream.

"The auction is on! Hip #268, Somebeachsomewhere. Sired by Mach Three, dam is Wheres The Beach. What are you going to give me? Would you give me $5,000? Well then, give me $3,500. Would you go $3,500? I've got $3,500. Now give me $5,000. Would you go $5,000? I've got $5,000..."

No one knew better than the car salesman from a small rural town in Canada that the Lexington Selected Yearling Sale in Kentucky was for serious harness racing people with deep pockets.

"The sale average for the first few nights was approximately $100,000," says MacGrath. "Lots of the yearlings were going for $50,000 up to $400,000."

MacGrath held his breath as the bid climbed higher.

"I kept thinking, I don't have $40,100," says MacGrath. "I have $40,000. If he goes for that, I own him."

"*Wouldyougo $20,000, wouldyougo $25,000, wouldyougo $30,000*"—the bids sizzled back and forth between the two men. Ultimately, MacGrath's rival teetered on the bid of $38,000. Chin up, heart banging, MacGrath bid $40,000. "*Wouldyougo, wouldyougo—*"

No, the other bidder would not go. He was out.

"*Sold! Hip #268, Somebeachsomewhere.*"

MacGrath was in such a hurry he beat the breeder, Stephanie Smith-Rothaug, from Rails Edge Farm, back to the barn. When she arrived with Beach, MacGrath was dancing with excitement.

"I had so many questions!" says MacGrath. "What was his personality like, did he eat well, what kind of hay did she feed him, what were the dam and sire like, was he okay being trucked? Stephanie was delighted. Breeders don't get a lot of people even coming back to the barn after they've made a purchase."

"Where is Beach headed for in Canada?" asked Stephanie, whose breeding farm is located in West Jefferson, Ohio. MacGrath noted the sad edge to her voice. Beach was one of her favourite colts ever, she told him. "He's special, you'll see."

"I told her we were going home to Nova Scotia," says MacGrath. "To the barns at Truro Raceway." Smith-Rothaug and MacGrath agreed to stay in touch.

MacGrath made the travel arrangements for Beach, his thoughts whirling on to the next set of plans related to the yearling. He'd already decided he would train the colt himself, as he'd trained other young ones at the very track he'd once managed for four years. It was something he loved so much, training the young ones, which he'd done in both Nova Scotia and Ontario. Yet despite the calming idea of working on his literal home turf, his heart was still thudding hard.

Why did this horse seem so different?

Years later, his wife Rhonda MacGrath would say that when he phoned to tell her the news about Beach, he was so delighted, "his voice was shaking."

And how did Rhonda respond to the news of a new, $40,000 horse?

"I was a bit in shock and I said, 'Well, what's his name?'"
Somebeachsomewhere.

"And I said, 'I like his name. I mean, of course I'm in with a name like that. We're east-coasters; we're beach people."

As for the ultimate quality and talent of the racehorse, she was certain Brent had chosen well. And it pleased her to hear him sounding so excited. No matter what happened, it was always good to have a dream to hang on to. Rhonda MacGrath, who had fought hard for her dreams, knew that better than most people.

But in those early moments of ownership of a horse called Beach, neither Rhonda nor Brent could ever guess how much spectacular change would soon come to their lives together, and to the lives of all who opted into Schooner Stables.

Brent MacGrath had indeed bought a horse. The inquisitive and easy-going colt would mature to have a body like a train engine. For Schooner Stables, he would be the horse of a lifetime—and would change the course of Standardbred horse history forever.

Chapter 2

HOME TO THE HUB

IT WAS A TWENTY-THREE–HOUR TRIP FROM LEXINGTON, Kentucky to Truro, Nova Scotia, with trucker Glenn Scargill at the wheel of the big rig. American-born Somebeachsomewhere was on his way to a new country and a new life as a pacer-in-training.

But where exactly was he going?

Truro is often called "the hub" of Nova Scotia. The town of about twenty-two thousand is set in the central part of the second-smallest province in Canada. The main routes east to Cape Breton Island, west to New Brunswick, and southwest to Halifax, all meet at Truro.

Most Nova Scotians know they're near to Truro when they start seeing the soaring silos, historic and commercial barns, and rolling hills that surround the town. They know they're *in* Truro when they pass the railway tracks and train station, which were first constructed between Halifax and Pictou in 1858. Truro remains an important transportation centre for Nova Scotia and points west.

At its heart and soul, Truro is a country town. Its agricultural roots are in beef and dairy farms, poultry and pork, sheep, and food farming of every sort—and the roots run deep. Organizations include 4-H Clubs and a horseman's club. Businesses, such as riding stables for English and Western riders, and feed and tack stores, flourish around the town. It also has the necessary infrastructure for equestrian competitors, such as large indoor and outdoor arenas and grounds for horse shows.

Horses, you say. *Tell me about the horses.*

Truro is horse heaven: farm horses, saddle horses, miniature horses, Western reiners, English hunter-jumper and dressage horses, racehorses—and lots and lots of harness racers. The harness racers run on a half-mile racetrack, Truro Raceway, one of the town's most beloved and historic features, located on the eastern edge of the town.

Truro Raceway opened in 1865, making it one of the oldest racetracks in Canada. One of three in the province, it is also Nova Scotia's largest harness racing track, and the only one on the mainland of Nova Scotia. Both the Inverness Raceway, in Inverness, and Northside Downs, in North Sydney, are located on Cape Breton Island, which is also part of Nova Scotia.

Truro Raceway typically offers live racing on Sundays and live simulcast races (which is a broadcast of a horse race that allows wagering at two or more sites) from top tracks across North America at its "Trackside Lounge" during the May through November racing season.

Rebuilt after a fire that began by arson in 1981, the grandstand and lounge areas are comfortable and welcoming. The lounge is nice enough, in fact, that romances have sparked there; more on that in a moment.

Harness racing is popular around the world, particularly in Europe, the United States, Canada, Australia, New Zealand, and South America. The sport has been a colourful part of life here in Nova Scotia for well over 150 years.

Naturally, not everyone knows the difference between a Standardbred (a trotter or pacer) and a Thoroughbred (a "galloper"), the two being distinct breeds.

Thoroughbreds were developed in England in the seventeenth and eighteenth centuries and race with a jockey aboard. Standardbred horses were first developed in the United States in the nineteenth century. They are used to draw "sulkies," or two-wheeled carts, while their drivers skilfully guide them down mostly half-mile or mile-long tracks.

Some researchers maintain that the ancient Akhal-Teke horse breed that originated in Turkmenistan provided the athletic foundation for most modern sport horse breeds, including the Thoroughbred. Others underscore the fact that every registered Thoroughbred can trace its lineage back to three founding Arabian stallions imported from the Middle East to England in the late sixteenth and seventeenth centuries.

The Standardbred derived from Thoroughbred and Morgan bloodlines. (The Morgan breed originated from one stallion owned by a schoolmaster named Justin Morgan in Vermont in the late 1800s.) And all Standardbreds date back to one stallion named Messenger (1780–1808), an English Thoroughbred bred by Richard Grosvenor and brought to the newly formed United States of America shortly after the American Revolution.

Some horse people call Standardbreds "brainiacs." All horse people know them to be highly intelligent and blessed with a tremendous work ethic and a consistent desire to please. Yet others refer to Standardbreds as "stoic." (Sadly, this characteristic has not always served them well. Unlike most horse breeds, they can survive, if not thrive, under hard circumstances.)

Within the one breed, there are two types of Standardbreds. These are either "pacers," who strike out with both legs of one side at the same time, or "trotters," who move their legs forward in diagonal pairs (right front and left hind, then left front and right hind). There are hardly any pacers in Europe, as they prefer trotters, but pacers dominate the North American racing scene.

Beach was a pacer.

And despite supernovas such as Somebeachsomewhere who come along now and then, Thoroughbred racing is still better known than harness racing to the average citizen in North America. Why is that?

Sports journalist Dave Briggs, who writes about both industries, has some thoughts on the subject.

"We'd have to get into a whole historical analysis of why," says Briggs. "[But in brief], and for whatever reason, the Thoroughbreds developed more of a following. There's a lot more pageantry in the Thoroughbred business and it has a lot more classic events that the average person understands. They know what the Kentucky Derby is; they don't know what the Hambletonian is. So that's helpful for Thoroughbred racing."

The Hambletonian is a major American harness race run annually at the Meadowlands Racetrack in New Jersey. Founded in 1924, the race is for three-year-old trotting Standardbreds.

The history of the two sports provides more insights.

"In the early 1900s harness racing was more popular in many places than Thoroughbred racing," Briggs says. "That was an era when people used horse and buggy transportation; harness racing was the racing equivalent of that. They could see all their neighbours had a horse and buggy and you go to the track and watch the fastest ones race. That made sense to them. As we got away from that, got into cars that people don't understand—then it was 'Why does the jockey sit behind the horse in a wheel buggy thing?' They [the general public] don't even know that they're called drivers, [not jockeys]. The consciousness isn't there."

But it most certainly is there in the Maritimes, especially on Prince Edward Island, and extra-especially during Old Home Week in mid-August each year.

"My one and only time going to Old Home Week," says Briggs, "I was amazed that you could walk into the family diner or the little variety store and the kids would be saying, 'Mom, can I go the races tonight?' I think to myself, 'This is not the experience I have in Ontario.' These kids, everybody, they all know what this is and they love it. I don't know why we got away from that. The most popular sport in North America in the early 1900s was horse racing. Then television came along. Horse racing was still the only legal form of gambling in most places. The horse racing industry said, 'Well, we're doing great. What do we need this television thing for? And if you compare the histories of say the National Football League to horse racing you see that pro football was not relevant at all to most people until it got on television, until they said, 'Hey, we're not a really well-known sport. We're going to jump on this television thing,' and the next thing you know they grew.

"And a lot of people say the problem is the young sports editors of the day grow up being influenced by what they see on TV. So in Canada that's hockey, that's curling, that's baseball sometimes, depending on what part of the country you're in. They don't see horse racing so they grow up without knowing about it unless their grandpa takes them or their dad takes them or their uncle takes them or their mom takes them, they don't go to the track. So we missed that opportunity."

How much responsibility belongs to the harness racing industry, to inform people, get them excited, to increase the pageantry, all the things you've been talking about here?

"Yeah, 100 percent on the industry," says Briggs. "The challenge therein is back when it was the only gambling game in town it didn't have a lot of competition. Now people can sit on their phones and gamble real money in most parts of this country; you can bet on sports. Not single-game sports but you can go and bet sports. You can go to casinos in most parts of this country, you can do the lottery.

"The challenge that people have had when they try to market this harness racing industry, is, 'What's my angle to get people to come to the races?' when they're competing with casinos and pro hockey and pro baseball and movie theatres that are quite different from decades back. Now there's stadium seating, 3-D movies, it's tough [to compete against all that]. So yes, the industry's had a hard time convincing people. How do we do this? How do we get people to come see our horses? And that *is* the attraction, the horses. Come to the track and see them up close; it's a spectacular animal."

"As society we're getting further and further away from animals and nature and all those things as we get into technology," Briggs continues. "It's the one hook that we have that's compelling, that most people can say they like horses. It's not everyone, of course, but horses are one of those animals that most people agree on. How do you not like horses—they're beautiful, they provided transportation for thousands of years, they're a key partner in human history."

Beach was a strong and natural pacer. The man who had just started to work with him, Brent MacGrath, was forty-seven years old. He had seen a lot of pacing Standardbreds in his time, had owned and worked with about thirty himself in both Nova Scotia and Ontario—so he could judge Beach's abilities with confidence.

A person has a better chance of doing that when they've spent their life around horses.

"My mother loved horses, and my father liked them," says Brent of his parents, Hazel and George ("Ted") MacGrath, of Truro. "My mum grew up on a farm; she didn't ride horses, but she was an animal lover, so we had saddle horses when we were young. We had a Standardbred broodmare. [Dad] also bought a foal at an auction one time, too. We looked after it."

One of four boys—brothers Gary, Barry, and Bruce were all older than him—Brent started out at the racetrack cleaning stalls and harness as a boy. "It was a great way to make cash when you're too young to work legally."

While there were any number of horsemen who watched over the young people coming and going from the barns, Brent tips his hat to Phil Pinkney, winner of the 2008 O'Brien Award of Horsemanship, whom he calls "an exceptional driver and trainer," and who was kind enough to teach him a lot about horses generally, and Standardbreds in particular.

By the time he was a teenager, MacGrath was fully involved with life at Truro Raceway. With dozens of horses coming and going from the racetrack to the barns, there was always need for groomers and "hot-walkers" to cool out, brush, feed, and water the horses after their races. Every day was an opportunity to learn, and the young MacGrath was all ears and eyes.

For example, it didn't take him long, to see how patient Standardbreds are—more so than other breeds. "Standies" as some people affectionately call them, are used to standing in cross ties (these are chains that are bolted on either side of the aisle in a barn or in a narrower tie-stall, and which have clips that attach to either side of the horse's halter), sometimes for several hours at a time, without making a fuss. Unlike the "hot" temperaments of their sometimes-taller Thoroughbred cousins, these horses are uncommonly even-tempered. They are also durable, consistently work hard, and have extraordinary stamina.

Then there's the subject of food. Unsurprisingly, these tough athletes love their fuel. Genial they may be, but the Standardbred enjoys his chow. Ignore at your own risk, the seasoned horsemen and -women say.

And fair enough. Standardbreds apparently exert about twelve times more effort than a Thoroughbred as they train to racing fitness, and on average, they are raced about three times as often. They also maintain that scorching speed for longer than "the runners" do. This, obviously, requires a higher overall level of fitness and stamina.

By twenty-one, MacGrath had moved from the barns to the offices beneath the grandstand, and had become the general manager, race secretary, and announcer at Truro Raceway.

"I worked at the raceway from 1980 to '84," he says. "I had a great time there."

He had earned his driver's licence for harness racing right out of high school, which, ready for work and adventures, he had left in grade eleven.

"I love jogging a horse," he says, of the daily warm-up rounds on the track that are so much a part Standardbred racing life. The boy who grew up in barns is never far away from the man who still frequents them, the two of them always happiest having a "hands on" experience with horses.

One day in the summer of 1982 MacGrath met a new bartender at the Trackside Lounge. Her name was Rhonda MacKenzie. Tall, restless MacGrath looked over at the petite brunette with the calm, gentle manner—and got a whole lot lost in her warm smile.

"On our first date we went out and he's talking about horses," says Rhonda. "I turned to him and I said, 'Do you like horses?' And he looked at me like I had just come from Mars and said, '*Like them? I love them.*'"

He also had big plans for his life, twenty-one-year-old Rhonda would learn. Brent, twenty-three, had already raced horses in New Hampshire, had taken a shoeing course as a young kid in Pennsylvania, and had worked as the race announcer in Saskatoon when he was nineteen.

Rhonda herself had just graduated from Mount Saint Vincent University in Halifax with a Bachelor of Arts in Child and Youth Study, and was planning to relocate out west in Calgary, Alberta, with the hope of finding work there, as so many of her co-graduates and friends had already done.

"About a week after that first date, Brent told me he was going to be rich, and he was [going to get rich from] training horses," she says. "I was like, okay, this sounds like fun. I'm just a young person from Nova Scotia planning to go to Calgary and, you know, have an adventure there, but this sounded like a pretty good adventure, too."

Raised in Truro with five sisters and four brothers, Rhonda had never been around horses until her summer job at the track. Perhaps she already knew it, but that dearth of equine company in her life was about to change—big time. Other happy changes were in the offing too.

Two years after that first date, Rhonda MacKenzie and Brent MacGrath were married. They had their reception—*of course*—at the racetrack.

"We got married in '84," says Rhonda. "But before we were married we decided that we were going to go to Ontario. It was Brent's dream to go and train horses, so we finished up the year at the track in '84 and moved to Toronto on January 1, 1985."

It was not a simple move, and the ups and downs in both their work lives and personal lives in the coming years would put great strain on the young marrieds. Toronto was a cultural universe away from the people they knew and loved best, and over 1,700 kilometres (1,050 miles) from the warm broth of the Maritime world in which they'd both been raised.

Undaunted, the MacGraths were going to give it everything they had.

Chapter 3

EARLY DAYS

"WE PUT OUR BELONGINGS AND THE HORSES ON THE TRUCK AND went to Toronto," says Rhonda. "We had two horses we co-owned that we took with us."

At the time, the Greenwood Racetrack was still operational. It was located in downtown Toronto, on the east side, near the area still known as "The Beaches." Built in 1874 and first called the Woodbine Race Course, the stadium was later demolished in 1994 and replaced by a residential and commercial development.

They'd called ahead and booked a couple of stalls, but they didn't know who they might meet when they first got to the racetrack. As it turned out, it would be one of the most important people in their horse-life-to-come: harness racing driver Paul MacDonell.

From the get-go, MacDonell, twenty-one years old and single, and the young, just-married MacGraths, got on well. Brent liked Paul's calm and respectful manner around horses, and appreciated his good reputation as a driver. Paul liked the MacGraths's lively energy and solid work ethic, and understood and supported their dreams of succeeding in the racing world.

None of them had any idea how far those dreams would take them.

Back on that first night in Toronto in 1984, the MacGraths were simply looking for a place to lay their heads.

The MacGraths admit they were a bit green at that point; it turns out their timing was not optimal.

"When we got to Toronto, the horsemen at Greenwood were on strike," says Rhonda. "We didn't know how to get our belongings off the truck. The track superintendent at Greenwood, a lovely man from Newfoundland, actually built us a ramp so we could drive the car off the truck. Then we drove the truck to his house and stored our belongings in his garage. We had never met him before but we had a rental truck that we had to return."

Rhonda laughs. "We look back and go, 'Oh, my God, what were we thinking?' Anyway, we quickly got into the early lessons of harness racing in Ontario, which is quite different than in the Maritimes."

Indeed. That difference is mostly about gambling, governments, and how the individual provinces choose to support or not support those involved in the harness racing industry.

Somewhat simplistically, one can say that harness racing in Ontario is big business. This remains true even after the loss of the "Slots at Racetracks Program," or "SARP," founded by one provincial government in 1998, and cancelled by another in 2012. This program infused the racing industry with 20 percent of the revenue from slot machines that had been placed at racetracks across the province. The cancellation of the program led to terrible upheaval, confusion, and a deep loss of revenue, businesses, and jobs in the racing world, and near-fatal hits to the province's breeding programs. On April 1, 2013, the Ontario government made a move to turn things around by starting a five-year, $500-million investment in horse racing. Industry analysts believe this has provided some stability to the industry in the short term.

There are numerous differences between Ontario and the other nine provinces. Ontario's purses are fairly large (in 2008, it was $1.5 million for the North American Cup, North America's richest harness race; it is now $1 million). Established in 1974, Ontario also has the lucrative Ontario Sires Stakes (OSS), which aims to improve the Standardbred breed and provide meaningful incentives for breeders, owners, and trainers to breed, buy, and race horses in Ontario. Only foals that are sired by a stallion registered and standing in Ontario are eligible for the program, which is now one of the leading sires stakes programs in all of North America.

> Unless otherwise noted, purses are expressed in Canadian dollars.

Atlantic Canada's harness racing industry is much smaller. With the notable exception of Prince Edward Island, where the sport is staunchly supported by its government and citizens—harness racing is, for the most part, a modest community event; the "crowds" are small and local, and the purses are relatively small as well. But this region, similarly, has an Atlantic Sires Stakes program, which has promoted the sport within its borders for over fifty years. An Atlantic Breeders Crown championship is held each year. The racing series, which is for two- and three-year-old pacers and trotters only, has six divisions. The races take place at five racetracks in Nova Scotia and Prince Edward Island.

All in all, the Ontario harness racing world posed a steep learning curve for the young couple from Truro, Nova Scotia, given that one of the pair hadn't known a horse from a zebra only a few years prior, and the other had only ever worked for other horse people, not for himself.

Veteran race-goers, for example, may be familiar with the term "claiming race," where the horses are all for sale for more or less the same, relatively modest, price up until shortly before the race. It is a buyer-beware scenario, as the horses are claimed before they run, and the claim is final. If the horse gets injured in the race, the sale still goes through.

"I think one of the big differences for Brent," says Rhonda, "is that he grew up around young horses, and although he'd also been around the racetrack and racing horses, his passion was working with the young ones. We went [to Toronto] with a couple of young horses, but at that time Greenwood was a lot of claiming races and racehorses, and overnight racehorses. It was a new game for Brent."

Overnight horses?

"Those are the horses that are non-stakes racehorses; they're usually older than two or three," explains Rhonda. "They race once a week. It's their job; it's what they do. You have a different program for the two-and three-year-old racehorses, and then you have a program with horses that race the Grand Circuit—and then you have your overnight horses. There are definitely different tiers of racing."

Grand Circuit?

Founded in 1891 and first held at only four tracks, the Grand Circuit is the oldest continuing harness horse racing series in the United States. Put on by the harness racing industry each year, it includes many of the most prestigious races for both pacers and trotters, such as the Little Brown Jug, for three-year-old pacers, and the Hambletonian, the first event in the Triple Crown for trotters. The circuit also includes the Breeders Crown series, which is a series of twelve races. These cover each of the traditional categories of age, gait, and sex. The Grand Circuit can visit as many as seventeen tracks.

No matter how many other jobs Brent had had, says Rhonda, "he'd always worked for someone else. He wasn't the trainer."

Now he was, and that was the whole new shining dream.

Rhonda worked at the Greenwood racetrack, too, as a "messenger bettor" providing table service for placing bets. (Racetracks no long offer this service.)

One of the horses Brent and Rhonda had brought with them from Nova Scotia, Whos To Blame, was claimed in a claiming race in his first race. Brent went on to claim some other horses after that, but there are no guarantees with horses, no matter how good your eye or how deep—or shallow—your pockets.

"We claimed a filly named Flying Abbey, and when she came off the racetrack she had a broken carpal bone," says Rhonda. "She never raced at all."

Instead, she was retired as a broodmare, which still left the MacGraths with a bill for the purchase of the horse, and then, with a bill for vet care.

"That was pretty much the nail in the coffin," says Rhonda, "for our stable experience."

It was also time to separate from their Nova Scotian backers.

"When we went to Ontario, we went with backing," Rhonda explains. "There were three people, plus ourselves, who had gotten together as owners and purchased the two horses. East Coast Stables, it was called. So even though the two horses were gone early, things weren't going that well. The partners didn't want to keep on, and we certainly weren't in a position to keep on by ourselves."

The MacGraths folded the stable, took on their part of the debt, and started to service that debt.

Rhonda, at this point, was working as a dental assistant during the day and at the racetrack in the evenings. "We were getting pretty desperate," she says.

Then Fate waved a friendly hand.

"Brent saw an ad in the newspaper that said, 'Earn $4,000 in bonuses in a month!' So he got up on a Sunday morning and he said, 'I'm going to go and see what this is all about. I've always thought I could sell something.'"

It would turn out to be the understatement of two lifetimes, at least.

"I don't think that he knew it was car sales that morning," says Rhonda. "Anyway, he went to a hotel in Toronto. The people there did some weeding out, and he was put into a two-week course. He finished, more or less knowing that there was a niche for him. He could do this—and he started selling cars right off the bat. I'm sure it made him feel a little more confident to walk on to that first car lot and say, 'I've been through this course.'"

Although confidence, as anyone who has met the over-six-foot cyclone of energy that is Brent MacGrath will tell you, is not a reach for him.

He was also able to instantly see connections between his main worlds of endeavour.

"Brent would take a truck and go down to the racetrack," says Rhonda, smiling. "He found a lot of customers that way." It kept him connected to that world.

"Brent liked selling," she adds. "In fact, he won an award his first year for truck sales in Canada."

If Rhonda was proud of that achievement, she was prouder of her husband's overall attitude, which he showed when the chips were down and the dreamscape had fogged over.

"Brent never looks back or has regrets," she says. "It's not his way." But nor had he given up on those dreams of theirs. "He never thought he was going away from racing completely, he was just focused on a new learning experience. He really enjoyed the people he was working with. He actually left that dealership [because it] required so much travelling, and went to another one that was closer. But he didn't like the working environment there and ended up returning to the original dealership."

It was from that first sales manager, Brent told her, that he learned how to sell.

"It was fortunate," says Rhonda. "Not only did Brent pick a good career for himself, but [his colleagues were] his kind of people—very out there, very aggressive and hard-working."

Rhonda says they were "doing okay" now, in reference to their working lives. However, other aspects of their lives were far more difficult.

"Life was not easy," Rhonda says quietly. "I had had a stillbirth. We wanted to start a family, but it's difficult in Toronto; you don't have your own family around to help you out. And so we were looking to go back east. A job opportunity came up, which we thought we'd check out."

Back to Nova Scotia they came. It was 1989.

For a while, Brent and Rhonda lived with Brent's parents in Bible Hill, a village near Truro. Soon they bought a house—and then the job they'd moved home for "did not pan out."

While they were thinking about what to do next, Brent met up with Rhonda's uncle, who was an accountant.

"He said to Brent, 'You're a salesperson, go work in sales, in the car business.' So he did."

Brent went to Pye Chevrolet and asked to speak to the owner, Garry Pye.

"Do you have any sales jobs open?" asked Brent.

"No, sorry, I don't," said Pye.

Rhonda's eyes have a glint of mischief in them. "Then he said to Garry, 'Here's my pay stub from a month of selling cars in Toronto, so I'm either going to work for you or against you.' And Garry said, 'Well, maybe I do have something.'"

As friends will tell you, Brent among them, soft-spoken, self-made Garry Pye is not a man to be intimidated; but nor is he one to miss an opportunity that he can work to his own advantage.

While things were looking up on the work front, the MacGraths were still struggling on the personal front.

"I had four more miscarriages," says Rhonda. "I was working at the mall, at a local store. I didn't go back to working in childcare until I actually had a child."

Had a child?

"Joshua was born in '91." The smile is wide, the dark eyes shine. "It was very, very nice. It was a long process. We actually almost adopted a child, but that fell through, and then it was shortly after that I was pregnant with Josh. It all worked out in the end."

Finally, Rhonda was able to use that good university degree.

"I got involved with the Bible Hill Village Preschool. It's been on the go now for almost fifty years. I was involved with helping out at the school, and, of course, then Josh went to it. After that, I went on staff."

And there she worked for over twenty years, eventually becoming the executive director of the preschool. "It was a lovely job; lovely."

When you flourish on home turf, as so many Maritimers do, there are few things better in life than to be there, with family and friends nearby, working in a world that you understand and enjoy.

Other adventures would soon beckon the MacGraths back down the highway to Ontario and there would be more extended time periods spent out of province, but from now on, Nova Scotia and especially Truro, would be their home base.

Brent MacGrath was back in a horse town. You know what happened next.

"Brent bought some local horses with Garry, Donnie Hall, and Al Atkinson," says Rhonda. "He wanted to be back working with young babies again, so he said to Garry, 'You should come in and be an owner.'" She smiles. "I don't think Garry had any interest other than the fact that, you know, maybe a happy manager makes for a prosperous dealership. But soon, he came to like going over to the barn with Brent. They had Maritime-bred horses for the first while. Then some other owners joined in, like Donnie Hall, who was a horse racing person and was as hands-on as Brent. So yeah, very quickly we had some babies."

Brent and Rhonda's own baby, Josh, came to the barn, too. He was soon comfortable around the large animals with their sweet hay-breath and shining dark eyes. The MacGraths were moving closer and closer to that fateful October 6, 2006, purchase—but they weren't quite there yet.

"Brent went to the Harrisburg Selected Yearling Sale and bought a filly that was not Maritime-bred," says Rhonda. "And then the next year he bought two fillies that were Ontario-bred. That would have been 2004, the year that Jamie Bagnell, Reg Petitpas, and Pam Dean got involved in the buying group."

Rhonda pauses, reviewing the important details. "They bought the two fillies; one was a trotter and one was a pacer. The trotter never made it to the races, but the pacer did; she went to Ontario. She was very small and she didn't have good success, so they sold the little filly. The trotter went to a farm and became a mama." She takes a breath. "Now we're into 2006, and that's when Brent decided he wanted to buy a better horse."

He'd also decided on a budget of $40,000 for that "better horse."

Brent MacGrath, Garry Pye, Jamie Bagnell, Stu Rath, Reg Petitpas, and Pam Dean—these, then, were the six members of Schooner Stables, registered in Bible Hill, Nova Scotia, and now the co-owners of a new and bonny bay colt.

"I knew there were six people," says Rhonda, "and I knew Brent had talked about $10,000 each, with the rest going for expenses, but even still, when he said we're getting a $40,000 horse, I remember thinking, 'Oh, my God.'"

What happened next?

Rhonda smiles. "Beach came home."

Chapter 4

PACER IN TRAINING

BEACH ARRIVED IN NOVA SCOTIA FROM KENTUCKY ON MONDAY, October 9, 2006, safely delivered by commercial trucker Glenn Scargill. Rhonda and Brent were at the Truro Raceway when the big truck tumbled down the road to the racetrack on the edge of town.

Was he going to look as impressive on Canadian soil as he did on American soil? Was it possible they had bought a champion?

Beach had to have been weary and relieved. Even horses with calm natures like Beach don't enjoy rocking down the highway mile after noisy mile, standing in their narrow slots with only enough room to move one step in any direction. Of course, there is hay in a hay-net right under their noses, and the good commercial trucks offer great suspension for a smoother ride. But any way you look at the trucking experience, it's not a relaxing one for the animal. All horses are glad to unload at trip's end.

But yes, Brent decided, despite the ill-effects of travel, the friendly, well-built horse looked just as impressive on the Monday, on simple Truro dirt, as he had on the Friday night, on the brightly lit auction stage.

"Rhonda," Brent beamed later, back at their house, when Rhonda came home from work at the preschool, "I think we have a contender."

Having not seen the horse yet, Rhonda wasn't sure what to think at this point. In the days to come, however, she would come to enjoy the

Two-year-old? Wasn't Beach purchased at a select yearling sale? And what is a yearling, anyway? Is that exactly a twelve-month-old horse? And what can these youngsters do at this point, when it comes to skills?

Actually, all Thoroughbreds and Standards have the same birthday: January 1. Beach was born on May 25, 2005, so he turned one the following January—2006. By the time Brent saw him at the Lexington Selected Yearling Sale, he was sixteen months old. If all went well, he would begin racing as a two-year-old, in the spring of 2007. And he would turn two on January 1, 2007.

horse's alert expression and friendly ways. Most of all, she loved to hear the happiness and excitement in Brent's voice. Brent had a baby to work with again—and nothing made him smile more.

"You know what," says Rhonda, thinking back on that day, "that's the way harness racing is, because they all love their two-year-olds. They're all about the hope and the dream and what they're going to do in the spring." She was happy for him.

Their two-legged "baby," Josh, was in grade eleven by then. He was happy for his father, too, but busy himself with school, a golf-course job, a part in a musical, and making use of his brand-new driver's licence—the kind that allows you to drive a car on the road, not a sulky on a track.

"We were both happy to help out at the barn," says Rhonda, "but, really, that was Brent's thing." At that point, anyway. Rhonda might have laughed out loud had she known how "horsey" her life was about to become.

Brent led Beach into his stall—"Just a regular ten-by-ten–foot stall," remembers Rhonda—and filled his feed bucket with pellets, his hay-net with fresh timothy, and made sure his water bucket was clean. As an extra treat, Brent filled Beach's feed bucket with carrots, too.

Lots and lots of carrots.

Horse wearing chifney bit. (MARJORIE SIMMINS)

To hold an attentive stance, harness horses are controlled in part by wearing a "chifney," which is also known as an anti-rearing bit, designed for young or temperamental horses. The grooms hold these by hand. A thin metal circle is visible in the horse's mouth. Inside the mouth, the bit loops over the horse's tongue and behind the chin. It is attached to a "sliphead," which is a single-strap headpiece that can be easily slipped on and off.

These bits do not hurt the horse; in fact, the grooms spend more time jiggling the chain-end of the lead shank to entertain the horses than they ever do pulling down on the bit, which would only be done in times of possible peril to either the handler, the horse, or bystanders.

Beach, in time, would munch his way through fifty pounds of carrots a week. His favourite kind? Bunny Luv, from California, ta muchly, the almost two-year-old might have said.

In terms of skills—as a well-bred and well-cared-for colt, Beach would have had, at this point, what's known as "good stable manners"—though apparently he could nip, which some stallions are prone to do.

But since birth, and intensely for six weeks prior to the sale, Beach and all the other yearlings going to the auction would have received basic training from the grooms who work at the various stables. They would have been taught to wear halters and to allow themselves to be led on a lead line by their handlers; they would also have learned to stand quietly and, when asked, to offer up their hooves for cleaning. When shown to potential buyers, the yearlings would have readily allowed themselves to be "set up," meaning they would stand squarely, head raised, with no moving about or fussing.

Beach often had visitors in Bible Hill because he was, as Rhonda MacGrath put it, "a people horse." Here MacGrath's niece Nicole offers Beach a bit of hay. (RHONDA MACGRATH)

Also in that six-week period before the sale, all the young ones are polished up like the Queen's silver. This grooming is far beyond your basic once-over with a stiff-bristled dandy and a soft-bristled body brush. Once the horse is brushed clean, the groom then rubs cotton cloths or chamois from stem to stern to bring out the coat's natural oils. Then the hooves are oiled, the ears trimmed inside and out, the facial hairs are trimmed, and manes, forelocks, and tails are conditioned.

Altogether, what they end up with are the shiniest, tidiest, cleanest and most desirable horses any bidder has ever seen.

That's exactly the kind of horse that settled down in his new stall that day in Truro.

But could he cover ground?

The starting gate at Flamboro Downs in Hamilton, Ontario. (DAVE LANDRY)

When it came time for the qualifying races in June, Brent renewed his expired harness driver's licence and was ready to start work with his gleaming colt.

On Beach's first day in harness—his first time with a driver in a sulky behind him—Brent introduced him to "the starting gate."

Harness races begin with the horses pacing behind a hinged gate, also called a "mobile barrier," mounted on a moving motor vehicle that leads them to the starting line.

And they're off and pacing! The truck roars away, taking the gate with it. For one second it seems as though the horses will have that gate in front of them for the duration of the race. Then the driver floors the accelerator. The truck pulls far ahead of horses, after which the wings of the gate fold in.

It often takes some time for young horses to get used to the starting gate, and there are different ways to train young ones to make them feel comfortable with the whole idea. Carl Jamieson, a respected trainer, a Hall-of-Famer, and a friend of MacGrath's from Wallace, Nova Scotia, had a particular way of training two-year-old pacers. MacGrath thought he'd try it out on Beach.

"We attached a starting gate to a pick-up truck and then tied Beach to the gate," says MacGrath. "I was in the back of the truck. I was talking to him, petting him; you know, just keeping him relaxed. I was only six inches away from him."

It's hard to imagine a better way to build trust than be *right there* with a young one as he learns a new skill.

"Pooker McCallum was driving the truck, and his brother Wink was on the cart behind Beach. I remember, in the first quarter mile of jogging, he was close to hitting the pace. I yelled at Pooker to stop; I wanted to jump off the truck and pull Beach's hopples up a bit," says MacGrath.

"Once we started back up again, I was quite sure if Pooker picked up the speed a little, Beach would roll on to the pace. So I yelled at Pooker to pick it up a bit and he yelled back, 'I am going thirty miles per hour, you know!' I said, 'A little more,' and he did—and Beach the pacer was off and pacing! That was a small preview of what was to come!"

Hopples are straps used to connect the front and rear legs on the same side of a pacer to help maintain their pacing stride. When MacGrath shortened Beach's hopples, the improvement was instant.

To put this into context, experienced pacers race up to 30 mph (48 km/h) at an awesome stride of twenty-five to twenty-seven feet. In the home stretch, their speeds can spike to over 35 mph (56 km/h).

So baby Beach was boogying.

It was also impressive that he was on the pace his first time out.

"Many horses are weeks, even months, figuring it out," says Brent. "And many horses, after they have learned how to pace, will jog on the trot, which is a more natural gait for a horse."

Harness Racing Language: The Basics

Pacing, trotting, pacers, trotters—the terminology can get confusing to those who don't own a Standardbred racehorse or frequent a harness racing track.

In the wild, horses have four natural gaits: the walk, the trot, the canter, and the gallop. The pace is not a natural gait, but it does come more naturally to pacing Standardbreds than any other breed because it has been bred into them for many generations.

Of course Standardbreds can walk (the slowest four-beat gait); trot (a two-beat gait, with the legs moving diagonally); canter (a fast, three-beat gait); and gallop (the fastest four-beat gait, which brings all four legs off the ground at once) just like the wild horses (which in North America, are mostly feral, not actually wild) or any other horse breed. Standardbreds will certainly walk and trot the first time they show up in harness to work, and they may well canter and gallop, too, if they are feeling nervous or perplexed. It takes time to relax into the pacing gait with harness on.

These are babies, after all, doing their best to be consistent. Hence the hopples, and for safety, the use of "blinders," which are firm leather squares or plastic cups attached to the horse's bridle or hood. Blinders cover the rear vision of the horse, allowing them to only look forward. As horses are emphatically "flight or fight" animals, blinders also reduce the risk of the horse being spooked and galloping out of control. (Ironically, the term for that is "running blind.")

Horses are also sensitive and reactive to noise, which is why many racing Standardbreds wear earplugs. When you hear a race announcer yell, "They've pulled the plugs!" what they mean is the drivers have literally pulled the earplugs out of their horses' ears, usually in the home stretch or final quarter of the race. You can see the drivers pull them with a kick of the foot, which releases them with an attached string. Generally this makes the horses step on the gas. Not all racers use earplugs; maybe half do. Beach wore plugs when he was racing, but not in training.

When a driver "jogs" a pacing horse, it may mean the horse trots, or he paces. Essentially, the horse, like any athlete, is warming up. He is being conditioned by the trainer, because beyond the introduction of new gear, and getting the horse used to it, and working out which leg goes where and when and how fast, working with young racehorses is all about the conditioning.

"Pacers will jog on the trot," says Brent, "and I am not one to discourage that. As long as they are enjoying their work, jogging is basic conditioning. That's not the same as training."

And so, "We would jog one, two, three, and four miles," says Brent, of his early days with Beach. "Gradually we'd ask for more speed for the sixteenth of a mile, then the one-eighth, then the quarter. You're building them up, teaching them to have confidence." (Races are timed in segments. "Fractions," or times, are usually recorded at quarter-mile intervals in training miles and races.)

Beach was fitting into the MacGraths' lives like a hand in a glove. Brent was at the racetrack at 5:30 A.M. before he headed for work at the dealership, and Josh and Rhonda would go down to the barn on weekends with Brent and sometimes on their own. Everyone was enjoying the company of their new four-footed family member. Even their golden retriever, Lily, came along to hang out at the barn.

"Yes, it was family time. It was nice," says Rhonda. "But most of all, Brent's back with a two-year-old and he loves it—and he loves the horse. Every day he keeps saying, 'You know, he does everything right; he does whatever I ask him to do.'"

No doubt about it, life in and around the Truro Raceway when Beach first came home in 2006 was good. And the pacing lessons continued to go well.

Back in the Hub, the months after October ticked over, with trainer and colt getting used to one another and, day by day, developing a deeper bond. And then, as it will, the crummy weather came to Nova Scotia.

"I worked with him until Christmas," says Brent. "Then we took him to Pictonian Farms in Pictou."

If Beach thought he was going to be lolling about on a large country farm for the rest of the winter, he was in for a surprise. Owned at that time by Tony Zuethoff, Pictonian Farms is a serious Standardbred breeding farm, with serious infrastructure that includes an "exerciser." An exerciser is the Cadillac version of the "hot-walker" that has been around for many years—a mechanical merry-go-round to which several horses are attached by their halters so they can slowly walk until they are cool after exercise. The exerciser is multi-purpose, as good for rehabilitating injured animals with a controlled exercise routine as it is for providing reliable exercise to young horses in training.

But, unlike in the hot-walker, the horses are not connected to the machine by a halter and dropped-down chain—an arrangement many trainers felt was unsafe and potentially injurious to the head and spine. Instead, exercisers allow horses to move freely between a set of gates or "stalls" that travel inside a circular fenced track. This means the horse is moving naturally, but at a specified pace chosen by the trainer.

"The track at Truro was icy," says Brent, "so we couldn't use it for training. I think Beach missed us, but when he came back from Pictou in April he was fit, strong, and ready to work. That exerciser is a workout."

It was time to "put the watch on him."

Commonly, the first time a young horse trains, he might do a three-minute mile. That's approximately 20 mph (32 km/h). In subsequent weeks, the trainer aims to bring the horse down five seconds for the mile each week. At that point, the horse should reach a 2:40-minute mile, or a speed of 22 mph (35 km/h).

On Beach's first time out that spring of 2007, he did a mile in two minutes, thirty-five seconds.

"I knew we had a horse of talent," says Brent, straight-faced.

Translation: he was thrilled with the numbers he was seeing.

By May, Beach was down to 2/20—a mile in two minutes, twenty seconds.

And by June, it was time for Brent to "qualify" Beach at the Truro Raceway. A qualifying race ensures that a horse has the ability to compete with other equine players of comparable ability, within the qualifying standards established for age and other aspects. The qualifiers might be age-specific—for two- or three-year-olds, or for "mature" horses, which are over three. In terms of sex, the qualifier could be for colts or fillies only, or for both sexes. And, of course, the qualifying races are either for trotters or pacers.

MacGrath himself was more than ready to see what Beach could do in competition. It's probably fair to say that he hadn't had as much fun with a young horse ever, nor had he dared to hope he had a true "contender." But hope is free, and every time Brent MacGrath put Beach in harness, he thought about the possibilities of a whole new competitive world opening up for himself and Schooner Stables.

But most of all, he loved spending time with the colt, who in turn, loved the attention he received. The two were friends.

The first two-year-old qualifier took place on June 24, 2007, with MacGrath driving, as he would for all three of Beach's races at the Truro Raceway. In the same race were six other eager, good-looking colts and fillies, all with the fun names breeders love to bestow: Assuasive, Absolom, Risetotheoccasion, Dropdead Beautiful, Single Step, and Boxstep Hanover. (Naming racehorses is a complex art form, with byzantine rules and regulations—and many run-together words or phonetic phrases. See Appendix C – The Art of Naming Horses.)

Beach drew post position five, third on the outside. It's a tolerable placement, though most trainers prefer the inside or middle. The outside position is considered a disadvantage because it is so difficult to manoeuvre over to the rail and save ground, a critical racing tactic.

While all drivers are happy to draw the rail, the choice spot, known as the "pocket," is on the rail behind the leader. Amusingly, a horse in that position is said to have a "garden trip," perhaps because the race is then a "walk in the park" for horse and driver. (Some people suggest it's an allusion to William Shakespeare's "primrose path," meaning the pleasant route through life.)

And the least desirable spot on a harness racing track? That would be third on the rail, known on small tracks as the "death hole." Many a wish to win has died in that position. With horses on either side surging ahead in two converging lines, horses in the middle can get "boxed in," unable to take the lead.

Third on the outside was likely just fine for MacGrath. He had never doubted the colt's ability, and he never would.

And yet…an observer could be forgiven for wondering: would Beach get off the gate well, and stay focused for the full mile (1,609 metres) with six other horses and sulkies around him?

MacGrath remained focused on the training aspect of the qualifying race.

"My job as the driver was to teach Beach to do what I asked him to do: stay calm, get around the track safely, and have a positive experience," says MacGrath. "Winning was not on the radar. I wanted him to have fun coming down the home stretch. You're educating them, and making sure they're having a good time."

That was the hope.

The field of seven readied themselves behind the starting gate.

Beach passed the quarter mark at 33.1. He passed the halfway mark at 1:04.2, and he passed the three-quarter mark at 1:34.2. All was well.

"I just let him roll along until the last one-eighth of the mile," says MacGrath. "The home stretch." Beach, focused on the job, surged first over the finish line with a time of 2:04.3.

Beach got a lot of carrots that night. He got lots of praise, too, along with a prolonged grooming session and many head rubs. It was a good day to be a horse named Somebeachsomewhere, and a good day to be man named Brent MacGrath.

A week later, on Canada's birthday—July 1, 2007—Beach ran his second qualifier at the Truro Raceway. It was a smaller field this time, with Absolom in post position one, Wild Side in two, Beach in three, and Sudden Cam in four.

Smaller fractions for Beach, too.

30.4.

1:01.4.

1:33.1.

And a finish of 2:02.1.

"Race two, he went to the front in the first quarter," says MacGrath. And that was that. Beach never left the front.

The third and final qualifier was scheduled a week later, on July 8, 2007. Beach drew post position five and was racing against Atlanta Girl, Campco Spud, River Ryan, and Meadowvale Ingle. His fractions were again respectable and his final time the fastest yet, at 2:00.1.

"That time, I moved him to the front between the one-quarter and one-half marks," says MacGrath. And again, that was where the motoring colt stayed.

Three starts, three wins.

"I was impressed with his performance," says MacGrath. "And excited."

When MacGrath shared his news about the three qualifier wins with the five other members of Schooner Stables—Jamie Bagnell, Pam Dean, Reg Petitpas, Stu Rath, and Garry Pye—they were all delighted. The horse people in the group, which included Petitpas, who'd owned racehorses since he was twenty, Dean, who owns and shows Quarter Horses, and Bagnell, with his early history with Standardbreds, might even have felt their hearts skip a beat or two.

Who was this promising horse they'd come to own—and what would his future be?

It was time for Beach to move to Ontario, and this time, Brent and Rhonda would deliver him. As agreed on by the group, they were headed for the Baycairn Training Centre in Campbellville, where trainer Jean Louis Arsenault was stabled and renting stalls. Arsenault, a friend and colleague of Reg Petitpas's, would become the trainer-of-record for Beach's second year.

It was also time for Schooner Stables to start planning Beach's second-year campaign.

The first decision was to engage Paul MacDonell as Beach's driver. The second was to launch Beach's career at the impressively titled Battle of Waterloo—the signature event at the Grand River Raceway in Elora, Ontario. The elimination race was scheduled for July 30, 2007, which was less than a month away. (An elimination race qualifies horses for the final heat of the same race, often scheduled for a week later.) It would be Beach's first "lifetime race," meaning his first time racing for a purse. In this case, the purse was $24,000.

MacGrath loaded Beach easily onto his trailer, making sure the colt had a generous supply of timothy hay to munch on during the journey (which MacGrath would replenish, along with water, during the course of the sixteen-hour trip). Then Brent and Rhonda buckled up their seatbelts in the cab of their truck and set off west down the Trans-Canada Highway, toward the Nova Scotia/New Brunswick border, then through Quebec, and finally, into Canada's largest, most populous province, Ontario, home to twelve harness racing tracks—far and away the most in the country.

The MacGraths had a 1,098-mile (1,768 km) trip ahead of them—and the subject of Beach's future, and their own, was much on their minds as the miles whipped by.

Chapter 5

THE BATTLE OF WATERLOO

LIFE WAS ABOUT TO GET COMPLICATED FOR THE MACGRATHS—wonderfully complicated. Happily, bolstered by many fortunate events since they'd returned to the Maritimes, they were both up for the ride. Win or lose, those around them would support them as well. In addition to Rhonda's large family, Brent's parents and his three brothers had been cheering them on since Beach had come home to Truro.

Life was also about to get complicated and exciting for their old friend, Paul MacDonell, with whom Brent had been in contact regularly since the purchase of Beach. Paul hadn't hesitated when Brent had asked if he would drive Beach in the elimination race at the Grand River Raceway. It didn't conflict with his racing schedule and he, too, was affected by Brent's enthusiasm for the new horse; he hoped his old friend had found himself a serious racehorse.

Not long after the Battle of Waterloo elimination and final, though, Paul expected he would be driving a talented colt owned by Katherine Bardis of Sacramento, California, in the next big race, the Metro Pace.

"At the time, Paul was driving one of Canada's top two-year-olds, Deuce Seelster," explains Rhonda. "He was trained by an Australian, Darren McCall, and was being directed towards the Metro."

The $1 million Metro Pace, which takes place in Campbellville, Ontario, is the premier race for two-year-old colts in North America. The race takes place at Mohawk Racetrack. The elimination race was scheduled for August 25, 2007, and the final was scheduled for September 1.

Before this, however, Beach would be competing in the Battle of Waterloo, at Grand River Raceway, in Elora. The elimination race was to be held on July 30, 2007, and the final a week later, on August 6. The two racetracks, Grand River Raceway and Woodbine Mohawk Park, are about three-quarters of an hour apart by car.

So that was okay, as Brent has been known to say, as so many people do say in the Maritimes, indicating one part of a story has been told, with another soon to follow. *Because who could possibly say if Beach would do well at Grand River?* All the same, Brent was "paid into the Metro," or eligible, having made payments through the winter and spring, and was now ready to make the final, larger starting payment, should circumstances warrant it.

In that regard, Brent's confidence was about to be bolstered. The first time Paul took Beach out for training before the Battle of Waterloo elimination race, he took Brent aside. *Hope you're eligible for the Metro…*

Paul's comment only confirmed what Brent felt in his bones. His decision was firm. Unless something went terribly wrong at Grand River, Beach would race in the Metro.

And if Brent had his way, a certain driver by the name of Paul MacDonell would be driving Beach, not Deuce Seelster.

However, first things first, as the old adage goes.

It was July 30, 2007, and it was time for Somebeachsomewhere to have his career parimutuel debut (with parimutuel betting, bettors wager against each other and not against the racetrack, as they would via a bookie). Somebeachsomewhere went off in the Battle of Waterloo

A "length"—to oversimplify—is approximately eight to nine feet (2.4 to 2.7 metres), or the length of an average horse from nose to tail; the measure is used to indicate the distance that separates horses in a race. More strictly speaking, however, a length isn't really a unit of distance; it's a unit of time. The (sometimes-disputed) rule of thumb is that one length takes one-fifth of a second.

elimination race in a field of seven, as a second favourite—and won, by a tidy three lengths.

Beach's fractions were his fastest ever, as was his time of 1:54.2, a Canadian season record.

This was Beach's first start. The crowd, always up for a handsome and commanding newcomer setting a record, roared their approval. "We were so excited when he won!" says Rhonda.

The couple had driven to Ontario for the race, while their son Josh had flown up. Brent and Rhonda drove home to Nova Scotia the day after the race, but Brent flew back to Ontario almost immediately.

"By then, Brent's pretty sure he's got a contender for the Ontario Sires Stakes Gold Division," says Rhonda. "Beach is turning heads wherever he goes. We even got an offer, the night of the [Battle of Waterloo] elimination race, to buy him, right then and there."

And how much was the offer?

"It was for $750,000."

In ten months, and with only three qualifiers and one elimination race under his harness, Beach's price tag had shot up an astounding $710,000.

Were they tempted to sell?

"You know," says MacGrath, "if Rhonda and I had owned him, I might have thought about it. But as a group, we thought no, let's keep on. I mean, who knows what could happen, right? And none of us were stuck for that original $10,000 we'd put in; that was one of the stipulations. So it wasn't as though someone's kid couldn't go to school for lack of those funds."

Besides, things were just starting to get interesting, and people were *talking*—horsemen that other horsemen listen to.

"Ron Waples is a very successful driver," says Rhonda. "He comes from a family of successful harness racing people. He was a commentator the night Beach won. He turned to me in the winner's circle and he said, 'Nice horse you got there.' And he said it in a way that you could tell people had been impressed by what they had just seen."

According to Rhonda, that's not all he said. As a commentator for the elimination for the Metro, Waples had said, on-air, "I went into the paddock at the Battle of Waterloo and I took one look at a horse and fell in love. That horse was Somebeachsomewhere."

Journalist Dave Briggs reported in the September 2007 issue of the *Canadian Sportsman* that Waples had remarked on-air that Beach reminded him of racing legend Niatross (1977–99), a horse many argue is the greatest pacer of all time. As a member of the Canadian Horse Racing Hall of Fame, the US Horse Racing Hall of Fame, and the Little Brown Jug Wall of Fame, Waples knows a thing or two about horses. The MacGraths were thrilled by his admiring words.

There was no doubt about it: Schooner Stables had a contender. In a blink of the proverbial eye, really, everything had changed.

"That's right, things were changing," says Rhonda. "Brent didn't want to be too far away from Beach, so after the elimination race we drove back to Truro to drop off our truck, but Brent came back on a plane immediately. And, of course, if he did well in the final of the Battle of Waterloo, he's looking to be entered in the Metro."

It was all a bit dizzying.

The Battle of Waterloo final took place on August 6, 2007. It offered a plump $300,000 purse. It also had a crowded field of ten good horses: Fun of the Game, Believeinbruiser, Samurai Seelster, Keystone Horatio, Doctor J Holiday, Ratings Hanover, Sturges Hanover, Keep in Control, Allamerican Dice, and Beach.

One journalist of the day wrote that Beach had a "tougher trip" than he had in the elimination. Another wrote that he "romped to a two and a quarter-length victory in 1:55," and "was off to sport's stratosphere."

Paul MacDonell said of that second lifetime start at Grand River, "Beach was in the back stretch and the track was a little deep and he started to get a little 'steppy-gaited,' not as smooth-gaited as he could be. I had to correct him and let him get his feet under himself for a small portion of the race. He did collect himself and then he went on."

It's the only instance he can remember, MacDonell says, where Beach, "gave me any trouble at all." He adds quickly, "Even still, he was just so professional in every aspect—so professional."

The video of the race on YouTube shows that it wasn't an easy win. Beach starts off in post position seven on the half-mile oval, and twenty-seven seconds into the race, or at approximately the first quarter, moves into the fifth position, "in the middle of the pack." At the half-mile mark, the announcer says Beach "still has to make up two and a half lengths" to reach the lead horse, "and rolls out there three wide," meaning Paul MacDonell is looking for a clear path to put the pedal to the metal.

All the horses are pacing smoothly and it looks like it could be a win for any one of several horses, with Keep in Control, Fun of the Game, Believeinbruiser, and Samurai Seelster all looking strong.

Then, in the top of the stretch, the announcer's voice starts rising, the words separated for dramatic effect: "Here. Comes. Some. Beach. Somewhere! Paul MacDonell and Somebeachsomewhere have come on to take the lead!"

Thereafter, Beach is, "cruising down the stretch to win the tenth Battle of Waterloo."

He'd done it. Legs a bit confused for a few strides, but he'd done it, and well. In fact, he'd won by three lengths, in a time of 1:55. Fun of the Game, the favourite in the elimination, had come second, with Believeinbruiser third and Samurai Seelster fourth. Two-year-old Somebeachsomewhere, an unknown from Truro, Nova Scotia, had just triumphed at the Grand River Raceway, winning both the elimination and the final of the prestigious Battle of Waterloo, his crew pocketing $150,000 in the process. He and his shell-shocked owners, Schooner Stables, now had nineteen days to prepare for the Metro Pace Elimination on August 25, 2007, at Mohawk Raceway in Campbellville.

Meanwhile, Paul MacDonell was making one of the toughest decisions of his life: would he drive Somebeachsomewhere in the Metro, or would he drive Deuce Seelster? These were two hugely talented colts with two keen groups of people who wanted him to pick their colt. He must have wished he could clone himself so he could drive the two magnificent horses at once and keep it all in the family.

In the end, he chose to drive Beach. An honest man, MacDonell has said his friendship with MacGrath "certainly wasn't a deciding factor." Instead, being a competitive and highly successful driver, MacDonell chose the horse he hoped to bring into the winner's circle—to collect that aforementioned $1 million for the purse—$500,000 for the owners, and his own 5 percent, or $25,000. (The remaining purse money broke down as follows: 25 percent to the second-place winner; 12 percent to the third-place winner; 8 percent to the fourth-place winner; and 5 percent to the fifth-place winner.) There was just something…unique about Beach. So unique, in fact, he'd made his decision shortly after the elimination race, which had gone so well. MacDonell later joked, "It was as though Beach had an extra gear."

They all agreed: Somebeach was *some horse*, it was obvious. But could his luck and talent hold? And did he, as importantly, have what it took to prevail over the most talented field of two-year-olds that had been seen in many a year?

For Beach to win over that big, tough field, he would need something else—the heart and soul of a champion.

Paul MacDonell would be guiding Beach down the track for the Metro.

Chapter 6
"BIG MAC"

WHO WAS "BIG MAC," ANYWAY, AND WHY WAS HE SO RESPECTED as a driver?

One thing for sure, MacDonell was not a big man in the physical sense. He was trim and of average height. The nickname was more a term of respect and affection for the man who'd always had horses in his life and who would go on to become one of North America's top drivers.

As happens with most potential horsemen and -women, he was first taken to a barn as a kid—and the horses, magically and irrevocably, did the rest. For MacDonell, born in Oshawa, Ontario, to parents Mary Lou and Blaise MacDonell, it was his father who introduced him to horses. (Originally from Judique and Port Hood, Nova Scotia, Blaise and Mary Lou could never have guessed that their son would go on to be one of the most successful drivers in North America. MacDonell even raced in Norway and Sweden in 2010 and 2011, representing Canada with trotter Define the World.)

"My father worked at General Motors and had a couple of Standardbreds on the side as a hobby," says MacDonell. "He was a lover of horses from the time he was a kid growing up in Cape Breton. That passion followed him up here to Ontario.... So I started following him to the barns at a very young age, and that was my first interaction with horses. I was somewhere between five and ten years old."

Other young people of the time might have had saddle horses or even ponies, both of which come in all different breeds, colours, and sizes. But for MacDonell, the perfect horse was a long-bodied Standardbred, of medium height, most often a bay (having a reddish-brown or brown coat with a black mane and tail and black "points," or lower legs). He grew to love the sight of their refined heads, broad foreheads, and large nostrils. Some of these Standardbreds, even many of these, in those early years, had "Roman noses," meaning a muzzle with a convex profile. Perhaps his father lifted him up to stroke the horses' well-defined "withers," or the rounded ridge of bone at the base of the neck. Or perhaps, on his own, he reached up to pat the horses' strong shoulders and, as he grew taller, their muscular, slightly arched necks. These were the horses that said "just right" to MacDonell.

"Watching the races was always so exciting to me," says MacDonell. The youthful looking fifty-seven-year-old casts his thoughts back a half-century to those first, durable impressions.

"It was the pageantry of it all. You know, the drivers' silks, and the starting gate pulling away, and the excitement," he says. "I also had access to the barn area when I was fairly young. That probably combined to pique my interest and excitement."

By the time MacDonell was in his teens, he was starting to think a career as a driver might be "cool." Watching his father train and race made the daydreams all the more real.

"This is going back to the late '60s, mid-'70s, when most people drove and trained their own horses. It's morphed into a specialty thing now, where you don't see many trainer/drivers, you see just one person doing specialty stuff."

By his mid-teens, MacDonell was eager to apply for his trainer's licence.

"You had to get your trainer's first," he explains. "And you had to be sixteen years old to be a trainer." After the mandatory two-year waiting period, he completed the practical and written tests and received his licence at age eighteen.

Even then, when he was starting out, MacDonell says, he never thought it could develop into full-time work. "You think—maybe just try this and see what happens." He smiles. "But as it turned out for me, it was a full-time job."

He started out driving his family's horses and was soon asked to drive for other people. By age twenty-seven, MacDonell won his first Breeders Crown at Pompano Park in Florida. It was the first of eight Breeders Crown races that he would go on to win. These annual, prestigious harness races take place in both the United States and Canada. They cover each of the sport's twelve traditional categories of age, gait, and gender.

MacDonell has also won three Metro Pace stakes, five Confederation Cups, three Elegant Image stakes, and is the all-time leader in Ontario Sires Stakes Super Finals, with twenty-two wins. In 2008, MacDonell was honoured with the O'Brien Award as Canada's top driver.

By 2016, his "job" had led him to more than fifty-three hundred wins on the track and post earnings exceeding $116 million.

MacDonell easily conjures up his early races.

"I can remember my first few times being so intimidated by all the other guys that had been there for years," he says. "I guess after a year or so you start to gain confidence when you start winning races and having people ask you to drive their horses."

Paul MacDonell is 155 pounds and fit, and stands five feet eight inches; it's a fairly average physical profile for a harness driver who, unlike short and skinny Thoroughbred jockeys, can be any height and weight and still drive a sulky.

"There are no restrictions as there are in the Thoroughbred racing world," says MacDonell. "But I think you'll see the good ones, the very top drivers, are not very big at all. Usually they watch their weight. They're slender, they're fit, and they're athletic."

He grins. "I probably weighed 115, maybe 120 pounds when I started. I wasn't very big at all. As a matter of fact, I can remember some people saying to my dad, 'Are you sure your son's strong enough to be holding on

LITTLE BROWN JUG. 2:11¼.

(NNEHRING, ISTOCK)

Once upon a time, the legend goes, a driver wanted to be alone so he made himself a one-man cart. His wife told him that only a "sulky" man would ride alone.

to some of these big horses out there?' My dad was confident that I was good because we did a lot of training at the farms, and he knew I could handle a horse. So he would just kind of shrug it off."

In spite of the early doubters, MacDonell says he felt welcomed into the racing barns.

"People knew who we were, because we raced there all the time," he says. "They probably thought, when I started going for my licence, 'Wow, that fellow only looks like he's fourteen.'" He pauses. "There were some people that would try to intimidate you just like in [any] sport. It's a competitive business, but I was ready for that, too."

Like any young athlete, MacDonell had "idols," or drivers he respected and aspired to be like.

"It was mostly guys that were racing in Toronto when I was a kid. There was Ron Waples, Doug Brown, William Wellwood—names like that who had large stables and good horses, and you always looked up to those people. And I also looked up to my father, because he was teaching me the ropes as we went along. So I guess he would fall into the idol category, too."

As with talented racehorses, gifted drivers are rare. For the men and women who drive pacers and trotters, it takes a special combination of factors to succeed and to remain a consistent winner.

"I think a driver has to have a really good feel for a horse; they have to have that confidence in the horse and the horse has to have confidence back into them. I think you have to have a nice set of hands that a horse can feel your intention through the bit. I also think you have to be consistent."

MacDonell's voice warms with nearly forty years of in-the-sulky experience. "Actually, there are a million words I'm looking for; there are a million things that go into it. You have to be confident, you have to be consistent; you have to be gentle, you have to be aggressive. You have to know your horse, you have to know other horses' tendencies; you have to know other drivers' tendencies; you have to know what class of horse you're racing against other classes of horses. There are so many things that go into what a good driver does, and if he can kind of roll those things up into one ball and put it all together and carve out a career and be consistent with those characteristics, then that usually makes up a good driver."

MacDonell says he learns something every day. Then there are the totally unexpected events.

"With these horses, there's something called 'making a break,'" says MacDonell. "That's when they lose their stride [and] basically take you out of the race." He explains that Beach was a pacer, so he wore "hopples" to help him stay laterally gaited. "Some horses lose their gait. They could be lame; they could have a foot problem…. Sometimes, they come to an abrupt halt, and if you're not prepared for that…" He stops for a moment, collects himself. "We're sitting in sulkies with wheels and those wheels—if you ever get pitched out, it's trouble. So that's part of it, too, as far as knowing your competition, because the longer you can stay healthy, the longer your career's going to last."

You might think that only young, inexperienced horses make these dangerous "breaks," but you would be wrong.

"Sometimes the older horses that have raced so many starts, they start getting aches and pains and they might do something unexpected," says MacDonell.

And what does that break actually look like?

"Basically, we go from a pacing gait to a gallop…and when they try and run in hopples some of them can't do that. So now they do a quick stop and that's when the trouble starts," he says. Breaks happen for other reasons, too. "They could hook a piece of equipment—even a shoe, for that matter—and trip. I've seen lots of things. We used to have hub rails…"

Two words that strike fear into a driver's heart.

"Hub rails were wooden rails on the inside of the track to keep horses [off the infield]," MacDonell explains, "just to keep the guide lane. I was in a race one time at Toronto, and a part of the wood was sticking out of the hub rail. We were going along the back stretch and a guy's wheel hit the big part sticking out. [It] pitched him right out in front of another driver and the other guy went right over top of him and broke his hip."

All kinds of things can happen, he says—even to skilled, careful drivers.

"Knock on wood, nothing really serious for me," says MacDonell, with obvious relief and gratitude. "I broke my wrist years ago and I had a fractured ankle one time, but nothing lately."

Broken wrist, fractured ankle, but nothing lately…

"But," continues MacDonell, "I've seen drivers with all kinds of pins and stuff in them."

Or who have been terribly injured, like John Willie Beaton, also from Port Hood, Nova Scotia, who, in 2016, broke eight ribs when he was tossed out of his sulky and another sulky's wheel went over him at the Northside Downs racetrack in North Sydney.

"Oh, yeah," says MacDonell. "John Willy was in bad pain for a long time." He brightens. "But he's back driving, isn't he?"

Yes, in fact. J. W., as he is known to family, was indeed back to driving the season following the accident. At the time, he said he was glad the accident happened on the last day of the season, so he'd have a full year to heal up. A part-time driver, J. W., now in his sixties, is closing in on his one-thousandth career win. A few broken bones aren't enough to interfere with that goal. And the cherry on the sundae to this story is that J. W. was inducted into the Cape Breton Sport Hall of Fame in February 2020.

Just as the drivers need to stay fit and mentally prepared, so, naturally, do the horses. This makes the warm-up process, which is particular to the individual trainer, important.

"When the horse gets to the track, people do it differently," says MacDonell. "Some people take their horse out twice before the race; some people only take them out once. They dress them up, put all the harness on them that they're going to race in, and take them out for a jog."

While the horses always race to the left, they can warm up going both ways. Again, it's up to the trainer to go "the jog way" (to the right, on the outside) or the "the right way of the track" (to the left, on the inside).

So you have your horse ready to race. He's sound, well bred, warmed up, and keen to race, and you're hoping for a win. But isn't there something else he needs?

"They need fight," says MacDonell. "When a horse gets in a race, particularly in the later stages of the race, or when they get tired, some horses can dig down deep and fight and try—they'll go right to the well for you." Others won't. "They're individuals; they're like people. They all have their personalities, and some of them will fight till the end."

In Thoroughbred racing, it's often called "heart."

"Heart and soul," says MacDonell. "Exactly."

Like the other "Mac," Brent MacGrath, Paul MacDonell liked Beach on sight. And while MacDonell had the privilege and joy of driving Beach in all twenty-one of Beach's career races, he also drove (and still drives) many other horses, sometimes for one race only.

So how does he build a bond with a horse that he may only drive once?

"That's a difficult thing to do," says MacDonell. "I would try and get as much insight as I could from the trainer or the owner…and get a gauge of what I should know or shouldn't know. Also, by this stage in my life I can tell how the horse is moving on the track—whether he's free and sound and happy and sharp and all the rest of it."

And if you're lucky, you continue to build a bond with a horse you drive regularly.

"I think getting to know tendencies of that horse really helps," agrees MacDonell. "I drive a lot of two- and three-year-olds at this stage in my career—a lot of younger horses—and sometimes those two-year-olds do one thing this week, [then] they've got something new for you next week. So you have to be ready for every little detail."

He says the breeding of the horse makes a big difference, and now that he's often driving the offspring of horses he's known, he has a sense of what they might be like. And other times it's just luck, says MacDonell. Luck is an odd creature, even dictating which driver a horse likes more than another, and who he will work harder for on the racetrack.

How do you get that horse on fire going down the track, anyway?

"Some will give you a hundred miles an hour right off the gate, but the race is a mile long so…you have to be able find the right trip. Have you heard that term at all?"

He explains that trip scenarios come into play in every race. Sometimes a horse goes to the front and no one challenges him for the first three-quarters of a mile, leaving him more energy for the last quarter-mile. Another trip scenario involves two drivers who think that they can out-lead each other and one of them gets "parked out," meaning "he's taking on all the air on the outside of the track," which usually sets up an opportunity for another horse to come from behind.

MacDonell smiles ruefully. "That's something our business needs to be better at. For a person who's new to the track, maybe they've been five times, but they might not have heard some of the terms that the announcer's using and they don't know what the hell he's talking about. In my opinion, we need to put it in layman's terms, be a little more explanatory. I mean we've got an audience that's captured that are diehard fans that know these terms, but they're not the only ones watching the races."

Or you can simply attend the races with someone who does know the lingo. That's an option, too.

With thousands of races to his credit, MacDonell could be forgiven if he mixed up his horses in his memory a bit, even superstar Beach. But he can readily characterize his relationship with the friendly stallion he came to know very well.

"I had a very nice relationship with Beach," says MacDonell. "Beach made life so easy for me. He had the strength, the power—all of the necessary attributes that a great horse would have."

As a powerful, playful, and, at times, bossy stallion—did Beach ever give MacDonell a hard time, on the track or off?

"Nope. Honestly he didn't."

Horsewoman and Schooner Stables member Pam Dean once commented that Beach was not easily overwhelmed, even as a young horse at a big, noisy track for the first time. It spoke to character and maturity, she thought.

MacDonell agrees.

"Keep in mind, when Beach came to the tracks he was racing against other two-year-olds," he says. "But he was way more mature than they were. I have a friend who remembers watching him walk into Grand River Raceway. He remembers looking at the horse and saying, "Beach just kind of looked around and said, 'Okay, let's get this over with.'" He was just so ready to get on with racing."

Physically, mentally, and even emotionally, young Beach was ready to take on the world.

Chapter 7

"MARITIME METRO MONSTER"

DESPITE TWO STELLAR WINS, BEACH WAS THE SECOND FAVOURITE, not the favourite, in the Metro Pace elimination. The favourite was a big brown colt by the name of Dali, owned by Uncirculated Stable, headed by Aaron and Isaac Waxman.

There was a lot to like about Dali, and a lot to respect. The son of Real Artist debuted in June 2007 at Mohawk Racetrack. Fans cheered full-on as "the brown speedster" took a come-from-behind, six-and a-half–length victory, crackling over the finish line in 1:51.3. He went on to win at the Meadows Racetrack in Washington, Pennsylvania, and then at the Meadowlands track in New Jersey. But the race everyone was still talking about was the Woodrow Wilson Pace, again at the Meadowlands. On that day, August 3, 2007, Dali claimed victory with a cyclonic 1:50.2, for a $415,000 (USD) purse.

Small wonder Dali was the 1–9 favourite for the Metro elimination on August 25, 2007. Beach himself was being sent off at 5–1 odds. (For more on this, see "Understanding Odds," page 263.)

Shadow Play was also causing serious chatter. He'd made his racing debut on June 21, 2007, at the Charlottetown Driving Park in

61

Elimination Races

As the word implies, elimination races were designed to eliminate some racehorses from the finals of a particular race, as we saw in the Battle of Waterloo, Somebeachsomewhere's first lifetime race. There will always be more horses that seek to compete in the large-purse races than will be allowed or are qualified.

"It's like a round-robin tournament in junior hockey," says Brent MacGrath. "The winners advance to the next division. You might face a tough division or an easy one. We always want to move the horses into the next division of competition."

Charlottetown, Prince Edward Island. Owner/trainer Dr. Ian Moore (a veterinarian and instructor at the Atlantic Veterinary College in Charlottetown) was in the sulky. Together they'd beat a field of maiden pacers by four and a half lengths. Shadow Play had continued to place well since being shipped to Ontario.

Altogether, Beach was racing against a solid field of seven: Dali, Shadow Play, Legacy N Diamonds, Perseus, Handsome Prince, and Future Cruiser. Every horse in the race was a possible winner and every owner believed their horse was the best—proper thing, when you know how hard these horses train and, yes, how much they want to win.

Harness racing people sometimes refer to top harness racers as "bred to the nines" (which seems to be a variation on the English idiom "dressed to the nines," meaning dressed to perfection, high class), or "royally bred," or even "bred in the purple" (the colour once reserved for royalty only). But it's not only flashy looks and careful breeding that make a racehorse: it's their competitive drive.

So on August 25, 2007, Mohawk Racetrack was humming and crackling with activity, owners, drivers, and grooms on the run, jogging in and out of barns and tack rooms and then leading horses onto the track for warm-ups. Vendors worked the concessions, and bettors and racing enthusiasts collected food and drinks and found seats in the grandstand. Everyone was psyched: ready for horse-racing action.

Finally, the post call for the Metro Pace elimination, the purse for which was $40,000, sounded.

Beach had the number three post position; not ideal. Right beside him was his main rival, Dali, in the "four-hole," or post position four. On his left, in number two, was Legacy N Diamonds.

MacGrath never stood with the other owners, or even his family, at race time. He preferred to watch the race from high in the grandstand in the open bleachers. That way, he could walk along and view the horses as they raced on the track far below, and he didn't have to listen to the questions, opinions, and chatter of other onlookers around him. The former announcer knew exactly what was going on in any given race, but wanted to concentrate on the action.

A horizontal blur of dark horses streaked down the track. Beach had no trouble finding his full pounding stride this time; he was able to hold off both the fastest two-year-old colt of 2007, Dali, and the talented Shadow Play. Into the home stretch they came, and out came the earplugs. Paul leaned back in the sulky: *Time to go, my friend.* Beach soared ahead of the field and won by three and a half lengths, in 1:52.1.

Dali came in second and Shadow Play, third.

In the bleachers, a racegoer had watched in surprise as a tall fellow near him hollered and danced in place.

"You must have had him bet," he laughed.

"No," said MacGrath, "I own him."

"Really? Can I get a photo with you and The Beach?"

"Sure!" And off the two men ran down the steps, onto the track, and into to the winner's circle.

It was starting to look like it was going to be a bad year for any pacer of distinction if Somebeachsomewhere took to the same track.

Not everyone in the grandstand expected to see Somebeachsomewhere in the winner's circle that day; in fact, a good number didn't. But, as the expression goes, "anything can happen in a horse race," and upsets are often the norm.

Some claim that the term "upset" joined the American sports lexicon in 1919, when a horse named Upset beat the mighty Thoroughbred racehorse Man o'War at the Saratoga Race Course in New York. It was the only race that Man o'War, also known as "Big Red," would lose in a career of twenty-one starts and twenty wins. And yes indeed, Samuel D. Riddle, Big Red's owner, was upset, as was the red colt's legion of fans.

And why did Man o'War lose that day, after six previous wins?

He had made a bad start at the tape barrier (no starting gates in those days), and lost a lot of time. He was also "handicapped" by weight in order to bring up the odds for the other horses, carrying fifteen pounds more than the favourite, Upset.

Those are the most probable reasons.

But mostly, as any horse person will tell you, Man o'War lost because horses aren't machines; they have good days and bad, just like humans do. And finally, ask any athlete: the factors that go into a win are numerous and complex.

All the members of Schooner Stables knew was that their wonder boy had had a good day, and had "done it" again. Now they had a week to prepare Beach for his next race, the final of the Metro Pace. If he came first, he would capture a cool $500,000—half of the $1 million purse.

Beach may have slept well over the next several days—he was apparently a deep and contented sleeper—but it's a good guess that his humans did not.

The MacGraths were still travelling from Truro to attend Beach's races. Brent still had to log hours at the Chevrolet dealership; he was the general manager, after all. "We'd fly up to Ontario from Nova Scotia on a Wednesday," says Rhonda, of the two-hour flight between the provinces. "Then Brent would train him on Thursday at Jean Louis's barn, where he was stabled. Jean Louis would jog him on the days we weren't there. Then Beach would race on Saturday nights, then we'd go home again."

The airborne hours were definitely adding up. And again, "that was okay," if exhausting, for Brent in this time of change and excitement. A bit of travel be damned. What was going to happen next was the more important question. MacGrath would have been happiest, it seemed to most, if he could have been glued to his horse's side.

There's a telling story about Jean Louis Arsenault in the September 13, 2007, issue of the *Canadian Sportsman*. Long-time editor and sportswriter Dave Briggs describes Arsenault's jittery state before the Metro Pace final, which was set for September 1, 2007. As horsemen do, he was feeling superstitious in the hours before the race. Some superstitious people will not turn over a calendar month before sundown on the last day of the month. In Arsenault's case, he wanted the calendar to stay on August even after the month had passed.

"I said, 'Leave it on August. You can mark a *32nd* in the next box, but don't change it.' The month was just so great," Arsenault said. In June and July he'd had no luck at all, but, he told Briggs, "The last four, five weeks have been unbelievable." Arsenault had won the prestigious Gold Cup and Saucer in Charlottetown, Prince Edward Island, on August 18 with Silent Swing (co-owned by Reg Petitpas). He had also co-trained, with Brent MacGrath, the horse that took the Battle of Waterloo elimination and final—Somebeachsomewhere. He was not going to jinx that same horse, the one that *everyone* was now talking about. Not on his watch, *M'sieur. Et alors, touche-pas le calendrier!*

And so the calendar stayed on August—and at last, it was time to gather in the grandstand for the final of the Metro Pace.

Moon Beam, Santanna Blue Chip, Deuce Seelster, Dali, Shadow Play, Weekend Gambler, Lonestar Legend, Its That Time, Alard Hanover, and Beach made ten for the field.

Beach was in the four-hole.

It was another powerful "purple" assembly, with every horse keen for, and capable of, the win. Of particular concern to Schooner Stables were the flashy and lethally fast Santanna Blue Chip, in lucky post position one; the fleet Deuce Seelster, who drew post position two; the outstanding Moon Beam, in post position three; the hurricane-force Dali, in post seven; and the serious speedster Shadow Play on his right, in eight.

"Ten on the gate and here they come, they're off and pacing!" cried the announcer. Several seconds of jockeying and stabilizing went on before he spoke again.

"And into the first turn, it's MacDonell who fires off the wings of the gate, setting Somebeachsomewhere off to the lead."

To look at MacDonell's move to the rail on video, it seems like a simple bit of steering, right to left. It's more of a float than a pass. The rising speed, however, is evident.

"At the first quarter it's 26.3!"

The floating had stopped, and the powering had commenced. The announcer's voice was getting tight, his words spilling faster.

"So up the backstretch MacDonell's got them all in the palm of his hand as Somebeachsomewhere fires to the front! Somebeachsomewhere is leading by two lengths."

At the half mark the number came in at 54.2 seconds. Shortly thereafter, "MacDonell is stepping on the accelerator!" By this time the announcer's voice was electric.

"At the three-quarters and it's 1:21.4! *Unbelievable*! And it's Somebeachsomewhere putting up *some kind of fractions*!"

A heartbeat later, it seemed, and they sailed over the finish line.

"Somebeachsomewhere and Big Mac scoop up to the big bucks to win the Metro Pace!"

Dayenu, as the Passover song says: It would have been enough. It would have been more than enough, more than anyone could ever have expected from the young colt with only three stakes races to his credit. The young colt who, when he wasn't racing, liked to have a hanging ball in his stall to play with, and who seemed to love carrots as much as he loved his people. *Dayenu*.

But it was not enough for Beach, who decided he may as well put a thick layer of icing on the sumptuous cake.

"It's a *world record performance* in the final of the Metro Pace! Somebeachsomewhere has done it in 1:49.3!"

Beach had set a new global standard for two-year-olds.

Eardrums must have popped that Saturday evening. The crowd was hollering to the skies, and on their feet clapping as though they'd all won the race themselves—which, in a way, they had, by being there, by witnessing greatness in all the contenders, by calling out the victor's name—*Somebeach, Somebeach*—over and over again.

That night, Garry Pye, Jamie Bagnell, and Stu Rath of Truro, and Reg Petitpas of Shediac Bridge, New Brunswick, sat in the clubhouse at the Mohawk Raceway and watched open-mouthed as their horse won the richest race for two-year-olds in Canada.

In the process, they, along with the sixth member of the syndicate, Pam Dean, became the first Maritime horse-owners to ever win a $1 million race.

In his four lifetime starts, Beach had already won $682,000. And he was yet to race in an Ontario Sires Stakes (OSS) program.

What was Schooner Stables going to do next?

Start planning for Beach's future, said MacGrath. *That's what we were going to do.*

And what do you suppose the headline in that September 2007 issue of *Canadian Sportsman* said?

"MARITIME METRO MONSTER."

"I never really liked that," says Brent. "I know why they used that word and that phrase, but he wasn't a monster; that wasn't him at all."

What was he?

"A horse of a lifetime. Beach was a horse of a lifetime."

Chapter 8

A BUGLING BABY BOY

THERE IS SOMETHING IRRESISTIBLE ABOUT STEPHANIE SMITH-Rothaug's smile, which shares the same sunniness and softness as her voice and manner. This horsewoman, originally from Saint Louisville, Ohio, sees the good in life, no matter how many personal challenges come along—and there have been a number of those.

Smith-Rothaug is the owner of Rails Edge Farm in West Jefferson, Ohio, and breeds Standardbred trotters and pacers. She bred one pacer, in particular, that people still talk about.

Somebeachsomewhere.

Currently, Smith-Rothaug has twenty-four horses at her farm: fifteen broodmares, one filly, eight yearlings, and one retired mare. Some of the horses are Beach's "relatives."

"I have an older mare whose name is Remis Rocket. She would be the half-sister to Wheres The Beach [Beach's dam]," she says. "She is pregnant and going to have a baby for me this year. But that's probably as close in blood to Beach as you can get here now. Then I also have…three daughters by Somebeachsomewhere. That lineage is going to carry on that way on the broodmare side."

Beach's half-sister, says Smith-Rothaug, is "an older gal."

"When Somebeach really started to make his claim to fame, a lady from out west called me and said, 'I've got a half-sister to your mare, would you like to own her?' and I said absolutely. I love this mama, so I bought Remis sight unseen." She pauses. "It's good, because I lost Wheres The Beach, so I still have some of that special family."

Wheres The Beach passed away June 13, 2014. Her name, too, will linger on in the Standardbred racing world. Smith-Rothaug says she calls the mare "Beach," too, because, after all, she came first.

"Wheres The Beach was about sixteen when she passed," says Smith-Rothaug. "I thought she had a lot more years, but…"

Smith-Rothaug bought Wheres The Beach when she was in foal. "She had two previous foals for Tara Hills up in Ontario," she says. "Those foals weren't quite to racing age, and they sent Wheres The Beach through the Harrisburg auction. She was in foal to a stallion called Astreos. He was a very good horse. Wheres The Beach had that foal and I sold him at Lexington. He was just grand, a stellar individual. He sold really well. Then the following year, again with Astreos as the sire, Wheres The Beach gave birth to another colt. His name was Stars On The Water. Then, after him, was Somebeach, who was sired by Mach Three."

Stars On The Water, Somebeachsomewhere—someone likes country and western music.

"I love music," Smith-Rothaug admits. She always plays music while she's working in the barn, and believes the horses enjoy it, too.

The full story of Wheres The Beach's arrival in Smith-Rothaug's life is a fateful one.

"Wheres The Beach was for sale because she wasn't a good fit for Tara Hills's breeding program, so they put her through the auction," Smith-Rothaug explains. "I was at Harrisburg working with my sister, Senena [Esty]. *For* my sister, actually. Her farm was Spring Haven Farm. We were at the end of the yearling session and we were out there to witness that. Then it turned into a mixed session after the yearlings were all sold, so we had a lot of horses to get ready…and there was Wheres The Beach. She was a beautiful picture, but she was in my sister's consignment to sell.

"I felt conflicted. How can I want to buy this horse if we're selling this horse? [I was] supposed to be working, not buying horses.... So I just didn't do anything."

Smith-Rothaug is enjoying this story.

"I was standing beside Ernie Martinez," she says. "He's an agent for a lot of people, and he was standing by [Peter] Heffering, who owned Tara Hills. We were watching, and I said, 'I like this mare here,' as we're comparing the catalogues. I think the mare's name was Movie Star Legs. Then I said, 'I [really] like Wheres The Beach, but she's in our consignment.'

"Ernie said, 'If you want her, go after her,' and I said, 'No, that would be a conflict.' He said, 'Well, she's a much better mare than Movie Star Legs. Just march over and ask that guy right there then, he'll tell you if it's a conflict.' So I went over and I told Mr. Heffering who I was, and I said, 'Would you object to me bidding on one of your mares?' and he said, 'Well, that's what she's here for.'

"That's how it came to be. I didn't have a whole lot of money. I was newly engaged and that money was supposed to be going to the big wedding that I was hoping for. Instead, it went to buying Wheres The Beach."

Said no horsewoman ever.

There are strange and resonant parallels between her story and MacGrath's: when Smith-Rothaug saw Wheres The Beach for the first time, she was smitten; when MacGrath saw Somebeachsomewhere for the first time, he, too, was smitten. MacGrath had only just decided he was going to buy a colt at the Lexington Select, and many strange and wonderful factors came together to make the purchase of the exact horse he wanted possible. With Smith-Rothaug, she was working the day destiny knocked; she wasn't supposed to be thinking about buying a horse, and she was supposed to be saving funds for a big wedding.

And yet she saw Wheres The Beach and was pulled to the elegant mare as if by magnetism. At the centre of both experiences was the abundant charisma of both Wheres The Beach and her colt Somebeachsomewhere.

"Wheres The Beach had a presence about her," says Smith-Rothaug. "She was kind. I didn't know that about her when I first met her, but she was big and strong [and] had a kindness about her. [Some mares]…go at the bars of the stalls. They gnash their teeth, or they lay back their ears. Wheres The Beach was easygoing about everything."

Life carried on. Eventually, after the successful arrival of Stars On The Water, Smith-Rothaug began wondering about whom to breed Wheres The Beach to next. She was interested in Mach Three, but considering the upcoming wedding, and the fact that she was in the process of buying a farm with her fiancé, she was reluctant to pay the $7,500 stud fee.

"When I bought the mare out at Harrisburg, I had asked Mr. Heffering, 'If by chance I get her, could I get back in to one of your stallions, preferably Mach Three?' He said, 'Yes, absolutely.'" As the breeding season drew closer, Mach Three's book was getting full. Ernie Martinez, who was agenting for Heffering, pulled some strings. "He called it a wedding gift to me from Mr. Heffering."

The fuller story, as Martinez told *Harness Link* at the time, was that Martinez had a Mach Three promotional breeding, given to him by horseman Joe Muscara and agent John Curtin, for work he had done. Martinez then generously gave his gift to Stephanie. Everyone was pleased with the outcome.

Of course. It is another enchanting detail in an enchanting tale. The breeding that Smith-Rothaug wanted for her beautiful mare, Wheres The Beach, but couldn't afford, was generously arranged for, and gifted to her on the occasion of her wedding.

It simply came to be because Somebeachsomewhere also needed to come to be—needed to be born from that sire and that dam at that time to that breeder. The pixies waved their dust in the air…and along came a colt that would change the course of Standardbred pacing history.

Considering Smith-Rothaug's strong tie to Wheres The Beach, and her delight in the robust and energetic colt named Somebeachsomewhere, it must have been hard to contemplate handing over the youngster's lead shank to a stranger at the Lexington Select auction. MacGrath, however, made that transition far easier than expected.

"Back then," says Smith-Rothaug, "it was not common for people to be so excited after a purchase. Maybe the owners that are buying my horses now are a little bit more like that. But then, it was just unheard of. We had sold horses for years and years, and people wouldn't hightail it back to the barn. You know, they might have a few drinks up at the auction block with everyone else."

And here was Brent, who actually beat her back to Beach's stall, he ran so fast from the arena to the barn.

"Brent wanted to know what the horse ate, what kind of hay I fed, what his program was at home. It was exciting for me, because you work for well over a year getting this product grown and you hate to see him go to people who [are blasé]. There were times when the owners wouldn't even come back to the barn to see what they bought; they'd just leave it to the trainers…. It was exciting that somebody, hopefully, cared as much as I did."

Smith-Rothaug, who does not have children, has long said that the foals are her "babies." This makes saying goodbye difficult.

"It's terrible," says Smith-Rothaug. "It's very hard to do, but if it's a good group, or if it's a good person and you get that vibe that they're going to care, it's easier…. I knew that Beach was going to be okay."

Still, Smith-Rothaug cried every time she saw Beach race.

"It was pride," she says. "I know you're not supposed to be proud and boastful, but just knowing you created that; that was your baby—and look at him! It's just like a parent going to watch their kid at a football game or a track meet and your kid's blowing everybody's doors off."

Stephanie bought Wheres The Beach in 2003. In 2004, Stephanie and her fiancé, Paul Rothaug, were married. Then in 2005, along came Somebeachsomewhere. That same year, Paul, a veterinarian, was diagnosed with melanoma.

"At the time, my husband was going through a cancer treatment," says Smith-Rothaug. "I think that's why the tears came more easily; it was the pride of raising that horse, but also what we were going through. That was a little bit of a reprieve from the cancer."

A gentle, humour-filled pause comes down the telephone line from rural Ohio to rural Nova Scotia. "On the other hand, there are horses that race now that…only win in 1:58, but…I still cry. Maybe I'm just that kind of person."

A horse person, you mean? A person who loves the beauty of a powerful, well-trained horse doing the best they can do, at whatever they've been asked to do, bred to do, and knowing that with luck, behind each one of those horses there is a caring human who helped them into the world—and who, one day, may also help them to slip away from the world?

At the North America Cup, June 14, 2008, Paul Rothaug and Stephanie were there in person at Mohawk Raceway to see Beach come away with his share of the $1.5 million purse. "Beach walked out on the track and it was almost like he took a bow. People said he did! There was so much hype, there was so much excitement over him, and it was the first time that I saw him after he'd won a race."

And what she saw was the foal she'd raised.

"I used to call him 'Bull' when he was a baby, because he was big and he'd just come right up to you and almost run over you like a bulldozer. When I saw him, I said, 'Bull,' and he knew me. He put his head right on my chest like he always used to, and we breathed for a minute—and then he took his head and shoved me, just like he used to."

Smith-Rothaug has firm opinions on the matter of animals and memory.

"People say that animals don't know one person from another, or they don't remember individuals, but I have to disagree with that 100 percent. He knew who I was, and it was an amazing thing. He was such a special horse. He impressed you every time you saw him. He never let you down."

Smith-Rothaug has some ideas about what made Beach so special.

"The night he was born I was camped out in the barn. That was before my days of having a foal alert where you could actually go in and eat a meal and not have to just live with the horse," she recalls. "I delivered him, and it was a quiet, beautiful night, about ten o'clock. As soon as I pulled him out and laid him beside his mother he let out the biggest whinny I've heard a baby do." A bugling baby boy.

Stephanie Smith-Rothaug at the Harrisburg Yearling Sale, November 2019. (AUTHOR PHOTO)

She lay down with the two of them as the mare cleaned her foal. "He actually got up before mama, as though he [was saying], 'Okay, lady, it's time go,' and he started to nurse. He was tall and he was so correct as a little fella. Some of them are all gangly legs," she says.

"Not Beach. He was up on all corners. He was bright and alert and there was something about his coat. It was fabulous all the time. I don't know how to explain it, but some of them come out and they're woolly. He came out and even though he was just a wet little baby, he just was perfect."

She says the growing horse was inquisitive about everything. "He was raised with other colts, but it seemed like he was growing, like, double what the other kids were growing. He was always the first one in the feed. I set him out in the field and he was always the first one up there; he was always the one initiating the exercising. As a specimen, he was always muscular.

"A lot of the farms put their horses on wheels and exercisers. He was just grown naturally, with free choice exercise. They were turned out all the time. The only time we'd bring them in was at sales-prep time, to get them out of the hot sun. Then they're turned out at night so that they can kick and play and do whatever they want to do." And the "bumping" stories had nothing to do with aggression.

"He wanted you to know he was there," says Smith-Rothaug. "Sometimes in a group of colts there's one that chases the others. You know—one that has his ears laid back and goes after them. What Beach would do is, he'd sneak up on his buddies and he'd bite one or nudge one and then he'd take off. He was just like, 'Okay, it's time to exercise,' so he'd bite them and then he'd go as hard as he could in front of them. He'd never want to be the one chasing them."

She later saw this quality in him when she watched him race. "He always wanted to be in front. You were asking about when they race and why I cry. I guess, partly, [it was] because I would see him as a little guy doing the same thing. He'd be clear out in front of everybody just scatting along, and then I'd think, 'I remember him like that as a little kid.'"

Stephanie Smith-Rothaug is a woman of faith.

"I don't know if this sounds corny," she says, "but I think God gives you what you need in your life at that time, and he gave me and my family that horse…. My brother was diagnosed with cancer about the same time as my husband was, in 2008. My brother and my father were full-time farmers, and I bought all my hay from them. So their hay fed Beach. If I needed someone to feed for me, my family was there.

"That [horse] was our joy through all that. I think that you're given that bright light at that moment, and he just carried us through, and he still does, every day."

She would ultimately lose both her husband and her brother to cancer.

"Beach gave us so much. As I said, I think the good Lord just gives you that when you need it. Every day I'm grateful to have known a horse like that—to have been there at the start of his life, anyway."

Stephanie Smith-Rothaug loves long, and well.

"You know the day you first called me? I think it was the day Beach passed away," she says. "I didn't know if I could even talk to you about him then. I think he passed on January 14th, wasn't it?"

It was indeed January 14, 2018, when Beach died—and he had turned thirteen only days before, on January 1.

"Yeah…I thought maybe that's why you were calling. I didn't know if I had it in me to talk about him that day."

Today, though, Smith-Rothaug wants to talk about Beach—two Beaches, in fact.

As a lifelong horsewoman and widely respected breeder from a family of horse people and breeders, Smith-Rothaug has had many horses come and go from her life. But as horse people know well, there are some that are known as "heart" horses. Their memories are particularly cherished.

"I hope that I can love two horses like I loved those two," says Smith-Rothaug, of Beach's dam, and Beach himself. "I thought I was going to die when I lost her."

In a lifetime of horses, why was it so hard to lose this one mare?

In the hours shortly after her husband died, Smith-Rothaug took herself out to the barn. She wanted to check on Wheres The Beach, who was in foal.

"I don't think she was really close to foaling," she says; she just wanted to see how she was doing. The top half of the mare's stall door was open and latched back and she had her head sticking out.

"She was the first one I saw that morning. I went over to her stall and—you know how I told you her son Beach put his head in my chest?" *Yes.*

"She put her head on my chest and she did not move for, I'd say, five minutes. That mare grieved with me. She didn't move. It was almost like she didn't even want to breathe; she knew that, in my heart, I was so sad. And Beach was like her in that way. I had her for all those years."

Beloved person or cherished horse, there are never quite enough years. *And oh, those heart horses, they are rare, and greatly missed.*

"But you know what? If I don't have another one, what a blessing to have grown a baby like him, and what a blessing to have a mare like her in our life."

It seems an obvious moment to say that Beach came into everybody's life and made it better.

"Absolutely," says Smith-Rothaug. "And so did his mama."

Chapter 9

PERFECT SIX FOR SIX

IT WAS AFTER BEACH'S WIN AT THE METRO FINAL ON SEPTEMBER 1, 2007, that the "Beach Parties" started up. These were the brainchild of Ashley Tibbitts, a parimutuel clerk at the Truro Raceway, who promoted the Beach Parties at the racetrack when simulcasts of Beach's races were programmed. The parties quickly spread to other Canadian tracks (and in time, to American ones), and in short order, at tracks large and small, hundreds of fans were gathering to watch the big-boned colt's races. To attend the parties, all you needed was a love of harness racing, a love for "The Beach," and a strong pair of lungs to cheer him on. Beachwear optional, of course. Everyone in Canada was thrilled that "the colt to watch" was theirs.

On September 8, 2007, Beach was ready for his fifth career race, which was also his second Grand Circuit race: the Champlain Stakes, at Woodbine Mohawk Park. The purse was $115,884.

Alongside Beach would be some wicked competition: Santanna Blue Chip, Upfront Hannahsboy, Todd J H Hanover, Weekend Gambler, The Mohegan Pan, Reconciliation, Allamerican Fargo, and Bandolero.

Lady Luck smiled on Beach, giving him post position one. MacDonell settled his fingers on the reins one last time, adjusting his seat-bones in the sulky seat and his feet in the horizontal stirrups. Forget the noise from the crowd, forget the ricocheting, splintered energies of eight other drivers, all envisioning themselves first over the line. All MacDonell needed to think was, *Am I driving the fastest colt here today? Yes, yes I am...*

The language of the race announcers is pure sports poetry. Lean in for the Champlain Stakes, 2007, because this is how it played out:

> "*And they're off!* From the outside, Weekend Gambler and Santanna Blue Chip both flash early speed. Coming down the centre now is Upfront Hannahsboy and away at the rail in fourth is Somebeachsomewhere. Dropped into fifth as we move to the quarter pole station is Todd J H Hanover, then it's back to Reconciliation. The final three in the field are the long shots, Allamerican Fargo, The Mohegan Pan, and Bandolero trails.
>
> "...Into the first turn and at the opening quarter-station, which pops up in 26.3, it's David Miller on the lead with Upfront Hannahsboy. Pocket-riding from second there is Weekend Gambler. In at the rail third is Santanna Blue Chip. Up and driving fourth now is Somebeachsomewhere as MacDonell summons up speed from the son of Mach Three, who went from fourth to first in about a 1/16th of a mile.
>
> "And on the outside now here comes Somebeach-somewhere to clear off the top! Back into second now rides along Upfront Hannahsboy and sitting at the rail from in third is Weekend Gambler, fourth inside Santanna Blue Chip. The half was 56 seconds. In at the rail fifth is Todd J H Hanover. The first to move from the backfield is Reconciliation; riding his cover is The Mohegan Pan. Locked up at the rail is Allamerican Fargo and the trailer tipped out is Bandolero....
>
> "There goes Weekend Gambler to go after Somebeachsomewhere! MacDonell again with that second-quarter speed of 29.2. He'll pick up the tempo in this third

Beach's fifth career race: the Champlain Stakes at Woodbine Mohawk Park, September 8, 2007. (CLIVE COHEN)

station with Somebeachsomewhere. He rolls him over there in a 1:25 at the three-quarters.

"They're off the turn and into the stretch and the one to chase down is Somebeachsomewhere, *the fastest freshman the sport of harness racing has ever seen!* Somebeachsomewhere kicks away by two lengths now. Back in second towards the inside is Upfront Hannahsboy. Jamieson launches a late attack on the outside with Santanna Blue Chip, but it is Somebeachsomewhere, to win again, by four lengths—a perfect five for five and 26 seconds on the end of it! He's home in 1:51! And that…is a Champlain Stakes *record*!"

Another win, another record—and the principals of Schooner Stables were yelling loud enough to be heard from their homes two and three provinces away.

Beach on the way to a win at the Nassagaweya Stakes, September 15, 2007, at Woodbine Mohawk Park. (CLIVE COHEN)

Next up, the Nassagaweya Stakes, held on September 15, 2007, again at Woodbine Mohawk. Against three known competitors—Deuce Seelster, Santanna Blue Chip, and Weekend Gambler—and some new ones—Roman Rocks, Mcapulco, Go West Young Cam, Brimsheen, Allamerican Dice—Beach was competing for the $145,300 purse.

They were, said the announcer, "a fine group of freshman pacers."

Beach took the lead from the quarter-pole on, had a three-length lead nearing the half-pole—and kept that lead to the end. In that home stretch the announcer had his eyes pinned on pacer number five.

"*And it's all Somebeachsomewhere!* Coming to the 7/8th mile marker, it's Somebeachsomewhere and Paul MacDonell! The beat goes on for the pacing son of Mach Three who's going to stride away and win the Nassagaweya Stakes, a *perfect six for six* to start his career and he's home in 1:51and 4/5."

As it turned out, Somebeachsomewhere was not eligible to race the Breeders Crown or Governor's Cup. The Breeders Crown, which wouldn't take place until mid-November 2007, a full two months after the Nassagaweya Stakes, was an expensive race in which to stay eligible to run, although for a modest fee, MacGrath did keep Beach eligible to run it as a three-year-old, should they decide to do that. The Governor's Cup came even later in November, which was really stretching out the year for a two-year-old colt who'd run a perfect six-for-six with some world and track records thrown in for good measure.

Brent further explains his reasoning at the time. "I could keep him eligible as a three-year old for one $300 payment as a two-year-old. If I wanted to race him as a two-year-old it would have cost about $10,000 to stay eligible. The race was late in the year and at the Meadowlands, which has a long season and was a long truck ride away."

Also, Beach's white blood cell count had been elevated to one small degree or another since before the Metro Pace. He'd been given some small doses of antibiotics for the unidentified infection, which was possibly respiratory in nature, before and after his races. But when MacGrath "pulled blood" on Beach after Nassagaweya, the white blood count was still elevated. It was time for a larger dose of antibiotics—and a close to the season.

It was also time for the colt and the MacGraths to go home to Nova Scotia, where Beach could enjoy "a well-deserved rest," says MacGrath.

"At that point, it was far more important for us to start thinking ahead and prepping Beach for his third year racing," he says. "But before that, we wanted him to rest up physically, mentally, and emotionally."

But Beach, being trucked home to Nova Scotia by Jean Louis Arsenault, barely stopped in Truro. "That very first day that he got home, we took him right to Tony's in Pictou," says Rhonda. Once settled at

Pictonian Farms, Beach grazed in the still–summer-lush fields to his heart's content.

For the MacGraths, the conclusion of the racing year meant a return to their home in Bible Hill—and many family conversations around their kitchen table. Somehow, someway, Somebeachsomewhere had entered their lives and turned them wildly, happily, irrevocably upside down. Decisions needed to be made about Beach's future, and about their future as a family with Beach in it.

How, for example, would they actually live their day-to-day lives, meeting their regular commitments, while providing top care for this abundantly talented but still-developing horse? And what about the details of Beach's three-year-old campaign? Exactly how ambitious should they be for him? Should they maybe even aim for the Pepsi North America Cup—the richest harness race in Canada?

They also had to consider the most common question posed to MacGrath, as the spokesman of Schooner Stables, right about then.

Is Beach for sale?

"No, he's not for sale," MacGrath would answer again and again.

There had, however, been some talk of selling Beach after his dizzying win at the Metro. Greg Blanchard reported in the October 2007 issue of *TROT Magazine* that Schooner Stables "had talked to several farms," thinking they could perhaps sell part of Beach, or as Brent MacGrath had put it, "at least his stud career, and we'd manage his racing career."

But, MacGrath had added, "The more I talked to people, the more I could see it was not going to work. I could see that any potential buyers would want to have a hand in the racing side of it, and we didn't want to give up control of that."

With just a wee bit of an edge, and a wee bit of pride, MacGrath closed the subject of the syndicate selling Beach.

"I really think the industry thought we would probably sell him to one of the big owners and the big trainer would get him," he told Blanchard. "This is one for the little guy, and I think it gives some of the horsemen who haven't had a good or great horse hope that there is a shot out there."

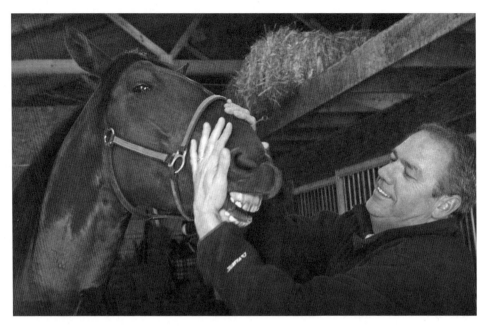

Brent and Beach had a special bond, which is clearly seeen here as they kid around in March 2008. (ANN MACNEILL)

And of course, MacGrath being MacGrath, he put Beach first in any equation. The rest of Schooner Stables backed him unreservedly.

"He is a colt that has never been hurt, never been sick, or never been stressed," MacGrath was quoted as saying. "So, if he stays healthy, he should make a heck of three-year-old." That was the hope, and a reasonable expectation.

But a number of human lives would need to change course for at least a year for the good tidings to keep coming in. And, of course, Beach would have to do what he had to do, as only that horse could.

Accordingly, six weeks after Beach had come home again to Pictou, Nova Scotia, MacGrath brought him back to the modest stables at the Truro Raceway.

But Beach's stall had been...upgraded.

"Of course he's 'Beach' now, so we had to build a new stall," says Rhonda. "Brent ripped out two stalls and built one and put on a locking gate, and we just kind of fancied it up a little bit for him."

The two friends, Beach and Brent, were together again for daily companionship and training. In many ways, things were the same as they had been the previous winter. Brent MacGrath was "hands on" again, in the barn and on the track, doing what everyone knew he loved best in the world: jogging a young horse, "putting the watch on him," and dreaming dreams of *what if, why not, and hell yes.*

But things were different, too. In particular, MacGrath was also readying himself to take a leave of absence from the car dealership for a year, which he was doing with boss Garry Pye's blessing. The reason for the leave of absence was simple: MacGrath was determined to become Beach's full-time trainer.

"Starting out, we didn't know what we had," says MacGrath. "We didn't realize we had a world champion. We thought we had a nice horse, but he had never been in a race when he left to go to Ontario. Well, we knew very shortly after his first race—once we got him on the big track up there—that we could have something special. Think about it—the first time he saw the starting gate he set a Canadian season record at Grand River." MacGrath says he received a call before he was even out of the winner's circle with someone offering $750,000 to buy Beach.

Beach went on to set a world record for earnings as a two-year-old, making $900,000 for the year. He was voted 2007 Two-Year-Old Pacing Colt of the Year in the US—and he had never even had a race in the US. Beach also tied for 2007 Horse of the Year in Canada.

That's when MacGrath decided to step in as trainer.

Jean Louis Arsenault had been the trainer of record for Beach's freshman year, but MacGrath had been flying back and forth from Nova Scotia to Ontario for every training session, and says he was very involved in the decision-making.

The Grand Circuit

Started in 1871, the Grand Circuit, also called "the Big Wheel," is a group of harness racing stakes races that take place in the US. The races are run on one-mile, half-mile, and seven-eighths–mile tracks.

The OSS

According to oss.ontarioracing.com, the objective of the OSS program is to improve the breed and provide viable incentives for breeders, owners, and trainers to breed, buy, and race horses in Ontario. The program has evolved into the leading sires stakes program in North America.

MacGrath spoke on the record about Arsenault in the March 2008 issue of the *Harness Edge*. "Believe me, this is no reflection on Jean Louis. He did a great job for us and if something was to happen that I could not train him, then the horse would go back to him. No ifs, ands, or buts about it, he did a great job. He did everything we asked him to do and went above and beyond the call of duty."

As a group, Schooner Stables ultimately decided to give Jean Louis a percentage of Beach's three-year-old earnings for looking after Beach on race day.

"He's a horseman," says MacGrath, of Arsenault—that wide, ringing phrase that covers so much territory but certainly implies that he would understand how the owners might feel about the improbability of having a superstar horse. "He understood how things had changed and why I chose to train Beach."

"Jean Louis was very gracious," adds Rhonda, "and he would have done the same thing had Beach been his horse. The idea had been that if

Paul MacDonell takes Beach for a jog at the Truro Raceway in March 2008.
(ANN MACNEILL).

Beach had been an Ontario Sires Stakes horse, then he probably would have raced right up until the end of November and he would have been with Jean Louis as the trainer, but that's not how it went. Beach went into the Grand Circuit and then came home. Jean Louis stayed on as his caretaker and the person who would paddock Beach on race days. Jean Louis was very good at details and he was very good to Beach. He's a nice guy and we got along great with him."

Nonetheless, not all horse people did agree with the decision, as was noted in magazines of the time. As enthusiastic as MacGrath was, as knowledgeable as he was about the harness racing industry, he could still not be called a full-time, successful trainer. His years at Greenwood, working mostly with claimers had taught him a lot, though ultimately, he'd had to work as a car salesman to get himself and Rhonda out of their horse-related debt.

At Truro, too, he'd enjoyed being a trainer of young pacers, but none had gone on to bring him fame or fortune. *Was he really up for the job?* many trainers and owners may have thought when they heard the news that MacGrath would be Beach's trainer for his third-year campaign.

Even Schooner Stables member Reg Petitpas fiercely disagreed with MacGrath on this issue, stating that MacGrath had "broken his word" to Arsenault, who Petitpas thought should resume training duties for Beach's second year of racing.

MacGrath, however, was immovable. That same horseman who had somehow known from the first glance that Beach could be "a contender" was determined to care for, condition, train, and develop Somebeachsomewhere—and for as long as possible, on Maritime turf. Brent MacGrath would watch and safeguard Beach's every step, believing the shining rocket of a pacer might even become one of the most famous Standardbred stallions of all time.

There was no point in standing in MacGrath's way. He'd been dreaming on a horse like this all his life.

Chapter 10
LOOKING TO MAKE HISTORY

MACGRATH WAS FOND OF SAYING ABOUT BEACH, "HE LIKES TO win, and I like to talk about him winning," which made MacGrath laugh, made the press laugh, and made everyone else connected to Beach laugh. Truer words were rarely spoken.

By March 2008, MacGrath was on the cover of the *Harness Edge* magazine. The photo was a close-up of the beaming, blue-eyed car salesman from Truro, Nova Scotia; the headline read, "Brent MacGrath—Looking to Make History."

With only one racing season to his credit, Beach had already become the fastest two-year-old in history, was a double Canadian O'Brien Award Winner (Horse of the Year, 2007, tied with Tell All; and Two-Year-Old Pacing Colt of the Year). In the US, he had won the Dan Patch Award for Two-Year-Old Pacing Colt of the Year, and the Nova Award for the same. On top of all this, horse people around the world were still talking about his stunning performance at the million-dollar Metro Pace in September 2007.

In the March 2008 issue of the *Harness Edge*, publisher Harold Howe interviewed Brent MacGrath. Howe asked MacGrath if Beach could dominate his class and "possibly even go undefeated."

To which MacGrath replied, "I am extremely confident about that prospect."

Both men knew they were talking about the possibility of Beach making harness racing history. How did MacGrath feel about that?

The answer was vintage MacGrath: "I don't feel any pressure at all or think about it. Every day I go out on the track with him he feels totally awesome. I don't sit there crossing my fingers that he comes back. I'm confident that he's going to come back well. I have no trouble sleeping at night.... If it's meant to be, it will be."

Beach was the first horse of such weighty prospects to call the East Coast of Canada home, which was sweeter than sweet to the men and women of Schooner Stables, and to the rest of the harness racing community in Canada.

So when Brent MacGrath and Garry Pye trucked Beach back to Baycairn Training Centre in Campbellville, Ontario, in mid-April 2008, the two men were likely talking about the possibility of more wins for their young superstar horse.

Once again Beach had been conditioned by MacGrath through that spring (as soon as the winter snow was gone and the track was clear of ice) at Truro Raceway. Magazine photos of the time show MacGrath helmeted and dressed in puffy winter coveralls, sitting in a blue sulky, Beach practically airborne above the track at Truro, and the centre field on their left still piled high with hard-compacted, dirty snow. The sun is shining, but the landscape does not look warm. Beach has a "mud-tail," the long hairs folded under and then twisted around into a tidy looking bun of sorts, which is meant to keep the tail from getting dirty.

On that same Truro track, on March 31, 2008, MacGrath trained Beach in a time of 2:04, with a "back half" of 58 seconds and "a piece."

Not too shabby for early in the year.

Paul MacDonell was also eager to start work again with Beach, flying out to Nova Scotia early in March. When MacDonell trained Beach, it gave MacGrath the opportunity to keenly observe the colt during workout sessions; likewise, MacDonell could observe MacGrath in the cart when he drove Beach. Later, the two men would compare notes on Beach's overall fitness and his attitude toward work—to which he remained as committed as ever. They also consulted on the upcoming three-year-old campaign.

They weren't the only two people watching Beach at that track on those chilly days.

"At that point," says MacGrath, "there would have been a big crowd on hand."

That crowd included horse people from all over; racing fans; Truro residents who knew little about harness racing but a lot about a big bay who was putting them on the map; after-school kids with their mums or dads; young men and women thinking about careers as grooms or trainers or drivers; staff from the raceway; friends and colleagues of Schooner Stables; and, of course, photographers and journalists. Most braved the cold, lined up along the fence near the grandstand to watch Beach being jogged. Others only came out of the clubhouse or surrounding barns when they put Beach "on the clock," as the horse people love to say.

But at some point, everyone wanted to be close to Beach, and to engage "the two Macs," as the press was fond of calling the two friends, in conversation.

And of course, *What's the plan for this year?* was the biggest question everyone in the crowd wanted an answer to. That, they would learn, was still under discussion.

What's his first start going to be, Paul/Brent?

That, in fact, was going to be a qualifier, scheduled for May 5, 2008, at Woodbine Mohawk Park, in preparation for the Burlington Stakes, scheduled for May 31, also at Woodbine.

Brent MacGrath takes Somebeachsomewhere for a jog at the Baycairn Training Centre in Campbellville, Ontario, in spring 2008. (DAVE LANDRY)

Racing fans and the racing industry were pumped about Beach's appearance, but a number of American trainers weren't lining up to bet exclusively on Beach just yet, despite his extraordinary first year of racing. Among them were Americans Ed Lohmeyer, George Teague Jr., Blair Burgess, and Kelly O'Donnell, who still believed, "for the most part," that Beach deserved number one billing, but who also happened to have firm opinions on other gifted pacers to watch that year and beyond: Santanna Blue Chip, Roberts Rage, Duneside Perch, Moon Beam, Dali, Badlands Nitro, and Deuce Seelster—along with thirty or so others.

Undeniably, 2007 was an exciting year to have a two-year-old harness racer.

Beach—along with MacGrath and MacDonell—had his work cut out for him.

But the "variable" of MacGrath in the role of trainer and manager was causing some low mutterings in the harness racing ranks. The *Harness Edge*'s publisher, Harold Howe, in the magazine's March 2008 issue, was unapologetically direct on the subject. "There are plenty of armchair quarterbacks who will be very critical of your decision and will point to the fact that you've never managed a horse like this before, among other issues," he said to MacGrath.

And Brent MacGrath, who had never, by a long shot, had any coaching on how to deal with the media or how to nimbly answer a negative question by turning it into a positive—except by being a "half-full" kind of person by nature—didn't skip a beat.

"I did manage the horse last year and things worked out fine. At the end of the day, the horse will do the talking so I don't need to say much. I know the horse better than anyone, and I think if he stays healthy and happy things will turn out fine. If he doesn't, then it won't matter who is training him; it just wasn't meant to be. He's going to get whatever he needs, and I will keep my eye on everything. He has to stay healthy and we need to have some luck."

Howe pushed harder. "Those same people are probably critical of you stopping with the horse after just six starts. They say you left a lot of money on the table."

It's never a good idea to question a car salesman about numbers: they work them every day and they know how to quickly and accurately calculate a profit, so MacGrath responded with alacrity. "I guess that depends on your definition of 'a lot of money.' All that we left on the table was an Ontario Sires Stakes Gold, and possibly the OSS Super Final. We would have had to stretch him out nearly two months, as his last race was September 15, and the OSS Super Final was November 11."

MacGrath managed the entire and lengthy Q & A well; he was direct, articulate, and never got rattled.

As for Howe, a well-regarded and seasoned journalist, he was simply asking the questions to which everyone in the industry, and the wider world, wanted to hear the answers.

MacGrath and Pye left with Beach for Baycairn Training Centre on April 15, 2008. They made one stop en route, in Montreal. All three were grateful and happy to roll into Jean Louis Arsenault's establishment in Ontario on April 16. Beach, as always, was a champ about being trucked—and chomping at the bit, as the expression goes, to get back to work. They had nineteen days to train and prepare for the qualifying race on May 5, 2008. The plan was for Beach to have his 2008 debut in the Ontario Sires Stakes series on May 17.

It was a good plan, they thought—as horse people always do. After all, what could go wrong?

PART II

THE THREE-YEAR-OLD CAMPAIGN:

"The Glamour Boys"

Chapter 11

BEACH THE UNBEATEN

IN EARLY 2018, THE LONG AND STORIED ERA OF STANDARDBRED racing in Toronto came to an end. Harness racing in the city had begun nearly 150 years prior, on the fairgrounds at the Canadian National Exhibition. Then it moved to Thorncliffe Park Raceway, which closed in 1953. Toronto's Greenwood Raceway, inaugurated in 1874, also hosted harness racing from 1875 to 1894, and then again from 1954 to 1993. Later known as "Old Woodbine," Greenwood closed late in 1993.

From 1994 on, Standardbreds raced at "the new Woodbine," located near Toronto Pearson Airport. Woodbine had opened in 1956 and was Thoroughbred-only until harness racing joined it in 1994, again, with the closure of Greenwood. Woodbine is once again Thoroughbred racing only. It has three tracks of varying lengths and surfaces.

Year-round harness racing is conducted at Mohawk.

Back again to 2018, when many race people took it badly to see the twenty-five-year-old Standardbred track torn up at Woodbine, and a second grass course for Thoroughbreds put in its place.

Darn those gallopers, anyway.

But in fact, the fun was beginning anew for harness racing fans in the province, which saw Woodbine Entertainment move the action for harness racing to the rural community of Campbellville, Ontario. There, at the renovated Mohawk Park, re-christened Woodbine Mohawk Park, harness racing was exuberantly back in business.

Most horse people simply call the track "Mohawk." Historically, the track has been the summer location for harness racing since 1963. In 1994, Standardbreds were brought to Woodbine following the closing of Toronto's Greenwood Track in the city's east end.

In April 2018, Mohawk had a celebratory reopening after a $10 million renovation to the track's grandstand and paddock. On March 1, 2020, Mohawk had more exciting news, with the announcement of a $1 million dollar (USD) race for trotters to be held every September.

Now the "Mohawk Million" has a unique format. Nine slots are available for owners to purchase, at a cost of $110,000 each. But the purchase isn't static. No horse is named until near the race day, and the slots can be sold, traded, or leased. Some compare it to buying commodity futures. As the race is obviously for the well-heeled in the industry, others compare it to taking a chair at the poker table with your own kitty in hand.

Here's where it gets really interesting: a tenth slot is reserved for the winner of the William Wellwood Memorial, which runs two weeks earlier. This provides an opportunity for a horse racing person who is not as wealthy to take part in the race.

The idea comes from the Thoroughbred racing world, which offers the similarly structured Pegasus World Cup at Gulfstream Park in Hallandale Beach, Florida.

Bless those gallopers, anyway.

The Mohawk Million is a real boost to the harness racing industry in Canada, which vies for the gambling dollar among myriad competitors, including lotteries, slot machines, card tables, and "VLTs," or Video Lottery Terminals.

There's no way around it—to boost interest, attendance, and betting, the industry will always need superstars such as Somebeachsomewhere, too, or his trotting cousin—also huge in the first decade of the new millennium, Deweycheatumnhowe. (He was named after a comedic parody of the name of a fictional law firm; *Do we cheat 'em and how?* is the phonetic reading.) A gorgeous, big-boned trotter, Dewey's claim to fame came from being the first-ever undefeated horse to win the million-dollar Hambletonian, named after Hambletonian 10, one of the Standardbred breed's foundation sires.

But it's not 2018, and it's not 2020. It's a decade-plus earlier, May 5, 2008. And the subject at hand is the "Glamour Boys"—because that's what the top three-year-old harness horses are called. As two-year-olds, they've competed hard in that first, or "freshman," year of racing. Usually, they've won some and lost some, but all of them have learned a lot and will put the knowledge to good use in their second, or "sophomore," year of racing.

As well as feeling more confident, these three-year-old colts and fillies also look more mature and, well, glamorous. They've built up muscle, they're taller and heavier, they move with authority and power. Their coats, as always, shine like sun on the water.

In those three-year-old campaigns, the Glamour Boys will compete against one another at equally glamorous races: the Hambletonian at Meadowlands in New Jersey and the Kentucky Futurity in Lexington (both for trotters); the North America Cup at Mohawk in Campbellville, Ontario; the Meadowlands Pace; the Messenger Stakes at Yonkers Raceway in New York; the Cane Pace, held at that time at Freehold Raceway in New Jersey; and the Little Brown Jug at the Delaware County Fairgrounds racetrack in Delaware, Ohio. The races are all for pacers; the last three comprise the Triple Crown of Harness Racing for Pacers.

And if your name was Somebeachsomewhere, and you were six for six unbeaten in 2007, your freshman year, and now, it's 2008, your sophomore year...

The focus on Beach at the start of his third-year campaign was unceasing. Magazines, newspapers, television, radio, and the internet all hummed with Beach stories and speculation about the year ahead. *Was he really that good? Was he Niatross reincarnated? And who in blazes was this Schooner Stables—had anybody heard of it? What about the trainer, Brent MacGrath? The colt—word had it he was as big as a barn door; Ontario-sired, Ohio-born, and developed in...Truro? Where the heck was that, anyway?*

Regardless of the noise, Beach and his "team"—trainer Brent MacGrath, groom Jean Louis Arsenault, driver Paul MacDonell, and the members of Schooner Stables—were all feeling confident. And why wouldn't they? They were about to qualify Beach the Unbeaten for the Burlington Stakes, they were certain.

There he was, then, at the "summer track"—Mohawk. Beach was up against a fine field of pacers: Legacy N Diamonds, Dinneratartsplace, Real Nice, Great Intentions, The Jay Rock, Third Fling, Casimir Homeboy, Million Dollardown.

Around them, a crowd of 150 people—about three times the normal number for a qualifying race, which sees no money won or lost, unless it's a private bet—were ready to see some smoking fractions, and something more than that, too. They wanted to see if all that hype was merited, if the first race of Beach's third-year campaign could possibly be as heart-thumping as his races in the preceding year. Come Monday morning, back at the office, would they have something to brag about to their co-workers? *Yeah, that's right, I saw The Beach's qualifying race out at Mohawk. Won by a country mile! Amazing!*

Which sounded great, didn't it? But would it happen?

It happened.

Beach won his qualifying race by ten and three-quarter lengths. He roared over the mile in 1:51 1/5, and seemed ready for more. A *Globe and Mail* journalist of the time, Beverley Smith, said of his last half-mile: "Beach barged home...in 54 4/5 seconds—and he's just beginning."

Gotta love that verb "barged."

Smith also wrote, "He's a Maritime-owned Standardbred horse that quite easily could shift the sands of the sport, and become perhaps one of the greatest pacers in history… You can't miss Somebeachsomewhere. He's a giant of a horse."

She added, "And he has one more asset: he has Mohawk-Woodbine Paul MacDonell as a driver. MacDonell, who drove him on Monday, has been known for upturning apple carts, winning Breeders Crown races with long shots. But this year, it looks as if everybody else will be chasing him."

Statements like these fanned the flames of excitement.

If anyone thought the comparisons to Niatross would slack off after that qualifier…they were wrong. Ontario fans were on their feet clapping until their hands stung, and it seemed more than reasonable to think the rest of North America might be following suit soon.

Beach's first start was still planned for May 17, 2008, in the first Ontario Sires Stakes Gold Elimination, also at Mohawk. The plan was to race him for the following four weeks, which would bring him up to the $1.5 million North America Cup in June.

But one week later, Beach stepped on a stone while turned out in his paddock at Baycairn Training Centre in Campbellville and bruised the coffin bone in his hoof.

This was a serious matter. Horses and their hooves are always a serious matter.

Large or small, all horse hooves share the same brilliant design.

Hooves are made of keratin, a durable protein (which is why many dogs like to chew on the hoof shavings left by the farrier) that is like human fingernails and hair. Both the hoof and the "frog," the soft triangular part on the underside of the hoof, absorb immense amounts of shock when an 800- to 1,000-pound horse takes a step. This absorption prevents the impact from travelling up the horse's leg bones.

The frog also pumps blood to the hoof and up through the leg with every step. The horse's hoof flexes and expands as the horse moves, particularly at faster gaits.

Apart from the rather large matter of keeping a horse upright, the hoof's central job is to shield and protect the coffin or "pedal" bone, the bottom-most bone in both the front and rear legs of horses.

In short, it's very bad news when a horse breaks his coffin bone. (Or any bone, ever.) It's also not good to see that coffin bone bruised, which Beach had done—severely.

"It was a bad, bad bruise," says MacGrath of that May 10, 2008, misstep. Beach's owners were concerned—and wanted answers fast. "We had him MRI'd that day and the results came in at eleven o'clock that night," MacGrath says.

For this procedure, a horse has to be tranquillized. It's a long, physically awkward bit of testing. But, as always, Beach was stoic and willing, and he trusted his owners to do well by him.

It was disappointing, but Schooner Stables didn't hesitate to scratch Beach from the May 17 race. Instead, and hoping for the best, MacGrath anted up for the Burlington Stakes on May 31 at Woodbine Mohawk Park in Campbellville.

Now came the tricky part. How was Schooner Stables going to keep Beach in shape for the racing season—while giving him the time he needed to heal?

"Lots of ice, lots of walking," says MacGrath, of the first part of the get-better/stay-fit regime. "Then we went jogging."

As it turned out, Baycairn was the ideal place for Beach to have been when this misfortune happened.

"They have trails on the property that go through the woods," says MacGrath. "Soft trails, built up with the wood chips from cleaning the stalls. I'd take him out in the cart and jog him for three or four miles."

But despite this bit of good fortune, and despite crafting a careful plan for recovery, the injury was stubborn.

"Beach would be lame, then okay, even on the chips," says MacGrath.

MacGrath assessed Beach day by day, and after a final thumbs-up from the veterinarian, Schooner Stables made the decision for Beach to compete in the Burlington Stakes on May 31, 2008.

"From May 5 to May 31, Beach hadn't had a single training mile," says MacGrath, underscoring once again that jogging is one thing; training is quite another. "But we had faith in him."

As added protection, Schooner Stables elected to have a bar shoe—a shoe with a closed heel that provides added support for the entire hoof—put on Beach's injured hoof. With everything in place to safeguard the hoof, it was time for the Burlington.

The Burlington Stakes originated in 1964 when the Ontario Jockey Club created a spring event for three-year-old pacers. The race has since become an important fixture on the Canadian harness racing scene. (In 2018 it was renamed the Somebeachsomewhere Stakes.)

The purse for the May 31, 2008, Burlington Stakes was $100,000. Beach drew lucky post position one. In a "talented field of ten," the horses included Santanna Blue Chip, Shadow Play, On the Brink, Trade Editor, Lets Getit Started, Genesis Showtime, Valentowner, My Time Hanover, Lucky Man—and Somebeachsomewhere, of course, who was looking for his seventh straight win.

As predicted, Santanna Blue Chip was soon "flashing hot speed from the outside," and from the inside On the Brink broke fast, as did Shadow Play. Beach was fourth on the inside. The frontrunners passed the quarter at a leisurely 28.1, but shortly thereafter, things began to change.

"Paul MacDonell calls on Somebeachsomewhere to shoot out of fourth," said the announcer, and then, "he's third, he's second, he is making an all-out acceleration to come after Santanna Blue Chip!"

By the second quarter, MacDonell had reached the front, with a successful charge to the lead, hitting the half pole at 55.3 seconds.

Meanwhile, Santanna Blue Chip had gone from "pacesetter to pocketsitter," and Beach cruised by the three-quarter pole with a length-and-a-half lead. Match to the gas by then, Beach paced the third quarter in 27.4 and led the field into the stretch. Santanna Blue Chip "rode in his pocket-draft, but he was a length and a half in arrears."

Now the announcer's voice was rising. "It's Somebeachsomewhere and Paul MacDonell and he hasn't lifted a line!"

It was true MacDonell hadn't lifted his whip, which he rarely used on Beach anyway. He did occasionally lay the whip on Beach's back, which was enough to make the colt surge a wee bit faster.

By then, the soft-spoken announcer was shouting. "It is *Somebeachsomewhere* in a *stunning* sophomore debut to win the second division of the Burlington Stakes!"

And Beach was "all wrapped up in 1:51:3," just an eye-blink—two one-hundredths—slower than the qualifier's finish, at 1:53.1.

He'd also thrown his fancy new shoe. Right into Paul MacDonell's... well, lap.

"When they were coming into the winner's circle, I saw blood all over Beach's hind leg and blood splattered on Paul's white and red silks," says MacGrath. "I wondered what in hell had happened."

Driving speed had happened.

"The nails in the bar shoe snapped off," says MacGrath. "The shoe flipped between Beach's hind legs and one of the nails that was still in the shoe stuck in Beach's hamstring. It hit a vein and [he] was bleeding profusely."

Jean Louis Arsenault, Beach's groom, took care of Beach's bleeding leg in short order.

As for MacDonell, who was in fact totally unharmed, MacGrath couldn't stop laughing about the shoe in his lap. "I said to Paul, 'If it had to be your balls or Beach's, I'd go with yours!" says MacGrath.

It is reported that MacDonell, ever the gentleman, did not clock his old friend with the offending horseshoe.

All in all, it was a grand and giddy start to the Three-Year-Old Campaign.

Brent MacGrath had one week to ready Beach for the elimination race leading up to one of the biggest races of his career, the Pepsi North American Cup, year twenty-five, held at Mohawk. The elimination race was to take place on June 7, 2008, with the final scheduled for June 14.

The purse for the elimination race was $50,000. Beach flew across the finish line at 1:49, with the accomplished Art Official placing second. Two other crowd favourites, Shadow Play and Legacy N Diamonds, came in a disappointing eighth and ninth, while On the Brink, who'd placed third in the Burlington Stakes, was sixth.

In six more days it would be time for the final of the Pepsi North America Cup.

Chapter 12

THE PEPSI NORTH AMERICA CUP AND "CANADA'S HORSE"

WITH A HEFTY PURSE OF $1.5 MILLION, THE PEPSI NORTH AMERICA Cup is the richest harness race for three-year-old Standardbred pacers in North America. The race was originally held at Greenwood Raceway from 1984 to 1993. From 1994 to 2006, the Cup was held at Woodbine Racetrack in Toronto.

But in 2008, the Cup was taking place at Mohawk. A first-rate field of ten was assembled to race the one-mile trip around the seven-furlong limestone oval: Somebeachsomewhere, the 2–5 favourite; Badlands Nitro (6–1 second choice); Santanna Blue Chip; Mucho Sleazy; Lennon Blue Chip; Sand Shooter; Art Official (9–1 third choice); Dali; Deuce Seelster; and Keystone Horatio.

It was a Saturday night and the racing conditions were as good as it gets: clear skies, no wind, a fast track, and temperatures hovering around 21°C (70°F). Beach was now eight for eight, undefeated.

And yet despite these fine omens, some in the crowd had a certain top Thoroughbred on their minds, by the name of Big Brown. Only a week prior, Big Brown, who had earlier won both the Kentucky Derby and the Preakness Stakes, had been the favourite to win the Belmont Stakes, and hence, the Triple Crown of Thoroughbred racing. Instead, he suffered his only defeat at Belmont. He, like Beach, had "foot problems," which many said was the reason for his heartbreaking loss. Howls of disappointment went up around the globe when Big Brown lost, the world feverishly looking for only the fourteenth winner of the Thoroughbred Triple Crown since 1919.

The crowd of eleven thousand at the Pepsi North America Cup on the evening of June 14, 2008, did not want to feel similarly bitter emotions. They wanted their hero, Beach, to be heroic.

The trainers present noted the "head nod" Beach exhibited in the warm-up to the race. It was a small bob of the head, indicating that the coffin bone bruise was still tender. MacGrath, watching Beach with hawk eyes, was relieved to see that the nod disappeared shortly after that.

"It's post time," said the race announcer. "The field of ten is settled on the gate for the twenty-fifth edition of the Pepsi North America Cup." One bated breath later: "Here they come!"

Racegoers that day saw that quickest off the wings of the starting gate, angling in from post six was Mucho Sleazy. Badlands Nitro fired up the centre, with Santanna Blue Chip in third. In fourth as they came to the quarter station was Beach. Keystone Horatio was starting to pour on the speed, but no one was watching him or the others anymore.

"And MacDonell starts the Big Fellah up! Here comes Somebeachsomewhere out of fourth, and he is third, he is second, and...Mucho Sleazy gives way...and Somebeachsomewhere rolls to the front."

At the half pole, Somebeachsomewhere looked relaxed but powerful. MacDonell's whip appeared to be draped over his shoulder; for a $1.5 million race, he wasn't even bothering to lay it on Beach's backside, though he would, not hard, in the home stretch.

At the three-quarter pole, though Beach was still leading, the announcer sounded worried.

"Somebeachsomewhere still not getting his cue from MacDonell. He still leads by a length and a half...and he's coming into the stretch...now he's leading by two lengths."

Beach, driven by a relaxed-looking Paul MacDonell, crossing the line at the final of the North America Cup at Woodbine Mohawk Park in Campbellville, Ontario, June 2008. (DAVE LANDRY)

It was as though the announcer was being slowly tortured, waiting for Beach to burn rubber. In fact, Beach was doing just that.

"*Here comes MacDonell; here comes Somebeachsomewhere!* He's big and he's strong and he's *got it going on!* Two and three-quarter lengths! Cup twenty-five goes to Canada's Horse! He's home in 1:49!"

"Canada's Horse"—now didn't that have a ring?

The crowd sure thought so. Loud from the get-go, now it was a jumping, hollering wall of sound. Young girls screamed Beach's name like he was a rock star out there performing on the track; in fact, that's exactly what Beach had done—perform—and exactly what he was—a star. Older fans bounced their homemade signs up and down—"Go, Beach, Go!" and "We love Beach!" Even normally staid horse owners and horse racing people, who had stood on the apron during Beach's warm-ups and after the race, came to the paddock to see Beach close-up.

Once past the wire, Paul pulled up on Beach. Then he turned him back down the Mohawk home stretch again, giving the crowd what they wanted: Beach The Unbeaten, on yet another victorious night.

Paul MacDonell and Somebeachsomewhere took *five curtain calls*, and still the crowd howled and stomped and spilled out of the grandstand and onto the track. When Paul made a pointing gesture at Beach's neck, to indicate the hero of the night, the crowd roared.

In videos of the time, Paul MacDonell, then forty-five, looked calm, even stunned, post-race, at least until a grinning, lanky Jean Louis Arsenault and another groom appeared from the sidelines, grabbing onto Beach's bridle and bringing him to a halt. Then the winner of forty-three hundred races was all smiles. It was, after all, MacDonell's first "NA Cup."

It was also his twenty-second wedding anniversary. What a day!

Soon after the race, reporter Greg Blanchard approached MacDonell, jogging alongside the sulky. "Paul, have you ever heard an ovation like that at a horse race coming to the finish?"

A visibly dazed MacDonell answered, "No, it just sent chills up my spine. I could feel everyone behind him. I've had so much support this week from everybody right across the country and the United States. They just love this horse. He's the whole show, this horse."

"He still looks like he wants to go," laughed the reporter, the footage posted on YouTube. "Was that 1:49 as effortless as it looked?"

"Once he got to the half at 54:4, he was pretty much on air," said MacDonell. "He got a breather he needed and I just let him pace down the lane; let him stretch out."

Because that's all you really need to do with a champion—*just let them stretch out.* That is, if every other bit of luck, weather, mood, soundness, strength, courage, and will all come together, along with a driver who has soft hands, a sharp mind, and a believing heart. Then, and only then, can you hold aloft the stunning gold, red, white, and blue North America Cup trophy, made from Royal Crown Derby Imari china and say, "We did it."

The cover photo of the June 18, 2008, issue of *Horseman and Fair World* magazine shows a smiling Paul MacDonell, dressed in his signature red and white racing suit, holding that same classy cup. In the background,

The winner's circle at the North America Cup. From left, Stuart Rath, Jamie Bagnell, Louise and Reg Petitpas, Paul MacDonell, Brent, Rhonda, and Josh MacGrath. (DAVE LANDRY)

there's another photo of Paul showing off Beach to his fans, who are packed into the grandstand. Beach is "flying," of course, all four feet off the ground, exactly as any mythical creature should cover ground.

Inside this same issue, a landscape photo shows a thick throng of people surrounding Beach, who wears a white cooler that covers him from head to haunches. His black "head number," with a yellow number two on it, indicating his post position, is attached to the crown of his bridle.

On the far right of this same photo is a close-up of Schooner Stables. Everyone is beaming, their joy evident.

But it is "the two Macs," Paul MacDonell and Brent MacGrath, who look about to sprout eagle wings and fly, alongside magical Beach. MacDonell holds the trophy with both hands, a huge grin spread across his rosy face. MacGrath, with his right hand cupped onto MacDonell's shoulder, and his left holding Rhonda close, has his head thrown back and is laughing in pure glee. *Did you ever, ever think something this wonderful would happen?* The caption might have read.

Odds are, if you'd asked Brent that actual question, he would have said yes.

Other odds are, if you'd asked Paul MacDonell, he would have said, *Knew it from the start.*

And Jean Louis Arsenault, who'd seen luck come and go so many times over a horseman's career? He might have said, *Shh—let's not talk about it at all. Amuse-toi bien!*

"When I think of how great horses overcome trials, I think of that night at the North American Cup," says MacGrath, twelve years later. "Beach was still dealing with that coffin bone bruise, but like all great athletes he reached way down and found what it took to win. With luck and greatness, he won."

Chapter 13

THE MEADOWLANDS PACE

DESPITE BEING DECLARED THE TWO-YEAR-OLD PACING COLT OF the Year in the US in early 2007, Somebeachsomewhere had never raced in the United States.

On July 12, 2008, that was about to change when Beach ran in the elimination for the Meadowlands Pace, a harness race for three-year-old pacers held at the Meadowlands Racetrack in East Rutherford, New Jersey.

Opened in 1976, Meadowlands is a near-mythical racetrack, popularly known as "the Big M." It offers both harness racing and Thoroughbred racing. Meadowlands has a structure common in the United States, with a main dirt track that is a mile long, offering sweeping curves and wide stretches, and inside this, a turf course which is seven furlongs, or 7/8 of a mile, used only by the Thoroughbreds.

And the best design feature? In the middle of the smaller track is a lake, intended to resemble the state of New Jersey.

The tracks' widths are equally impressive, at ninety feet for the main one and eighty feet for the turf course. Like Red Shores Racetrack in Charlottetown, Prince Edward Island, and like most tracks, Meadowlands is equipped for racing at night and the majority of its races are held in the evening.

Also like Red Shores, and in the way of all top tracks, the modern "Meadowlands Racing and Entertainment Complex" offers live race streaming and race replays for those who wish to access these on their mobile devices, as well as restaurants and bars on-site.

Since 1981, the Meadowlands also has been famous as the home track for the Hambletonian, which is the first leg of the Trotting Triple Crown; the Yonkers Trot, held at the Yonkers Raceway in Yonkers, New York, and the Kentucky Futurity, held at The Red Mile in Lexington, Kentucky, are the other two. In 2015, the Meadowlands also became home to the Cane Pace, the first leg of harness racing's Pacing Triple Crown. The other two are the Little Brown Jug, held at the Delaware County Fair in Delaware, Ohio, and the Messenger Stakes, held at Yonkers Raceway in Yonkers, New York. To make things interesting for racegoers, the Cane Pace for pacers is run on the same program as the Hambletonian for trotters.

But it had never been MacGrath's plan for Beach to try for the Triple Crown for pacers. In his opinion, the Little Brown Jug, with its series of heats in a single day prior to the final being run, was just too gruelling for his young horse.

"My position was there was no upside to the Triple Crown," says MacGrath, "and lots of downside."

MacGrath received a good deal of criticism for this position from the wider harness racing world, which views the Little Brown Jug as not-to-be-missed. It is a race for champions, the horse racing people say, a race that a horse such as Beach should compete in.

Once again, MacGrath was ruffling feathers near and far, but in his view, he had thought the matter out carefully. He was firm and unapologetic. The Little Brown Jug was indeed a great race; but no, Beach wasn't going in it. Too many heats, and relatively small purse money, when contrasted with races like the Pepsi North America Cup, the Meadowlands Pace, and the Messenger Stakes. As well, MacGrath wanted to try to set a world record at Lexington with a fresh horse.

And so, the plan for that point was the Meadowlands Pace Elimination on July 12, 2008, and the final, worth $1.1 million (USD), a week later, on July 19.

In the field of eight for the $50,000 elimination, Beach may have recognized some familiar friends—Art Official, Badlands Nitro, Mucho Sleazy, Moon Beam, and Weekend Gambler—among a few new competitors, Meant To Be Me and Grab Your Keys. Beach drew post position five.

With a few "whip taps from MacDonell," Beach soon made a grab for the lead. By the first quarter, secured in 27.1 seconds, Beach was in the lead; he passed by the second quarter in 55 seconds, leading by one and a quarter lengths.

Art Official began applying pressure on Beach from the outside. He was, said the announcer, "breathing down his neck now." Beach passed the three-quarter pole at 1:22.1, with Art Official still pushing hard for the lead.

But it was not to be for Art Official.

"Into the stretch drive, Somebeachsomewhere scoots away here—with the whip tucked away! Somebeachsomewhere just kicked sand dust in Art Official's face on the far outside. Badlands Nitro is trying to make it up. *Hello!* Somebeachsomewhere is a perfect ten!"

A perfect ten?

Of course: Somebeachsomewhere had won ten races in a row.

It was plain for all to see at the Meadowlands Pace elimination that Beach remained undefeated with plenty of gas in the tank at the finish line, finishing in 1:48.3, by four and a half lengths.

This didn't mean, however, that Art Official (bred in Canada; sired by Art Major, from Naughty Shady Lady) hadn't "raised his stock" with his two second-place finishes to Beach—at the North America Cup and the Meadowlands eliminations. While his intervening seventh-place finish at the NA Cup final was disappointing to his owners at Sawgrass Farms of Illinois, Art Official and his young driver, Ty Buter, were still "ones to watch" at the upcoming Meadowlands Pace final.

And they weren't the only ones. At the elimination race, Badlands Nitro had come third and Mucho Sleazy had come fourth. The other six contenders for the Meadowlands Pace Final were Share the Delight, Sand Shooter, Tiz a Masterpiece, Atochia, Bullville Powerful, and Dontloseyourdayjob. (Dontloseyourdayjob scratched on the day of the race, leaving a field of nine.)

If ever a race win looked promising for a three-year-colt named Somebeachsomewhere, this was it: the Meadowlands Pace final, July 19, 2008, with a beckoning purse of $1.1 million (USD). The heavy 1–9 favourite, Beach, was sound, fit, and full of fight. Beach's driver, Paul MacDonell, and every member of Schooner Stables were all, quite reasonably, expecting good news. They might also have been envisioning, by day's end, holding the event's stunning, swirling silver trophy of a pacer in full flight. Bring on that eleventh win! The team was ready.

Beach's loss at the Meadowlands Pace is *still* a subject of conversation among horse racing people and race fans today—twelve years after the fact. Back then, it caught just about every headline and editorial for months.

"Somebeachsomewhere Loses for the First Time." *Globe and Mail*, July 21, 2008.

"Art Official Upsets Meadowlands Pace." *Harness Link*, July 20, 2008.

"World Record Needed to Upset Somebeachsomewhere." *CBC.ca/sports*, July 19, 2008.

Wait a second—*world record?*

Correct. To beat Beach, Art Official and his driver Ron Pierce had to set a world record for three-year-old pacers.

Here's how the race unfolded:

July 19, 2008. It was almost 90°F (31.7°C) that day in East Rutherford, New Jersey, with high humidity. It was a field of nine. MacDonell and Beach drew post position two; Art Official was in post position six. In retrospect, it seems clear that every driver who entered in the race that day had decided to go flat out from the start instead of rating over the four quarters of a mile, as is the usual way, and then asking for it all in the home stretch.

Schooner Stables had been warned: There was a lot of money at stake, and these competitive American drivers weren't going to give Beach even a sniff of a chance to pull ahead. Therefore, to get anywhere near the front, MacDonell would have to take his shot early, on the backstretch, going three wide to pull ahead.

Meanwhile, Art Official and the correctly named Bullville Powerful were fighting for the lead. The two horses passed the half-pole in 51 and 4/5—"Probably never seen before," MacDonell would later say of the scorching speed.

They were pacing flat out. At that point, MacDonell couldn't clear them.

As Doug Harkness of *Atlantic Post Calls* later said, the whole field "ganged up" on Beach, in much the way hockey enforcers used to gang up on Wayne Gretzky, and still do bully Sidney Crosby.

MacGrath never did agree with this viewpoint. Beach was the winner of his elimination race. Due to this, Beach's team was allowed to choose his post position. MacGrath believed their choice of post position two had been a mistake.

"We would have done better with the four- or five-hole," he says. "We would have floated out from there."

Beach did get out front at the three-quarter mark, and he held the lead into the last eighth of a mile. But at the finish line, Art Official, who paced the race of his life, won by a neck, and for the very first time, Beach came second. Art Official's time of 1:47 broke the previous record for three-year-olds, set in 2002 by American Ideal at The Red Mile in Kentucky. Beach's time also broke that record.

Incredibly, the winning time was only six tenths of a second off the all-aged race record of 1:46.4. This was set by Holborn Hanover in 2006.

There are times when it's good to be a horse—and not a driver of harness horses. Paul MacDonell was devastated by the loss at the Meadowlands Pace, though being a class act both on and off the track he was gracious in defeat that day and thereafter—as so many people in the industry have noted. Beach had been magnificent; no one denied that, either. It was Art Official's day and all of Schooner Stables would tip their hat to him and to driver Ron Pierce and owner James Jesk.

And yet, so many years later, there are memories of the Meadowlands Pace that still make MacDonell uneasy.

"There was a scary moment at the three-quarter pole," he says. "Maybe it was at the 7/8s. That was the first time I ever felt him under a bit of stress. He was getting tired on me."

MacDonell was scared for Beach, because he'd worked so hard in that race—harder than ever before, he says—and was still only three years old.

"He went extra distance, way more than most horses that night just by the way the race went. If you bring up the race on YouTube, you'll see that Beach had to go three wide on the back stretch and clear to the front. Then there was a horse coming on his tail, which by the time we reached the three-quarter pole in most races I hadn't even asked him to pace yet…. He had gone quite a piece before the three-quarter pole and I wasn't sure how he was going to react, and that was a little bit scary," MacDonell says—especially scary, given that the eyes of most of the racing world were on him and Beach. *What if Beach broke stride? What if he were injured?*

MacDonell takes a deep breath and continues the story. "We're getting down to the nitty-gritty in the mile and this horse, Art Official, is inching. If you watch the replay, the horse just inched and inched and inched as hard as he could, and in the last two strides he got to Beach. That was it. Art Official won."

Heartbreaking, and yet MacDonell knows he couldn't have asked for one more thing, not one more "inch," from his horse.

MacDonell has happy memories of that race, too.

"Something really spectacular happened that same evening. I got off the horse and then Beach was walking back to the paddock. He had to basically walk in front of the grandstand towards the paddock at the Meadowlands, and the people were cheering him as he was walking. So that was even more heartbreaking."

MacDonell takes a long moment between his words. "Do you know people from the New York area? They're as hard a critic as you'll ever meet. They are *not* warm and fuzzy."

And yet that crescendo of applause kept coming—for the horse who *lost.* "He deserved it."

Some horse people will tell you a horse knows when he loses a race. But in this case, says MacDonell, "I don't think Beach knew that he lost the Meadowlands Pace final."

By a neck. How could Beach possibly know?

"Yeah, he raced his heart out and he was beaten, but it was like he never knew he was beaten."

Which, in a way, was fine, because he would never be beaten again.

"Exactly," says MacDonell, many years after that tough day. "There are lots of horses that have been through what he went through there. Most of them lose more races than they win. Obviously, Beach was an exception. But, yeah, some of them just lose confidence altogether. You'll see a horse, you'll look at his race form, and he hasn't won a race in twenty-five starts—and most of it is because of confidence."

Then do you think they know when they win?

"I think they do. I can rhyme off a whole bunch of horses that are feeling pretty good about themselves coming out of the winner's circle. They're bouncing and they're happy, especially if they win easily—like they didn't exert much energy and they're still full of themselves."

For Beach, though, there was no time to dwell on the defeat. The day after the Meadowlands Pace it was time to cross the border from the US back into Canada, and then travel to the Baycairn Centre in Ontario. His next competition would be the Three-Year-Old Open at Mohawk on August 3, 2008.

But Team Beach's real focus was Flamboro Downs and the Confederation Cup heat, with a purse of $50,000, and the final, with a purse of $493,000—both scheduled for August 17.

Chapter 14

ONWARD

THE PURSE FOR THE THREE-YEAR-OLD OPEN AT MOHAWK, HELD on August 3, 2008, was $50,000. It was an "overnight race," meaning a race put on by the racetrack, not a "stakes race," which the horse owners must pay into over a period of time to stay eligible to compete.

Gathered that day was a smaller field of six—Keystone Horatio, The Mohegan Pan, Deuce Seelster, Romantic Thriller, Roman Rocks, and Somebeachsomewhere.

Beach, in post position five, finished first.

One can only imagine MacDonell's happiness and relief to be steering the snorting and prancing Beach back into the winner's circle again—not to mention the relief felt by every member of Schooner Stables.

Finally, Beach was entered into his first Ontario Sires Stakes Gold Final, scheduled for August 10. This race was open to both three-year-old colts (stallions) and geldings. The purse was $180,000. There were familiar faces: Keystone Horatio, The Mohegan Pan, Deuce Seelster, Romantic Thriller, and Roman Rocks, and new faces: Lucky Man and Lyons Geoff.

Beach, in post position three, finished first.

However, Beach's owners hadn't quite uncrossed their fingers yet. The next race for Beach was the distinguished Confederation Cup, at Flamboro Downs in Hamilton, Ontario.

Founded in 1971, Flamboro calls itself "Canada's fastest half-mile Standardbred racetrack." Certainly, it has seen some of the fastest racehorses in the industry over the past fifty years.

The Confederation Cup actually meant two consecutive races at Flamboro: the heat and the final, both on August 17, 2008. Back-to-back heat races would be a whole new experience for Beach, as would racing on a half-mile track. He was one big horse to zoom around those tighter turns.

But hadn't Brent vetoed aiming for the Pacing Triple Crown and entering the Little Brown Jug because these races required two or more heats in a single day?

True.

So why agree to a similar format at Flamboro?

Because, Brent told the press, "We're prepping Beach for Lexington—for a *world record* in Lexington."

What's in Lexington, Kentucky? The Red Mile...a legend of a track situated in the Bluegrass region of Kentucky, an area famous for horse breeding and racing. The Red Mile, named for its mile-long track of red clay.

And that meant Beach had to be a whole new level of fit, which he could do by racing in Canada and only travelling those long and enervating miles when it was time to go to Lexington.

But first, Flamboro Downs. The purse totalled $50,000 for the heat and $493,000 for the final.

In an open draw, which MacGrath has gone on record to say he thoroughly dislikes, Beach drew the enviable inside post position two; the crowds yelled their approval. One of Beach's toughest rivals that day, fellow Canadian Shadow Play, from Charlottetown, Prince Edward Island, drew the unenviable number eight; the crowds groaned.

Good luck aside, Beach did what he came there to do. He won in straight heats on the half-mile track—in world record time. He ran the final, or "Cup 32" (the thirty-second Confederation Cup) in 1:49.2, which is a world record for a three-year-old pacing colt on a half-mile track. And he won by a decisive four lengths. The formidable field of Santanna Blue Chip,

In September 2008 Beach was scheduled to race in two three-year-old stakes races in the US, which meant he would need to spend at least two weeks in Lexington, Kentucky, allowing time for training and rest. Some owners do not turn their horses out during racing periods because of the risk of injury, but it was important to Brent MacGrath that Beach have time in the field, so he chose to stable him at ACL Farm. Beach went on to set the world record for a three-year-old on this trip. (RHONDA MACGRATH)

Brent MacGrath takes Somebeachsomewhere for a walk outside the Baycairn Training Centre in Campbellville, Ontario, in June 2008. (DAVE LANDRY)

Driver Paul MacDonell kisses the North America Cup in the winner's circle at Woodbine Mohawk Racetrack in Campbellville, Ontario, in June 2008.
(DAVE LANDRY)

Beach headed toward the finish during the Confederation Cup elimination at Flamboro Downs in Hamilton, Ontario, August 2008. (DAVE LANDRY)

A cheeky Somebeachsomewhere sneaks a snack before the Confederation Cup at Flamboro Downs with Josh and Brent MacGrath. (DAVE LANDRY)

Horse ownership isn't all fun and games—there's a lot of hard work involved. Rhonda MacGrath pulls her weight behind the scenes at The Red Mile in Lexington, Kentucky, September 2008. (DAVE LANDRY)

Somebeachsomewhere, with driver Paul MacDonell showing his impeccable form, en route to a world-record finish during the Bluegrass Stakes at The Red Mile in Lexington, Kentucky, September 2008. (DAVE LANDRY)

Rhonda MacGrath with Somebeachsomewhere. (RHONDA MACGRATH)

Paul MacDonell gives Beach a tap as they streak toward the finish at the Metro Pace final at Mohawk, September 1, 2007. (CLIVE COHEN)

A rapt crowd looks on at The Lis Mara (a division of the Tattersalls Pace) at The Red Mile, October 4, 2008. (CLIVE COHEN)

Two views of the same race—the North America Cup final, June 14, 2008, at Woodbine Mohawk Park. Above: immediately after the start gate. Below: Beach on his way to a $1.5 million finish. (CLIVE COHEN)

Brent and Rhonda MacGrath in silhouette with Beach, Baycairn, November 2008. (DAVE LANDRY)

Beach in fine form during the Confederation Cup final at Flamboro Downs in Hamilton, Ontario, August 2008. (DAVE LANDRY)

The Mohegan Pan, Keystone Horatio, Shadow Play, Deuce Seelster, Lisfinny, Anderlecht, and Tiz a Masterpiece came over the finish line in that exact order.

That was it?

No; amazing though the race was, there was more magic to come. Some fairy dust got sprinkled about on that day.

The 2008 Confederation Cup was the last race on the afternoon card (schedule) that day at Flamboro Downs. Usually, the crowd streams out of its seats in the grandstand as the horses come over the finish line for the last race. There may be a scattering of applause from some, and then off they go. The bettors who have won are headed to the box office. Those who have lost, or who didn't bet at all, are heading up to the bar to have a libation, or to the restaurants for supper, or out to their cars in the parking lot for the drive home.

But on August 17, 2008, this abrupt exodus did not occur. Instead, the estimated ten- to fourteen thousand fans cheered and clapped and clapped and cheered. They watched Beach come into the winner's circle and hooted and hollered as though they were at a rodeo, not a horse race.

"Love it, love it, love it!" A dancing and delighted Brent MacGrath compared the moment the racers had come into the home stretch to the huge swell of sound when a quarterback scores a touchdown.

But that hadn't even been the *very* best part. That was when Beach, in the winner's circle...*bowed* to that immense crowd, who roared to Jupiter and back with pleasure and surprise.

Did he really bow to the crowd?

You tell me. Facing the grandstand, Beach bowed his head until the crowd reacted with louder applause. As MacGrath later told sportswriter Dave Briggs, "He likes to bow his head and show them how good he is."

As he had done at the North America Cup, MacDonell jogged Beach up and down the tarmac a few times so everyone had a good chance to see the big stallion, and to express their admiration.

Some context: at this point, Beach had seven "sub-1:50" miles to his credit, in fifteen lifetime starts; his 1:49.2 mile trumped the previous three-year-old global half-mile mark of 1:50. Interestingly, that had been set by another Canadian-bred, Mr. Feelgood, back in 2006.

And where had he set that record, you ask? At the Little Brown Jug, in Delaware, Ohio. Brent was very much going against public expectation by not taking Beach to race there. It was not surprising that Reg Petitpas and others were disappointed.

For Paul MacDonell, that day at Flamboro was about as sweet as a day can be in the harness racing business. This was no less than his *fifth* Confederation Cup win.

And for this race, MacDonell had been able to give Beach a "breather in the second quarter," unlike the pounding, relentless pace of the Meadowlands Pace. That had to have felt better for both driver and horse.

Beneath the joy, beneath the pride, beneath the excitement and the vindication of the Confederation Cup win, Brent MacGrath felt determined

Caretaker Jean Louis Arsenault with Beach at Flamboro Downs. (DAVE LANDRY)

to prove to the world how brilliant and consistent Beach would continue to be. This was the bonfire beneath his desire to have Beach try for the all-age, all-time world record in Lexington.

In fact, MacGrath had been talking about the world record as far back as May 2008—and his focus hadn't changed one iota.

What would that record look like, time-wise? Take a deep breath, because the numbers are hard to believe. What MacGrath wanted for Beach was to pace a mile in *1:45*. That's one minute, forty-five seconds.

Was that even possible?

No one knew, and certainly not MacGrath or anyone else in or connected to Schooner Stables. The goal was, said Paul MacDonell, "unseen territory." But he was along for the ride—no doubt about it.

MacDonell, the gentleman, the believer, the friend to MacGrath, and the heartfelt supporter and driver of Somebeachsomewhere, offered his take to *Canadian Sportsman* in the September 4, 2008, issue. "I think Brent wants the horse to go down as one of the best ever. He doesn't want to have any doubters.... People say all the time, 'Oh, you're not as good as Matts Scooter [a Standardbred pacer and sire who was named Harness Horse of the Year in 1989], or Abercrombie [a world record–holding pacer who won the E. Roland Harriman Award for Harness Horse of the Year in 1978].' Everyone's got their opinion, but I think every time [Beach] sets foot on the track, he's knocking them down one by one."

The Beach Team had one more race in Ontario. After that, they'd be loading up the truck and trailer for the nine-hundred-mile drive to Kentucky.

For The Red Mile.

Chapter 15

THE RED MILE

ON SEPTEMBER 6, 2008, BEACH WAS SET TO RACE AT THE MOHAWK Racetrack in the second division of the Simcoe Stakes, which offered a purse of $132,326. Including Beach, there was a field of seven, with familiar friends and rivals The Mohegan Pan, Deuce Seelster, Dali, Anderlecht, and Legacy N Diamonds, and new rival, Stonebridge Magnum.

Earlier, in the first Simcoe Stakes division for three-year-old pacing colts, the two favourites in the field, Keystone Horatio and Santanna Blue Chip, had given their all, with the latter ultimately winning by a nose. The competitive duo had crossed the wire in 1:53.2. Get Out Of Dodge had come third.

The owner of Santanna Blue Chip, none other than MacGrath's friend Carl Jamieson, was delighted with his bonny bay colt's hard-won victory. He acknowledged the fine race run by Keystone Horatio and called the race "good prep" for the next one, in Ohio. That race, of course, was The Little Brown Jug.

One could bet with some assurance that after that first division run there would have been more mutterings about MacGrath's decision not to enter Beach into that most traditional of showcases for pacers, the "LBJ." Santanna Blue Chip was a keen and capable competitor. What a joy it might have been, many racing fans might have thought, to see the two big bays duke it out for the Little Brown Jug.

Meanwhile, back in Campbellville, Ontario, it was a cold night. The crowd in the Mohawk grandstand was small in number but warm in spirit. Bettors, not surprisingly, had firm faith in Beach, sending him off as the 1–9 favourite in his sixteenth start. He had, after all, fourteen wins to his credit, and only one loss.

From lucky post position number one, MacDonell drove Beach to the front immediately. The fractions had the crowd crying out and people pumping their fists skyward in the chilly air.

Beach clocked 25.3 for the first quarter.

He whirled by the half in 53.2.

He sizzled by the three-quarter pole at 1:20.2—the fastest three-quarters of a mile in Mohawk history.

Of the six other contenders, driver Luc Ouellette and his horse, Dali, were the only pair in contention for the win. The others trailed by six or more lengths during the course of the race. In the stretch, Beach was holding the pace, just. At that point, The Mohegan Pan upped the pressure. Despite this noble effort, which gave The Mohegan Pan the place spot, and despite the fact Beach didn't have his usual kick in the home stretch, he still had a clear victory. He finished in 1:50.1. Deuce Seelster came third, and Dali, fourth.

Beach had not, however, set a track record, a hope that the two Macs had shared. Blame the fact that the track had been "a little dead" and it was a cold night, as MacGrath told a reporter from *Standardbred Canada*. Also, it had been three weeks since the Confederation Cup final, perhaps a shade long to get the best performance.

There was other good news, however: at this point, three-year-old Somebeachsomewhere had earned his syndicate over $2.3 million dollars. Cheers, all, and bring on The Red Mile!

When horse racing people speak of the track known as The Red Mile, they use words like "hallowed." It was opened on September 28, 1875, by the Kentucky Trotting Horse Breeders Association. It is the second oldest harness racing track in the world, preceded only by the Goshen Historic Track in New York, which opened in 1838. The world might not get to see Somebeachsomewhere race at the Little Brown Jug, but it would most certainly see him thunder down one of the world's most famous red-clay tracks.

The Red Mile racing facility is also impressive in scope, with a two-story clubhouse, a round barn, and a park. The gaming facility simulcasts no fewer than 364 days a year, and is a beloved venue for horse racing people, gamblers, diners, and bon vivants from around the world.

Was this the venue in which The Beach would set an all-age, all-time world record for pacers? Or was MacGrath finally asking too much of his young colt—and would there be a price to pay? After all the caution, all the care and good management—was this the one lofty goal that should never have been set? And what about the weather—wasn't it on the cool side for a horse to set a world record? Wouldn't it be that much harder for the horse himself to warm up and pace his optimal best?

Racing at The Red Mile started at 1:00 P.M. that day—September 27, 2008. The Bluegrass Division for three-year-old colts and geldings, Beach's race, was scheduled for four o'clock. It was the fourteenth, and final, race on The Red Mile card.

A field of ten assembled behind the starting gate: Mystery Chase, Dali, Blue Claw, Goddess's Justin, Upfront Hannahsboy, Riggins, Major Hottie, MCA, Tiz A Masterpiece, and Somebeachsomewhere—the big stallion himself in post position three.

MacGrath started in his usual perch high up in the grandstand, but this time, when the gate pulled away, he darted into the finish-line box and got a front-row seat, eyes riveted on the horses.

"And they're off!"

The next words out of the announcer's mouth surprised no one: "Somebeachsomewhere paces out strongly and has already crossed over against the pylons well before the opening turn."

In Thoroughbred racing, jockeys wear coloured jackets representing the owner of the horse they are riding; in harness racing, drivers choose their own colours, which are then registered so they can't be duplicated.

This meant that Beach and Paul MacDonell had already taken the rail position.

At the midpoint of the opening turn, Beach was two lengths ahead. But Blue Claw was in second, ears flattened and pacing hard.

Just whose race was it going to be?

Videos of the race show what looks like an impossibly relaxed-looking Paul MacDonell, dressed in his customary silks: white trousers and a red-and-white jacket. The whip, more decorative than active, appears to be resting on MacDonell's shoulder. The sulky is bouncing just a bit as its wheels roll over the clay surface of the track. Beach is motoring down the track, his flawless gait never faltering.

Beach and MacDonell reach the first quarter in 26:4 and the second quarter in 52:4. By this point, Beach has extended his lead to three lengths. The determined and powerful Blue Claw hasn't fallen back, though, is pushing hard to tighten the margin.

It's altogether too cozy for Beach, who begins to draw away. He quickly opens up the space between himself and Blue Claw to four lengths. There is less than three-eighths of a mile to go. And here, finally, evidence of MacDonell's nerves show—or is it merely his racing experience? Either way, he glances over his shoulder to see exactly how close the still-in-second Blue Claw might be.

Clearly, it's too close for both Beach and MacDonell. By the three-quarter mark, Beach has pushed out the lead to three and a half lengths, blazing by the pole in 1:19.2.

The infield clock at The Red Mile, showing Beach's winning time—the fastest mile ever in a race by a three-year-old pacer, and equal to the fastest mile ever in a race in the all-age category. (DAVE LANDRY)

It's possible, it's just damn possible, Beach is going to get that all-age, all-time world record—and you can hear it in the announcer's voice, which is more staccato by the second.

Beach streaks past the finish line. "One forty-six and four—*equals the world record!*" the announcer yells with everything he has, microphone be damned.

Just a minute...*equals* the world record? Didn't Beach *surpass* the world record at The Red Mile?

Brent MacGrath clarifies. "Beach's time was and is the fastest mile ever in a race by a three-year-old pacer, and equalled the fastest mile ever in a race in the all-age category. Beach didn't have the fastest mile ever, though, in the all-age category."

That honour had gone to Cambest, a striking black pacer who, on August 16, 1993, had clocked the fastest mile in Standardbred history in a time trial. (Time trials are not races, as the horse is attempting to beat

A jubilant Garry Pye on his way to the winner's circle at The Red Mile. (DAVE LANDRY)

its own best time in a non-competitive event.) He did this at the Illinois State Fair in Springfield. On that day, surrounded by galloping horses or "prompters" pulling sulkies, which are used to push a horse to make its best effort, five-year-old Cambest paced a mile in 1:46.2. The record stands today.

MacGrath points out that Beach's record stands today as well. "Fastest three-year-old ever. Period. And the fastest race mile in history, too, tying the all-age mark set by Holborn Hanover in 2006, and he was five."

One can't help wondering if three-year-old Beach might just have had that all-age win had the weather been more clement.

"That's right, it wasn't ideal conditions for an all-age world record," MacGrath agrees. "It was around 72°F [22°C]; it should have been warmer."

MacGrath and MacDonell had had a game plan for the race and stuck with it, quarter by quarter. The plan didn't include seeing Beach

Brent and Rhonda MacGrath take Beach for a leisurely jog at ALS Farms in Lexington a few days after his world record win at The Red Mile. (RHONDA MACGRATH)

"staggering over the wire," says MacGrath. No one wanted to endanger Beach by pushing him too hard.

"Besides," he continues, "we had the Lis Mara next. We were considering taking another run at the world record then."

Chapter 16

REFLECTIONS FROM SCHOONER STABLES

BRENT MACGRATH, GARRY PYE, JAMIE BAGNELL, REG PETITPAS, Pam Dean, and Stuart Rath were the six members of Schooner Stables; the six co-owners of Somebeachsomewhere. They started as a one-horse stable, and remained so during Beach's lifetime.

Some members, such as Reg Petitpas, had spent a lifetime around harness racing barns, and owned other successful racehorses apart from the one owned by Schooner Stables. Others, such as Pam Dean, didn't know a great deal about harness racing, but did know about saddle horses; in Dean's case, she rode Western on her own well-schooled Quarter Horse. In Jamie Bagnell's case, he was breeding Standardbreds when he was a teenager, but had been away from horses for many years.

Then there was Garry Pye, Brent MacGrath's partner and boss at the car dealership, who chipped in for a lark, and Stuart Rath, a local businessman, raised on a farm and quite happy to be off it. Both men knew little more than that some horses were "nice colours," and others, mostly brown and black, pulled a cart with a driver in it around a racetrack in their own hometown of Truro. Pye and Rath thought being a racehorse owner would be great fun, if not particularly lucrative.

All Schooner Stables members were successful business people, and most had done business at Pye Chevrolet, in Truro.

They all loved Beach—and they never dreamed their $40,000 horse would forever change the course of Standardbred racing history.

And without Brent MacGrath, the central human character in this tale, there would be no Schooner Stables at all.

GARRY PYE

Garry Pye has a lot of titles. He is the president and owner of Pye Chevrolet Buick GMC, a car dealership in Truro, Nova Scotia, and of Truro Toyota, Amherst Toyota, and Summerside Toyota; he is chairman of Blue Water Group (a marine industrial supplier) and CEO of Andy's Tire, Ltd. On this day, he speaks as a proud member of Schooner Stables II. He is also the husband of Mary Lou Pye. Leaning across his desk at the Chevrolet dealership, Pye's expression is earnest and his voice is pitched low.

"In my mind, the story's very much Brent MacGrath's story," he says. "Brent grew up in Bible Hill here outside of Truro and spent some time at the racetrack learning how to look after horses and shovelling what had

Schooner Stables owned Beach during his racing career. When Beach went to Hanover Shoe Farms to stand at stud, the Somebeachsomewhere Syndicate was created, with the original six members of Schooner Stables retaining about 80 percent ownership of the stallion. In 2011, Schooner Stables II was born. The current members are Brent and Rhonda MacGrath, Stu Rath, Jamie Bagnell, and Garry Pye. Still based in New Brunswick, Reg Petitpas remains as involved as ever in the harness racing industry. Pam Dean still rides her own horse and remains a harness racing fan.

to be shovelled and cleaning stalls in those days. …He came to work for me, and that's how I became associated with him in terms of being able to be a partner in something I know almost nothing about—the horse racing business."

"It's sort of a Maritime thing: you partner up with a couple of other guys and buy a horse or two, but in most cases the partners would hire the local trainer and a local driver. In Brent's case, he did the training, which is really unusual," Pye notes.

"Brent had a depth of knowledge about racehorses that none of the rest of us had, and most of the other owner-investors didn't have. So when it came to the idea that we should spend a little more money, go to the US, and buy a really well-bred racehorse, that was all right with us. When Brent went to the horse sale to see what was available, he could tell one horse from another, which most of us couldn't."

While Pye's sense of humour is evident, there is more than a grain of truth in what he is saying. Schooner Stables comprised roughly half horse-knowledgeable people and half newcomers to the sport of harness racing.

But MacGrath's knowledge of Standardbreds has never failed to impress Pye.

"I've listened to Brent MacGrath talk to veterinarians who make their living in the racehorse industry, and he will name the muscles, ligaments, and joints the same way they will," he says, adding that he always felt confident with MacGrath's decisions related to Beach.

"Brent's judgement was always impeccable when he decided if Beach should go in a race or shouldn't go in a race," says Pye, noting that part of the strategizing was not over-racing the horse so he wouldn't be too spent to give his best effort at the final races.

Pye also admired MacGrath's ability to resist pressure from others in the industry to run Beach in certain races. "Brent always looked after the horse's welfare first," he says. "He refused to put him in the Little Brown Jug and people were calling him [out on that].… Brent withstood the pressure."

Pye points across his office to a horseshoe hanging on the wall. He cites a number that he's long had memorized: "One forty-six and four [1:46.4]—the all-time world record by a three-year-old harness racer; that's one of the shoes he wore that day."

Pye is also convinced that, without MacGrath, the Beach story would not have worked out as spectacularly as it did. "Yes, we did have a world champion athlete, but without the way he was trained and the way he was treated...I don't know if the horse would've risen to his athletic [potential] or not. I'm sure Brent was really important to this."

REG PETITPAS

Not all of the members of Schooner Stables are from Truro. Reg Petitpas and his wife, Louise, come from Shediac, New Brunswick, a two-hour drive north of Truro. The Petitpas' are owners of Larca Enviro, an environmental services company that specializes in oil-spill cleanup and remediation. The couple owns and operates other businesses in New Brunswick, including an assisted-living facility and an apple orchard.

It's an interesting mix. "We're pretty diversified," says Reg.

Reg Petitpas was born in the town of Dieppe, New Brunswick, and Larca Enviro is based in the city of Moncton, which is only twenty kilometres from the couple's home in Shediac. All three places are in close proximity, which makes for a pleasant life.

A life which, for Petitpas, has almost always included racehorses.

"I lived five minutes from the old New Brunswick Downs," he explains. "We had a track in Dieppe at one time. I was there all the time. I was there after school; I wasn't supposed to go, but I was going anyway. My dad would tell me no, but I'd go."

Good luck to any parent trying to keep the kids away from the excitement of a nearby racetrack. Like most kids, Petitpas was drawn to the beautiful horses and thrilling races. He bought his first horse by age twenty-one—setting his course as a lifelong horseman.

"A filly," he says of that first horse, fondly remembered. "Her name was 220 Sylvia." He and his wife, Louise, have always had horses. "We've had over 100 now, maybe as many as 160. Sometimes we'd own six or seven at one time. We've been going to sales for years and years and years. Sometimes we go to Harrisburg, sometimes Kentucky. There are also sales we go to in Ontario and the Maritimes."

The sales in the Maritimes are in Truro, Beach's old home turf, and on Prince Edward Island.

Currently, the Petitpas own two Beach babies, and also have a Beach broodmare in Sussex, New Brunswick. At the 2019 Selected Yearling Sales at Harrisburg, Petitpas bought an elegant grey colt, a Beach baby by the name of Somewhere in Verona.

"He's being trained in Truro by Emmons MacKay," says Petitpas. "The colt's doing good. It's too early to tell how good he's going to be, but he's doing everything right so far."

Reg Petitpas and Brent MacGrath go a long way back.

"We met at the dealership in Truro," says Petitpas. "I was buying trucks for my company. We bought trucks from him for twenty years."

Petitpas joined Schooner Stables in 2006, the year MacGrath purchased Beach.

And what did Petitpas think when he saw Beach for the first time?

"He was a good-looking colt," he says, "but nobody in their right mind ever thought he'd turn out to be the horse he was. We buy a lot of good-looking colts, but we've never had one like that. Nobody knows when that can happen."

Even now, Schooner Stables members struggle to describe the shock of the miracle that landed in their lives. A more common story is one of a promising horse that, for whatever reason, doesn't live up to its potential. Petitpas has seen a few of those, along with his winners.

STAKES RACES

There are different levels of stakes races, which, accordingly, have larger or smaller purses. Depending on the number of horses competing, or "divisions," there is also more or less money. In the Maritimes, the A level in harness racing is the top level, with B following. In Ontario, the top level is referred to as Gold (purses range from $80,000 to $180,000), and the second level as Grassroots ($20,000 to $25,000). Horses can be entered in either the Gold or Grassroots events, but not in both. The Gold Series consists of forty Gold "legs," or five events for each of the eight categories for age, sex, and gait. Horses earn points with each Gold leg, with the hope of qualifying for the Gold Super Final.

"I mean, you're going to go to the sale and you'll see a horse they paid $300,000 for," he says. "They're gorgeous and they'll never race. I saw one three years ago at the Harrisburg sale. Another gorgeous-looking colt, a Somebeach[-sired two-year-old], and he never raced. They paid $260,000 American for him. So you don't know.

"With Beach, we were all expecting to maybe have a horse that could race the B stakes [Grassroots] in Ontario or something. Even that's hard. We didn't have really big hopes."

Nor did trainer Jean Louis Arsenault, particularly, even though he was glad to see the good-looking colt come to Baycairn Training Centre in the winter of 2006. Arsenault, originally from Moncton, New Brunswick, was good friends with Petitpas.

"Jean Louis was my trainer," says Reg. "He had four horses in the barn for me already, and he had trained my horses for over twenty years in Ontario. So that was the connection—that if this horse ever made it, it was with Jean Louis...and Paul MacDonell was going to drive. That was the deal we had made early on, Brent and me."

Petitpas had complete faith in Arsenault's training abilities. "I had another horse that made over a million with him," says Petitpas. "So yes, I had pretty good faith in him."

Later on, when MacGrath stepped in as trainer after Beach's first big win, there would be some ongoing conflict between Petitpas and MacGrath, and some awkward times for Schooner Stables. But that was later.

Petitpas and his wife have had "some pretty nice horses" over the years, he says. Best-known of these might be Silent Swing, who made them $2 million, he says.

In 2006, Petitpas and David Shea purchased four-year-old Silent Swing from owner/trainer Jack Darling. The gelding had banked just over $460,000 in his first two years of racing. By 2009, at seven years of age, Silent Swing had gone on to bank over $1.5 million. This included major stakes wins in Canada and the United States. He won the Winbak Pace on Little Brown Jug Day. His lifetime mark of 1:48.4 was taken at the Meadowlands.

Despite Beach's early promise in the Truro qualifiers, seasoned horse racing people know all too well that *anything* can happen, or nothing can—that's the name of the racing game. So Petitpas was waiting, with great interest, to see what might happen when Beach entered his first stakes race.

"After Beach's first race at Grand River we got a call from a top trainer in Ontario," says Petitpas. "He offered us $750,000 for him after his first race. So we discussed it amongst ourselves. We're all business people and it wasn't going to change anybody's life once we split that money [six ways], so I said, 'Let's ride.' So we did."

Then things started to get really interesting—and lucrative.

"Beach won the Metro for a million dollars," says Petitpas. "We knew he was definitely the real deal."

Like MacGrath, Petitpas wonders—if Beach had been owned by an individual, would the outcome have been different? "Once people start offering money for a horse that you paid $40,000 for, I mean, you can't say no forever."

Then the offers got bigger.

"Shortly after his two-year-old career, we were offered $4 million for Beach. If I'd owned him alone, he would've probably gone at $4 million."

Indeed, a nice bit of lolly.

As it transpired, Schooner Stables was having a wonderful time. People were talking about the horse, people were talking about the money the syndicate had turned down—and everyone wanted to see what happened next.

"It was fun," says Petitpas. "My life didn't change personally, but it was great for all of us.... There wouldn't be a day that passed by that somebody wouldn't ask me, 'How's Beach making out? When's his next race?'"

A bit like owning...a rock star?

"Yeah, it was."

It was also, on a deep level, hard to grasp as a new reality.

"The chance of that happening to us.... I mean, it'll never happen again to any of us, for sure.... It's just a freak, right?"

That word again—this time, obviously, meaning impossible or unbelievable, or once in a blue moon. Not an event for ordinary people, living good and ordinary lives. Nor would there be a repeat.

"It's like a winning lottery ticket," says Petitpas. "What's the chance of you winning the lottery twice?"

Even now, many years after Beach's racing days and his years at stud, the Petitpas's still remember him with great fondness. "He was a very nice horse to be around," he says.

"It's been a hell of a ride."

JAMES BAGNELL

James "Jamie" Bagnell has been in and around the horse business for a long time.

"I started as a teenager," says Bagnell, who is married to Nicole Bagnell. "We had a hobby farm on the north shore of Nova Scotia near River John—Brule Beach. I became interested in the Standardbred racing business, and I became a breeder, probably before I was sixteen years old. I had quite a breeding operation over there, with five or six broodmares, and a stallion and yearlings running around. I did that for five or six years, breeding Maritime-bred horses; lost money every year except for one."

The young man, who would go on to become a successful businessman, was particularly fascinated by the business side of racehorses.

"The Standardbred operation was a lot of fun. I met a lot of interesting people, and got fairly involved in the industry," he says. "I was one of the founders of the Atlantic Sires Stakes, which was a stakes program for Maritime-bred horses. I did that for probably six or seven years, and then decided that was enough. I basically removed myself from the industry for years—never paid any more attention to it until Brent called me."

Oh, those casual phone calls from Brent MacGrath. Those calls can change lives.

Like Petitpas, Bagnell had known MacGrath for some time.

"I've been a customer here at Pye's Chev for many years," says Bagnell. "Brent called me and said, 'I want to buy a horse, and I want to form a group—are you interested?' and I said, 'Yeah, I'm in,' without hesitation.... So that's my horse background: I was in early and I got out, and Brent got me back in."

Born and raised in Truro, Bagnell grew up in a family business— Bagnell's Launderers and Cleaners—a laundry, dry cleaning, and uniform rental business. He started working with the company at a young age.

"I eventually took over as president, CEO in my mid-twenties," says Bagnell. "Then I started to diversify that company into the environmental services business. From that I founded and formed a company called Inland Technologies." The company provides special waste management as well as aircraft de-icing, glycol fluid recovery, and airport snow removal.

Now the CEO of a thriving company, Bagnell had indeed come a long way from his family's hobby farm in River John, where the family had spent weekends and summers. (Bagnell's father, John Edward Bagnell, known as "Jack," kept purebred beef cattle as well, making the "hobby" farm more active than most, with twenty or thirty beef cattle, and, often, twelve or fifteen horses.) Even considering his involvement with horses as a teenager, Bagnell's barn times must have seemed like a pleasant part of his past. No wonder he pounced on MacGrath's suggestion.

Like everyone in Schooner Stables, Bagnell became aware that his life was about to change substantially after Beach's first race.

"There'd been earlier indications," says Bagnell of Beach's promise, "but his first race brought that home." That, of course, had been the elimination race for the Battle of Waterloo final, held at the Grand River Raceway in Grand River, Ontario. Bagnell will never forget what he saw.

"I was watching the race from my place in Florida," he says. "At that time it wasn't quite as easy to get online and to watch races as it is today, but somehow I managed to [do it]. I was by myself in my office, and I'm watching this horse go around horses. The TV show had people commenting on the race afterwards. They were just amazed…. Just the way Beach circled around the field of horses to win the race was incredible."

Was he pinching himself, making sure he wasn't dreaming?

"Yeah, big time, big time. I couldn't believe how he performed during that race and how easily he won it. It was exciting!"

The next week was worth two big pinches—and a plane ticket.

"We'd had to earn ourselves into the Battle of Waterloo," Bagnell recalls. "The final is a $300,000 race. Obviously, by winning the elimination, our horse had qualified for the final. A week after, we went up to Ontario to see him race at the Battle of Waterloo."

When you've seen genius in motion once, expectations have a way or rising.

"All I could think was, 'Win! He's going to win.' Every race thereafter we went with the expectation that, 'This horse is unbeatable,' and he was, with one exception. And in my mind, that doesn't count."

Was there ever a loss that shone more victoriously than Beach's loss at the Meadowlands Pace?

"Beach was clearly far beyond anything else in that field. Maybe it's unfair for me to say, because I was out of the business, and I really wasn't following harness racing, but that was quite the performance."

As for the horse himself, Bagnell found him "playful."

"Especially with Brent and Rhonda," says Bagnell. "They babied him, obviously, but he was very friendly; very playful. He liked to nip at Brent all the time, which I thought I wouldn't let the horse get away with, but, you know, he'd just tap him and stuff. Brent has a way with horses. Part of the strategy is you want your horses to be happy, and it makes a difference. Beach was a happy, happy horse. He was fun to be around."

He smiles, thinking back. "I'm not an expert, but I suspect that if you take a stallion, or any sort of a horse at a very young age, and you deal with him like Brent did—baby, baby, baby, take him out for walks, you know—they're going to be happy. There's just no question about that."

A happy horse, many other horse people will tell you, is also a secure horse. And security comes from predictability and a patterned life—just as it does for many humans. Brent and Rhonda showed their caring for Beach each day, in many ways. One can only guess it was their gift to him, for all the gifts he'd given them, and for simply being in their lives.

After he'd missed that first race, Bagnell never missed another.

This is saying something for a busy businessman. Bagnell obviously added some hours into his already packed days. But he didn't want to miss as much as another millisecond of history in the making.

"It was pretty fun to walk on the airplane to go to the horse races knowing that you're going to win," he says, with a grin as wide as…a runway.

It was happy times for all, those mid-2000s, for Jamie Bagnell and his family, for the other five members of Schooner Stables and their families, and, of course, for Beach, the only horse in that one-horse stable.

PAM DEAN

Pam Dean's equestrian background involved riding horses, not racing horses. She got her own saddle horse when she was in grade six.

"I ride in the Western discipline," says Dean, who spent her early life in the Musquodoboit Valley, a rural area about an hour outside Halifax. "I did a little showing, but just at local shows."

It's a familiar story by now, but Dean and MacGrath met through business. She and her husband, Rod, had a construction company, Archibald Drilling and Blasting, which had started in the Musquodoboit Valley and later moved to Truro. The couple had bought vehicles from MacGrath in the mid-1980s, and eventually they all became friends.

Dean can't recall how the question of joining Schooner Stables came up. "I'm sure we were sitting across from each other over the desk at Brent's office, discussing business, and then he told me the story of his life with horses. He didn't know I liked horses, and I most certainly didn't know he did," she says. "He [probably] just said, 'I'm putting a group together to buy a racehorse. Would you like to come in?'"

So Pam and Rod Dean joined the syndicate.

What were their expectations?

"We didn't expect much," says Dean candidly, of a business not known for easy money. "And the first two or three horses cost us money, no question."

The pre-Beach years were lean, everyone agrees. MacGrath's earlier choices did not make money on the track, which is not unusual.

Two or three years ticked by.

Dean and the others, might have said, "Well, maybe this is enough for me." But they didn't.

"We wanted to support Brent. That's what it was. We didn't even consider saying no," she says, thinking back on the emotional framework of the agreement to all work together. "Every horse you bought, you thought, 'This might be the one.' You bought in on a dream as much as anything. And each time—you know, Brent's a very enthusiastic man."

You mean it was hard to resist his vision…?

Dean nods. "Brent was quite irresistible in terms of saying, 'Oh, no, this one's absolutely something.' He's very optimistic and he works hard."

A practical-minded horsewoman and a level-head businesswoman, Pam Dean still can appreciate the many unusual factors that came together to make the purchase of Beach possible.

Was it "meant to be" for this small group of people from the Maritimes?

"It did seem so," she says.

One thing is for sure: the group was agreed on the price—$40,000—and who would be the purchaser of the new, more expensive horse—Brent MacGrath.

Dean had no extra expectations at that point. "My goal would've been Brent's goal, which was to get a horse to the Ontario circuit. That would have been all [we hoped for]." She pauses. "[If it] paid for itself, that would be a perk."

When did she realize things had changed?

"For me it wouldn't have actually been until the second year of racing," says Dean. But there were strong indications before that, she agrees.

"Brent called me one morning when Beach was here in Truro and wanted me to come down and watch him; he was going to put him on the clock…. Brent took him out. The horse didn't look like he was going that fast," she says.

"Brent just showed me the watch. Beach had gone, probably, thirty seconds faster than what I thought he'd gone. That's how smoothly he moved. He moved differently than other pacers I'd seen. So I knew then he was different, though I wasn't quite sure how. He's a little bit like a freight train; the power's coming from the back, he's not digging like this"—Pam makes motions with her hands, like an animal raking the earth with its front paws. "Brent was excited about him, but Brent was positive and excited about every animal," she says.

"The next time I probably got a sense of Beach was when Brent qualified him here in Truro before he went to Ontario. There were four or five elderly gentlemen sitting behind me in the stands and they were talking about 'Brent's colt.' And when Brent brought him out of the barn, I listened to their conversation. These were gentlemen who had been around the tracks for a long time. I sensed, from their conversation, that maybe we had something special."

And all this was pre-Ontario, pre-first-race. "So then he went to Ontario and the Battle of Waterloo."

Before too long, Brent MacGrath would take a year off work, and he and his wife would move to Ontario.

"Beach was a very fortunate horse to have their 24-7 care," says Dean. "Brent was extraordinary there, too. That whole relationship, what Brent and Rhonda did to mix it up for that horse, to keep him happy, it was beyond imagining." She smiles. "They just drove him around to give him walks!"

Amid the early excitement in Ontario, Dean was having superstitious thoughts. "I think it became more of a 'When is it all going to fall apart?' feeling. I think I felt like that right 'til the end. It became a ride, then. I don't know if 'ride' is the right word; you're walking above ground a little. Every race you go to and you're waiting; 'Something has to happen here'—you know, he's going to get sick, he's going to get lame, something. I took it all as a gift, but I was disbelieving also."

Simply put, Dean was having trouble believing her eyes; believing her life.

Meanwhile, the facts were speaking for themselves. "The Metro Pace is the big race for two-year-olds," says Dean. "That probably set him among his peers—put him right at that level with the very best in North America."

It was a head-shaking moment, she says. "There were some wonderful horses that year, too.... They were always second to Beach. He was so superior. And if you were to talk to some of those drivers, they would tell you that, I'm sure."

Did it cause hard feelings toward Beach from the other drivers?

"Oh, no, I don't think so," says Dean. "Horsemen respect horses. I would've been shocked if there had been ill will. I know at the awards nights, or at other times, there was nothing but positives from other drivers and owners." She pauses, a horsewoman to the core. "Because next year, it could be them."

Dean likes to think back on the "Beach Parties," too.

Unfortunately, she says, "We never went to one, of course, because we were always at the live race."

Beach and his "humans," the six members of Schooner Stables, had a lot of family and friends who wanted to cheer him on—more with each race.

"He became the people's horse," says Dean.

Dean spares no praise for Beach's driver, Paul MacDonell. "He's a wonderful man. He's a gentleman. Very respectful and quiet." She says she never tired of watching Paul drive. "Beach was so fast. I was always a little bit nervous watching them go. Then I started to watch for what MacDonell asked, when he asked. I watched for when he might choose to let him go, or when he might choose to pull the earplugs."

She's also grateful for the way the two Macs carefully managed Beach.

"I believe he was managed without money in mind, per se. Excluding the three qualifiers in Truro, Beach only raced twenty-one races in two years. That's pretty low."

It was an exciting time—which passed quickly. "It was like a blur to me," Dean says. "When we went into the second year of racing, [I was] overwhelmed by the response of people. It would make me tear me up to see people screaming for Beach. It was as though he was bringing life back to something that was gone."

Bringing life back to something that was gone...

For most who are directly involved in harness racing, magic is a constant in their lives, from bringing a tiny foal into the world, to taking a new colt out on the track for the first time, to turning on the lights in the barn on a cold winter morning and seeing ten bright horses' faces turn their way, expectant of food and a good working day ahead. But beyond that, harness racing horse owners and harness racing fans are always hoping for the appearance of genius and star quality in their midst—that "something" that comes and goes as it will, and cannot be commanded into appearing.

That "something" that Somebeachsomewhere had, from his first rising "on all corners."

Dean says Beach's second year of racing became all about what he brought to the industry and to the audiences. "It's like you stepped into the centre of a rock concert or...something. It was that atmosphere." It would be that way for the entire second year of racing, in both Canada and the US.

"People loved him wherever he went." She thinks back. "You know, it probably started at the North America Cup, when Paul walked him down the front stretch. You could hardly get over to the winner's circle. There were people right from the fence to the building, all screaming and hollering for Beach."

And Beach lapped it all up, cat to the cream.

"Oh, yeah," says Dean. "He was a bit of a ham. And when Paul took that horse down that fence [with people hanging over it], people went crazy." She says people with any sort of connection to Nova Scotia would show up.

But there was no "big feeling," as a Maritimer would say, about how Beach was presented to the world and to the media, she insists. "Brent and Paul MacDonell made him a humble hero."

Dean detested the nicknames the press and others gave to Beach.

"They called him names that bothered me, like 'The Freak' and sometimes 'The Monster from the Maritimes.' They had names for him, but they weren't derogatory; I took them that they might be, but they weren't."

Dean makes a point that she believes is essential, related to the longevity and success of Schooner Stables. "The other side of this Beach coin is that none of this may have happened if we had been another group looking at this as an investment. It could have all been over [after the first race]. That's the way it is with horses. It could have been over at any point.... And if it all went south tomorrow, that was okay; we were all happy."

Curiously, Dean still finds the whole experience of briefly having had Beach in her life a little unreal.

"It was hard to believe it happened to us, that we were able to be part of this. I'm truly grateful."

STUART RATH

Truro businessman Stuart Rath, known to all as "Stu," is candid about his involvement with Schooner Stables.

"It was Brent's deal," he says, echoing many of the other members. "I just tagged along."

In Colchester County, the north-central area of Nova Scotia, home to the towns of Truro and Stewiacke, Rath's name carries a lot of clout, both in business and community circles. His influence spreads far beyond the county.

But in his earliest years, Rath was simply a country boy who grew up on a dairy farm in Camden, Nova Scotia, and attended a one-room schoolhouse in that rural community. While he loved the farm and the country, he decided on a career in banking, which he did for sixteen years before going into business for himself, first buying and developing Eastern Cablevision, then, with businessman John Bragg, purchasing Halifax Cablevision. He sold his part of the company, which is now Eastlink, to Bragg in 1995.

Rath's business dealings are numerous and diverse, and include investments in both commercial and residential real estate. He's heavily involved in community development, and he's received many community awards, including the Truro Chamber of Commerce's Lifetime Achievement Award.

Some would argue that on top of all these weighty and admirable life achievements, Rath's name, as with the names of all the members of Schooner Stables, is most firmly linked to a certain horse who liked to break world records and eat carrots.

Stu Rath and Brent MacGrath knew one another first through Pye Chevrolet, then had the secondary connection that Rath's son Duane was also in the car business.

In the spring of 2006, Rath's wife died from breast cancer. Rath admits he was feeling "pretty lost" that summer when MacGrath asked him to come to Lexington. That turned into an opportunity to become the sixth and final member of Schooner Stables.

"[Like everyone else], my investment was $10,000," says Rath. He smiles. "It was by far my *best* $10,000 investment." At the time, he didn't know Pam Dean or Reg Petitpas, but he did know Garry Pye and Jamie Bagnell.

A gentle, loyal man, he confesses to having had some guilty feelings about the transaction and its subsequent flowering because, he says, if his wife hadn't passed, it wouldn't have happened. But at the time, the invitation was a welcome distraction.

Rath trusted MacGrath as a friend and as a businessman, but especially as a horseman. Rath was not in the arena at the moment MacGrath purchased Beach, but he saw MacGrath soon after.

"He was excited," says Rath. "He kept saying, 'I can't believe I got him for that price.'" He grins. "We pick on one another, as guys do. Another one of the fellows with us that night at the Lexington sale was an accountant, Glen Smith."

Now Smith wasn't a part of Schooner Stables, but he was excited for his friend Rath that he'd joined the group. Later on, when Beach became successful, Smith used to say that Brent hadn't had much success with earlier horse buying groups, such as the early East Coast Stables, but when Rath came aboard Schooner Stables, he'd brought them luck.

Rath's grin widens. "I guess Brent and I were out somewhere another time, and I must've brought that up, [about being the guy who'd changed the group's luck], you know, rubbing it in, and Brent said, 'You liar, you did sweet nothing! You had no claim to our success.' I bring it up occasionally, in my business speeches or whatever. He's right, of course. I didn't have anything to do with how it all turned out."

But it's sure fun to rib an old friend.

And in fact, while Rath enjoyed teasing his friends about bringing luck to the buying equation, it seemed, instead, to be Beach who brought Rath luck.

"It turned out to be a great time for me," Rath says, of the period that followed the purchase of Beach. "I got into a new relationship fairly quickly, seven or eight months after the loss of my wife." His voice quietens. "You're not meant to be alone." Rath and Wendy Kaupp have been together ever since.

Rath, who may be a country lad, but is not a horseman, finds the world of horse trainers quietly amusing.

"Trainers are eternal optimists," he says. "They really are. Brent is the eternal optimist, and of course he was very optimistic [about Beach]. He trained him here in Truro in the middle of winter. He enjoyed every day."

Rath, meanwhile, was taking all the growing excitement with a grain of salt, though obviously he was glad things were going well. But even he could clearly see the steady upward trend of Beach's wins.

"You get pretty excited about it," he admits. "He only raced six times in that first year, but he won every race. By then, we knew we had something pretty special."

Interestingly, some of Rath's other friends were vocal in their amazement that Schooner Stables did not take the ever-increasing offers of money to buy Beach. "They thought we were crazy not to take it," says Rath. "But, fortunately, money wasn't an issue. We were all successful business people."

And with unwavering faith in MacGrath, Rath was happy to "tag along," as he termed it, for one of the grandest adventures of his life.

JOSH MACGRATH

Josh MacGrath is the general manager at Truro Toyota, a car dealership co-owned by his father, Brent MacGrath, and partners Garry Pye, and Richard Bowness. He lives in Truro, and recently bought a house with his fiancée, Christina Appleby, a musician and fashion designer, in nearby Bible Hill, the village where he grew up, and where his parents still live.

It's a Maritime story already, and it's only just begun.

"We were always an animal family," says Josh. "Horses, dogs, and other animals, but especially horses."

Josh remembers a certain routine from his younger days in the MacGrath family home.

"I'd be getting ready for school, sitting at the kitchen table having cereal, and Dad would come in the back door," says Josh.

Josh MacGrath and Beach at ACL Farm in Lexington, Kentucky, 2008.
(RHONDA MACGRATH)

Brent MacGrath had, of course, been at the Truro Raceway since the pre-dawn hours, where he might have been jogging one youngster, grooming another, and checking a third for soundness.

Josh would ask, "How are the horses?'"

"He was [always] cautiously optimistic," Josh remembers. But he also remembers how that changed with the arrival of Beach, as a yearling, to the Truro Raceway.

"Every morning we'd ask him, 'How are the horses?' and every morning, he'd say, 'Beach was perfect!'" says Josh. "No caveat. Looking back, I can see that change in the morning routine so clearly."

Josh was fifteen years old when Beach came along, and he remembers his father's growing excitement. "He started to have the most profound relationship with Beach and he was extremely optimistic about Beach's future."

Josh says he didn't have the same relationship with Beach, but adds, "I liked being around Beach, and I was the helping hand at the barn."

Another strong memory for Josh is how Beach behaved. "He was such a personality! He had so much character, and he was also calm and kind."

And Beach loved to play. "He was so smart," says Josh. "He wanted to have you engaged in whatever play he was doing. He made it easy to be close to him."

Sometimes, Josh can barely believe that he learned basic horsemanship—"how to groom, pick out his feet with a hoof pick, and bandage"—on what he calls "the best horse of all time. He was like the Wayne Gretzky of the horse world. He made it easy to feel connected to him."

This geniality, of course, is not the way of many stallions, some of whom can be short-tempered and reactive.

"Beach," says Josh, "wasn't like that."

Josh also spent two seasons helping out at trainer Freddie Saunders's barn at the Truro Raceway. Saunders taught him a bit about training and how to jog a horse. And while he's grateful to Saunders, Josh still says that without Beach coming into their lives, he would never have sat behind a horse in a cart.

But like any young adult, Josh eventually found his own interests. He moved to Halifax to study business and English, and then became serious about music, joining a band.

"I like to go to the track now and then," Josh says, "especially if a friend of mine has a horse in a race, or for the Atlantic Grand Circuit events. But overall, you might call me a 'fair-weather' race fan." (The Atlantic Grand Circuit is a week-long series of races for Atlantic Canada–bred harness racers, held at Truro Raceway.)

Josh also added a youthful touch to the Beach fan equation. He, along with Garry Pye's son-in-law, Glenn Roberts, launched and managed Beach's Facebook group, a site that has over thirteen hundred members.

When asked why his dad bonded so quickly with Beach, Josh has an immediate and astute answer.

"They share personality traits," says Josh, now twenty-nine. "Both are sharp performers, with grit. Brent and Beach—they both love to win. They were focused on the process, disciplined, and applied intense dedication to the improvement of the process of competing. They both want to perform."

The bond went yet deeper.

"I also think they had respect for one another," Josh says. "They were happy to see one another. They were both disciplined yet nuanced. I think they recognized that in each other. They had the same attitude of, 'We won't lose for lack of trying.' It was a similar energy—larger than life. And only one speed: go."

Josh also admires his parents' willingness to work together. "They were connected to one another, and 'on point.' Dad loves every aspect of the barn, every aspect of racing and preparing a horse for racing. Mom focused more on Beach's day-to-day care. But they were both up at 6:00 A.M. to feed at the barn, and went back again at 9:00 P.M. to see that all was well. They were equal contributors to Beach's success."

As a couple, says Josh, "My parents understand the dynamic of a two-person team better than anyone else I know."

But it wasn't all easy. "You have to remember," says Josh, "[the situation] with Beach was tumultuous. It was great, but in some ways it was hard, too. All of a sudden you've got the whole industry watching you. You'd better know how to handle yourself when a microphone gets shoved in your face."

Despite the pressures, says Josh, his parents did not allow all the upheaval to impact their marriage. "Both my parents were clearly focused on not letting that happen. Mum is such a great communicator and so emotionally intelligent. For them, it was a case of synergy—the creation of a whole that is greater than the sum of its parts."

It's something Josh hopes to see in his own married life—a gift, perhaps, from Beach, who was good at bringing out the best in everyone.

PART III

HORSE OF A LIFETIME

Chapter 17

FOUR GREAT RACES

IT WAS THE WORST-KEPT SECRET IN THE HORSE WORLD THAT Brent MacGrath and Schooner Stables wanted to broker a syndication deal with renowned Hanover Shoe Farms, the self-described "World's Leading Horse Breeder," for Beach to stand at stud there after he finished his racing season and career in November 2008.

At the post-race interview after the Bluegrass Division event at The Red Mile on September 27, 2008, MacGrath made the announcement that a deal had indeed been reached—and that both sides were thrilled with the outcome.

In the meantime, there were five races that Schooner Stables planned to enter Beach in before the end of his racing career. These were the Lis Mara at The Red Mile; the Messenger Final at Yonkers Raceway; the Ontario Sires Stakes Super Final at Woodbine Racetrack; The Breeders Crown Final at The Meadowlands; and the Matron Stakes at Dover Downs, in Dover, Delaware. The team had happy expectations for all of the races, but never forgot that the only way to take racing is one day, and certainly one race, at a time.

THE LIS MARA, THE RED MILE, LEXINGTON, KENTUCKY, OCTOBER 4, 2008

It was a sunny but cool day in the southern US, and Team Beach was a week past its glorious win in the Bluegrass Division for three-year-old colts and geldings at The Red Mile in Lexington, Kentucky, where Beach had set a world record for three-year-old pacers, at 1:46.4.

On that same red clay turf, a field of seven now assembled behind the starting gate for the one-off Lis Mara, a three-year-old "open" event, meaning it was open to fillies, stallions, and geldings, three years old and up.

The race had been sponsored by the owners of a stallion called Lis Mara who had retired to stud only the year before. The two-time world-champion had been a huge talent for some years, finishing his racing career with the distinction of being named the 2007 Aged Pacer of the Year in both Canada and the US.

The purse for the Lis Mara that day was $293,000 (USD). The seven pacers, Dali, Lonestar Legend, Somebeachsomewhere, Blue Claw, Riggins, Major Hottie, Upfront Hannahsboy—in order of post position—were all seasoned champions, well able to cross the finish line first.

That is, if six of the seven could edge past the powerhouse in post position three, who had that damn "extra gear," as his driver Paul MacDonell was known to say. And why not? Wasn't it finally time for another brilliant pacer to win?

"And they're off!"

Major Hottie didn't wait for any further invitation. The powerful bay in a field of other powerful bays floored it from the outside toward the rail. Lonestar Legend was even quicker from the rail, settling shoulder to shoulder with Major Hottie, while Dali powered into third.

Beach was in fourth.

As they approached the quarter-mile, Lonestar Legend shot into the lead. But not for long.

The announcer's words could almost be Beach's theme song, they'd been sung so often at Beach's races.

"*And here comes The Beach*! Somebeachsomewhere is *underway*!"

When Lonestar Legend passed the quarter-mile in 26.3, Beach was four lengths back, with a quarter time of 27.2. Moments later, Beach passed Major Hottie, and then, Lonestar Legend.

"The Beach is on the lead before the half-mile split!"

But Lonestar Legend was right behind him, determined as ever, as Beach passed the half-mile pole in front of him in 53.4.

Meanwhile, Dali had pulled ahead into third, but despite Lonestar Legend's tenaciously held position in second, Beach had stretched his lead to one and one-quarter at both the half and three-quarter poles.

And still Lonestar Legend gave it all he had, pushing to take the rail, eating into Beach's lead by half a length. With an eighth of a mile left, Beach and MacDonell flicked on the overdrive.

Beach won by three and a half lengths, in 1:47.4. He was followed by Lonestar Legend, Dali, and Blue Claw. Major Hottie, who had perhaps expended too much in the first two quarters, finished in fifth, followed by Riggins in sixth and Upfront Hannahsboy in seventh.

As always, the applause for Beach and Paul MacDonell was jubilant and sustained.

Overall, it had been a phenomenal day of harness racing at The Red Mile. Only a short time later that same day, superstar trotter Deweycheatumnhowe had won the first and final heats of the prestigious Kentucky Futurity, part of the Triple Crown of Harness Racing for Trotters.

Trained and driven by Ray Schnittker, "Dewey" had won ten for ten in his first year, 2007, voted in as Trotter of the Year to finish off. That year, 2008, had been no less spectacular, with his first seven starts completing a string of seventeen consecutive victories. He'd also been selected, unanimously, as Trotter of the Year and Three-Year-Old Trotting Colt of the Year.

Along the way he'd made $2,218,987 (USD) in earnings for 2008, making him, by a good margin, the leading money-making trotter in North America.

Dewey's victory in the Kentucky Futurity was a cause for joy and celebration for his owners, for his many fans in North America and around the world, and for the American Standardbred Trotting community.

But Somebeachsomewhere's resounding win at the $293,000 Lis Mara took its share of headlines and television clips, too—perhaps even the lion's share. Some of the press even said that Beach's seventeenth win in eighteen lifetime starts at the Lis Mara came close to "stealing the thunder" of Deweycheatumnhowe's exciting 1:53 win at the Futurity Stakes.

Politics aside, Schooner Stables was thrilled with their victorious pacing colt's performance, and relieved that they all had a bit of a breather coming up before Beach would race in the Messenger Final, at Yonkers Raceway, in three weeks' time.

There were those who might have thought it was getting late in the year, and that the next race day, in New York State, could bring cold and stormy weather.

MacGrath could have been forgiven for thinking there was no weather that could hold back his thunderbolt of a colt. Ever the optimist, he might even have thought they had an equal chance of decent weather and a fast track. It had been just that kind of a lucky year, hadn't it?

THE MESSENGER FINAL, YONKERS RACEWAY, YONKERS, NEW YORK, OCTOBER 25, 2008

"It was a dirty, miserable, windy night," says Brent MacGrath, so many years later. "The nastiest race night I'd ever seen."

In fact, hurricane conditions prevailed at Yonkers Raceway that evening. The track lights lit their own bases more than the track, it seemed, and the slashing rain came down sideways. The southerly winds weren't raw, but the temperature made little difference to the assault of the wind and rain. The horses came into the paddock wearing rain sheets. When these were pulled off, their bodies were drenched long before the post sounded. Underfoot, the track was packed, hard and wet.

But this is what top athletes do, both human and equine: they compete no matter what the weather, what the circumstances—giving the same supreme effort they would at any other time.

The first-rate field of six pacers resolutely made their way to the starting gate. They had been brought together to compete for a hefty $650,000 (USD) purse, and, abysmal weather aside, the racegoers were keen to see them race.

To Schooner Stables's dismay, Somebeachsomewhere had drawn the worst post position possible: six, on the outside. Legacy N Diamonds was in one, Brother Ray in two, Dali in three, Santanna Blue Chip in four, and fellow Maritimer and supreme rival, Shadow Play, was in five. Beach was the three-to-one favourite—but he had his work cut out for him on this wretched night, perhaps as never before.

"Here they come…they're off!"

Limestone and muddy spray flew up into the faces of both riders and horses as they took off. Santanna Blue Chip shot out from the mid-pack to take the early lead as the field headed into the first turn. Shadow Play and Beach followed close behind. By the opening quarter of 27.1, Shadow Play had muscled past Santanna Blue Chip and taken the lead. An "unhurried" Somebeachsomewhere stayed in third—until, at the 56.1 half-mile, MacDonell cued him. The pace began to pick up.

And still, "Shadow Play is the one to knock off!" shouted the announcer.

Inexorably, relentlessly, every splashing stride brought Beach closer to the front-runner. At the three-quarter mark (1:24.2), he was still "shadowing" Shadow Play, but his progress was like a kettle only seconds before it boils: racegoers knew it was about to get lethally hot on that track for the two champion harness racers.

"And Shadow Play is *all heart*! It's come down to these two in the Messenger Final!"

Rhonda MacGrath shares a treat of carrots with Beach at Baycairn in November 2008. (DAVE LANDRY)

So close, so heartbreakingly close, ran those two leaders, even stride for stride, and yet it was "Somebeachsomewhere—*some champion*!" who rocketed over the finish line first in 1:52.1.

Later, pundits would say the track conditions had slowed the footing by at least a couple of seconds. Even still, 1:52.1 was only a "tick" off Always a Virgin's stakes-winning local record, while the all-venue Messenger record, set by Allamerican Ingot in 2002, was 1:50.3.

Paul MacDonell would say, when he caught his breath after this, one of the wilder races of his career, that he got a "nice third seat" and a breather in the second quarter, and then had to come "first-over," a manoeuvre which means being the first horse to make a move on the race leader, moving up on the outside.

Of course Beach had endured a brutal first-over trip in the Meadowlands Pace—but had finished second, a "nk," or neck, behind Art Official. And if you don't think that uneasy memory flittered through MacDonell's mind the night of the Messenger, think again.

Fortunately, the bottomless pit of "heart and soul" MacDonell had once spoken of, which Beach had shown at the earlier neck-and-neck race, served him well yet again. This time, it culminated in a win.

But of course, horses don't know that they've won when it's that close—do they?

They certainly know when the whole wet crowd yells their name to the black skies above, and the humans spill onto the muddy track to be closer to the winner's circle. That's when the victor leans closer to their trainer, or their own humans, for a comforting pat on the neck, cheek, or nose, knowing a warm, dry stall, a rubdown with soft towels, and a feed tub full of carrots awaits them.

A photograph in the October 29, 2008, edition of *Horseman and Fair World* shows MacDonell, with a drenched Schooner Stables assembly, and Beach, sporting a neon-yellow rain sheet that covers his body and neck.

And the only thing as noticeable as that yellow sheet?

The huge smiles of all the people gathered in the downpour.

ONTARIO SIRES STAKES SUPER FINAL, THREE-YEAR-OLD COLTS AND GELDINGS, WOODBINE RACETRACK, TORONTO, NOVEMBER 15, 2008

All of Beach's races were special to the MacGraths—but this one had something both Brent and Rhonda cherished.

"For the Super Final at Woodbine, all of Rhonda's brothers and sisters, and their families, were able to come to the race," says Brent.

"All nine siblings," says Rhonda happily. "And altogether, about thirty family members. It was great."

It was also Beach's debut at the large and elegant track, complete with sparkling infield ponds. Small wonder the MacKenzie family wanted to be in Toronto that night. Not only was Beach's racing career drawing to a close, making this race one of the last opportunities to see the mighty bay in action at the top of his game, but it was a chance to experience Woodbine, too, which has a fascinating history and grand ambiance.

"The grandstand is huge," says Brent, "and the track is set way back from it. The whole facility is so impressive."

But beauty aside, if anyone in the grandstand had been hoping for better weather than at the Messenger Final in Yonkers three weeks earlier, they were sorely disappointed. There were no sparkling ponds that day; rain-puckered or ice-covered ones, maybe.

"It was cold," says Brent MacGrath, "about 0°C, going between snow and rain."

Ontario Racetracks: A Brief History

Informal Thoroughbred racing had its beginnings in 1797 on a sandy strip of land on the peninsula that once connected the Toronto Islands to the mainland of Ontario.

The first Queen's Plate, Canada's oldest Thoroughbred horse race, was run on June 27, 1860, at the Carleton racetrack in Toronto. The prize was "a plate to the value of fifty guineas." (Held every summer since, the Queen's Plate is now the oldest continuously run Thoroughbred race in North America.)

Greenwood Raceway was built along the shores of Lake Ontario in eastern Toronto. The track had a lot of names in its time: Woodbine Race Course, The Woodbine, Old Woodbine, and Woodbine Riding and Driving Park. In 1963, it became Greenwood Race Track.

Since 1956, Woodbine has been set on a grand 780 acres in Etobicoke, a former township that is now part of the City of Toronto. The modern and gracious facility has three tracks: a one-mile track with an artificial surface made from a composite product called Tapeta; the E. P. Taylor Turf Course, at one and a half miles long; and a 7/8 of a mile turf track.

Was Beach up for yet another demanding race on a weather-compromised track? It's not as though the competition had lessened. The hard-driving Shadow Play had fought every inch of the way that day in Yonkers, requiring Beach to dig deep for a champion performance. No cakewalk, that.

This time, including himself, he'd be competing in a field of eight. Some names were familiar as serious opponents Beach had run against before—Keystone Horatio, The Mohegan Pan, Deuce Seelster, Lucky Man—and some were new: Trade Editor, Dougs Fame, and Amillionpennies. All had more than enough speed and talent to claim their post positions.

Beach drew post position three. Paul MacDonell and Beach jogged purposefully to the starting gate.

"Here they come," said the announcer. "And a good beginning for Somebeachsomewhere as he's the fastest off the wings of the gate."

It was a good beginning for The Beach.

It was a good quarter pole (:27), half pole (:54.2), and three-quarter pole (1:21.0).

It was a good home stretch, with all his track-mates lined up behind him, stretched out like ducklings following their mama to one of those rain-pocked ponds in the infield.

Keystone Horatio was, according to the announcer, "a long-distance phone call back in second."

Not to mention how effortless it all looked, which of course, is what champions—both of the equine and human variety—do best. Paul MacDonell sat quietly in the sulky, whip set back over his shoulder, eyes straight ahead; Beach purr-paced ahead of him, as though he had a Porsche engine, fifth gear not yet engaged. At the wire, Beach was an extraordinary eleven and three-quarter lengths—roughly ninety-four feet, or twenty-nine metres—ahead.

The win also put Beach near the $3 million mark in career earnings.

"We were so very pleased with his performance," says MacGrath.

As well they might be.

For Schooner Stables member Pam Dean, the race was unforgettable, for many reasons.

Paul MacDonell driving Beach toward the finish line during the Ontario Sires Stakes Super Final at Woodbine in Toronto, Ontario, November 15, 2008.
(DAVE LANDRY)

"The weather that night was miserable," she affirms. "It was a blizzard—rain and snow and wind, and when we went down to the winner's circle it couldn't be outdoors because it was too nasty, so we ended up going back to the barns. There were probably 150 people there."

She remembers recognizing a florist she knew from Truro. "In Ontario! And that's where she had to be that night. Relatives of ours would show up. It was wonderful."

Schooner Stables was delighted, as were the MacGraths and Rhonda's family—and, of course, all the cheering and jumping fans in the immense grandstand, and on the track itself, and in the barns, and watching the simulcast across North America—everyone enjoying one of the best Beach Parties ever.

MacGrath's friend, Canadian Horse Racing Hall-of-Famer, Carl Jamieson, couldn't resist making a joke about the circumstances of the race.

"Now Beach has a world record in a snowstorm, too," Jamieson laughed.

Not quite—but considering the weather, it should have been. For Schooner Stables, the $300,000 purse no doubt added to the pleasure of the win.

BREEDERS CROWN FINAL, THREE-YEAR-OLD COLTS AND GELDINGS, THE MEADOWLANDS, EAST RUTHERFORD, NEW JERSEY, NOVEMBER 29, 2008

That Meadowlands Racetrack, in New Jersey—The Beach was going to race again on the same track where, as a three-year-old, he'd suffered his one and only defeat, to Art Official, at the Meadowlands Pace. Wasn't it somehow unlucky to come back there—to make this Beach's penultimate race? *What if, what if...?*

Or were questions of luck far, far behind the mature three-year-old Beach now? Could his speed and flawless gait blast him right through a poor post position, or help him overcome awful weather? Would that healed crack in the coffin bone stay healed, or would the bone break entirely, as, tragically, they have been known to do? Or would another shoe get thrown?

It's a horse race—that will always mean anything can happen. Luck is always a factor with the health and soundness of these powerful but fragile four-legged creatures. There are so many variables, so many ways for a horse to pull up lame or to spectacularly miss disaster.

And what about Schooner Stables? They'd won nineteen of twenty races with their amazing powerhouse of a stallion, and were now entered in a twenty-first race. Perhaps that group from the Maritimes was feeling cocksure, saw that $500,000 purse as having their initials on it—before the race even took place?

"Absolutely not," says MacGrath. "And we made no predictions for Beach, either. He'd lost there, after all. But sure, we wanted another good race and we hoped for the best."

Beach, in fact, had skipped the elimination race, taking "a buy" that was offered to the highest-earning winners for the year. There had been "rumblings" or questioning about this choice, MacGrath said; some horse racing people viewed it as unwise.

"Why do the $25,000 elimination race?" says MacGrath—typically, holding the same opinion now as then. At the time, MacGrath was determined to save Beach's energies for the bigger race, although MacGrath kept steady with Beach's conditioning work the week before. "As far as we were concerned, Beach was in good shape and ready to race the final."

And as far as everyone back home in Truro was concerned, the Breeders Crown was going to be one of the best nights ever—for The Beach, and for everyone attending the party held in his honour at Truro Raceway.

Organized by local businessman Bruce Kennedy, this party might indeed have been the most colourful and fun Beach Party to date. Staff wore Hawaiian hats and beads, as did many of the partygoers. The dining room at the clubhouse was decorated to the nines, and the event included a multi-course meal. Tickets for the evening sold out instantly.

"It was huge," says MacGrath, "probably one of the premier events ever put on in the grandstand. Everybody spoke very highly of it. The entertainment was a whole program of racing from the Meadowlands. They also had special races going on that night at the Truro Raceway."

There was a big purse and a big field for that Breeders Crown final. Oddly enough, Beach was given post position three again, the same position he had started from in his last race. Was that a good omen? Once again there were competitors old and new—Shadow Play, Dali, Blue Claw, Share The Delight, Lisfinny, Blueridge Western, Bettor Sweet, Mystery Chase, and Rudy Rednose.

Shadow Play had come so close to winning the Messenger Final, losing by a neck. Would he take sweet revenge this time out? Dali had been a noble competitor throughout Beach's career; Blue Claw, a more recent threat. And didn't every one of the nine want to see The Beach well back in their rear-view mirrors, so to speak?

Undeniably.

It was a good race. It was a race that showed the drive and courage and ability of ten top-of-the-line harness racing pacers. Shadow Play, in the pocket directly behind Beach for the entire race, did indeed keep Beach concentrated on the job, as did Blueridge Western, coming on so strongly, so gallantly, in the home stretch.

But it was Somebeachsomewhere, also in the home stretch, who poured it on and drew away. "Somebeachsomewhere goes out a champion!" the announcer cried. Beach won the race by one and three-quarter lengths, coming over the wire at a hard-driving 1:48.3, followed by Shadow Play, Blueridge Western, and Dali.

"With that 1:48.3, Beach broke the twenty-fifth Breeders Crown record—and it still stands," says MacGrath. "He was on cruise control. I was proud; we all were. Beach was as good the last race as he was in the first."

Hold it—wasn't there one more race to come? What about the Matron Stakes at the Dover Raceway, in Dover, Delaware? The last four races had been so much fun, and so lucrative, and Schooner Stables had paid into The Dover Stakes, as well—hadn't they?

"That's right," says MacGrath. "We all thought, 'This is great, why not go to Dover, pick up another few thousand dollars?'"

But as it turned out, Beach was running a temperature after the Breeders Crown.

"I was disappointed," says MacGrath. "But it was the right decision. Beach was a little bit sick. We all wanted him to finish well."

Nonetheless, it was hard for everyone in the harness racing community in North America and beyond to bid adieu to Somebeachsomewhere. Who wanted to think that they'd never see The Beach race again, never see the power, beauty, and awesome ability of one of the best pacers ever in the history of the sport—a pacer some said was the very best? Not...anyone.

But circumstances being what they were, it was time for Schooner Stables to accept that the excellent outcome at the Breeders Crown was indeed going to be the race to end on.

The tally of Beach's triumphs throughout 2008 defied belief. He'd won the United States Harness Writers Association's 2008 Dan Patch Horse of the Year and Pacer of the Year awards, and Harness Tracks of America's Nova Award for a Three-Year-Old Pacing Colt. He'd won Canada's O'Brien Award for Horse of Year—by unanimous choice—along with the Cam Fella Award, which honours meritorious service to harness racing in Canada.

He had been nominated for the Lou Marsh Trophy as Canada's Athlete of the Year—an award generally reserved for humans.

He had been a media sensation. The Canadian Broadcasting Corporation in Nova Scotia had named him their "Newsmaker of the Year." The *Halifax Herald* claimed his as their Sports Story of the Year, while his hometown newspaper, the *Truro Daily News*, announced him as their Newsmaker of the Year. *Canadian Sportsman* declared Beach the Readers' Choice Horse of the Year, and the magazine itself called him their Newsmaker of the Year.

It was all heady, heartwarming, and hard to believe.

But new adventures beyond the track beckoned. Somebeachsomewhere, the harness horse, had retired, victoriously, with a career of twenty-one starts and twenty wins. He had set four world records, including the fastest race mile in the history of the sport. He had also recorded sub-1:50 miles in exactly half his wins. With a bow to the grandstand, eyes bright with competitive joy, The Beach was now stepping back from a world that had hollered his name to the heavens over two glorious years of harness racing.

Somebeachsomewhere, the stallion, would leave for Hanover Shoe Farms in Pennsylvania in one week's time.

Chapter 18

A SPORTSWRITER'S DREAM

SCHOONER STABLES AND HARNESS RACING FANS WEREN'T THE only ones feeling somewhat off-kilter when The Beach retired. Sportswriters in Canada and around the world felt his departure keenly. Some of Canada's best, in fact, had been covering Beach's career since his first appearance on the track at Grand River, and may even have felt sad and deflated after his last race at the Meadowlands. And while those scribes would miss seeing Beach up close, and talking with Schooner Stables about their colt's latest win, they also knew there would be stories about his new career as a stallion, and, of course, stories about his sons and daughters, should any of them turn out to be chips off the old block.

Unquestionably, there would be more Beach stories—and that was something for which they could happily await word.

One of those sportswriters was Dave Briggs, who has a curriculum vitae any journalist would give a lot to call their own. The multi–award-winning Briggs has worked for a number of Ontario newspapers, both as a news reporter and a sportswriter. He worked as publisher and editor of *Canadian Sportsman*, a harness racing trade magazine, for nearly nineteen years. The periodical, which had been in existence since 1870, was the oldest harness racing magazine in North America. Sadly, it ceased publishing after the December 2013 edition.

Sports journalist Dave Briggs at the Meadowlands in New Jersey, 2009
(DAVE LANDRY)

Briggs has also worked as a columnist for *Horseman and Fair World,* published in Lexington, Kentucky, and as a features writer for *Hoof Beats* magazine, published in Columbus, Ohio.

He is the former editor of *Canadian Thoroughbred* and is currently the editor at the online publication *Harness Racing Update.*

Industry players know if they talk to Briggs, he'll get the story right, and he'll tell it well, with lots of energy. He is trusted and well liked. Overall, Briggs probably wrote more about Beach than any other Canadian or American journalist had done. The entire "Beach experience" is one he will never forget.

The Maritimes would love to claim Dave Briggs, but they can't— not quite.

"My family is from New Brunswick," affirms Briggs, "but I'm not. We've come from that part of the world going back to the 1700s; just not so much anymore." As a child, Briggs, who was born in Windsor, Ontario, visited his grandparents in Plaster Rock, New Brunswick—population 1,023—which only strengthened those Maritime bonds.

Anyone researching a book on racing legend Somebeachsomewhere quickly comes to see the quality of the sports writing connected to harness racing. The language seems particularly zestful when discussing the story of Beach. Those sportswriters, women and men, rock a keyboard.

"There's a decent bunch out there," agrees Briggs. "And I think Beach was a special story, so that's a big part of it. People put some more effort into it or followed him more closely because they knew that this was a once in-a-lifetime type of horse."

Beach's syndicate was also a once-in-a-lifetime gathering of people.

"Don't get me wrong, the horse was fantastic," says Briggs. "He obviously had talents that exceeded other horses' talents on the track. But it was the complete story that I loved—one man cobbling together some friends from the Maritimes and going to a sale and buying one horse and getting it for basically the last dollar he had to spend on that horse."

It was a story even the largest North American newspapers loved. "One Horse in the Stable, But He's One of the Best," read the July 17, 2008, headline in *The New York Times*. This may have been the inspiration for the oft-used phrase, "one-horse-stable." Journalists around the world came to love it—the implication being that Schooner Stables, the "little guy," was making the rich guys look bad for doing on a proverbial nickel what they couldn't do for a bar of gold.

It was true: Schooner Stables wasn't rich, not by horse-world standards.

"It's the improbability of the story; the fact that this wasn't the usual suspects. These were people from the Maritimes, where the love of horse racing and horses is very deep. I deal with the same kinds of owners and trainers and the usual wealthy people with the star horses every year, and I didn't know who Brent MacGrath was. I certainly knew who Paul MacDonell was, because he's raced around here and he's been successful for many years," says Briggs.

"Brent's an interesting guy on his own, and the rest of the Schooner Stables is fascinating, so it's all that. The more you delve into the story, the more improbabilities come out. How did these people end up with this horse?"

Briggs first saw Somebeachsomewhere race at the Metro Pace. It was also the first time Briggs met MacGrath in person.

Briggs was aware that horse racing people were talking about Beach's height and build, both of which were generous for the breed.

"I'm not a horse expert," he says. "I've been around a lot of horses, but these people work with horses every day. It's when the stars of the sport said, 'Whoa, you know, this is an unbelievable specimen here,'—that's when I took more notice of him."

He pauses, as though in confession. "To be really honest—and some people know this; Brent probably knows this—I was among the more skeptical people of Beach at two years old. I didn't really buy into all this [excitement] until he was three, and that was mostly because of previous experiences. I had seen countless horses that were the next 'great big thing,' and being fantastic as a two-year-old really doesn't mean a lot," he says, noting that this is because the competition isn't fully formed yet.

"You're dealing with baby horses racing against each other, and everybody's telling me this is the greatest horse [they've] ever seen. I even questioned voters making Beach tied for Horse of the Year in Canada…at two, because there was a three-year-old that year, Tell All, who went out and won all the big races…. I said, 'I know you people see that this horse is going to be great, but I want to see it at three.'

Briggs wasn't the only one who questioned the 2007 co-win with Tell All, who, over his racing career, was winner of many prestigious races. "Tell All was a gorgeous horse," says Briggs, "a Canadian horse that was going to the United States and winning the Little Brown Jug. Then he won the North America Cup here in Canada."

Briggs readily admits that, in the long run, he was wrong about Beach. "That realization came pretty quickly once Beach won the North America Cup and we all saw the way he dominated [during his third year]."

In fairness, it is Briggs's job, and the job of sportswriters generally, to be skeptical, and also to resist owner-as-head-cheerleader. "Brent's a good talker, right? He's very persuasive."

It soon became obvious, however, that MacGrath wasn't the only one feeling cocky—that, in fact, he and Beach were mirror images of confidence who brought out the competitive best in one other.

"It was Brent's obsession," says Briggs, of the focus on Beach. "Especially those two years that he took time off work and followed this horse around, at two, then at three. I know he sent him to Jean Louis Arsenault to train in Ontario, but it was basically Brent calling the shots."

Briggs didn't see all of Beach's races due to simple geography.

"I live two hours from Mohawk," he explains. "But I saw most of the key ones."

Briggs saw the Metro Pace when Beach was two years old, and the North America Cup when he was three.

"I was there for the Meadowlands Pace in New Jersey, too," he says. "That was a great one. I was at the world record mile in Kentucky, and I was back at the Meadowlands for the Breeders Crown. I was also at Mohawk for the Ontario Sires Stakes Super Final night during Beach's three-year-old year."

Briggs won't soon forget what the big pacer's presence meant to the harness racing industry.

"Beach was outstanding," says Briggs, pointing out that he was one of few horses to ever get mainstream media coverage. "To end up on CBC News, *The National*; to be considered, briefly, as a national athlete of the year against humans, with the Lou Marsh award; to get in the *Toronto Star*; to be on the cover of the *National Post* [headlined 'Canada's Greatest Stud']."

Briggs says Beach's unconventional story was part of the draw. "People say, 'Here's some Maritimers doing this incredible thing in this sport.' That's easy to sell, because it wasn't just a bunch of rich guys owning a horse and racing—and also, it's a really good horse…. Beach was instrumental in gaining attention outside of the sport and inside the sport."

Then, of course, there was the focus on Beach as a personality, a bona fide star.

Canadians, says Briggs, "adopted Beach really quickly." There were also regional ties at work.

"The Ontario people in the sport are always pretty big fans of the Maritime folks because they go to the Gold Cup and Saucer [held in Charlottetown] and they see the enthusiasm Maritimers have for horses and for harness racing. They also saw how connected Maritimers were to Beach."

The Americans, for good reason, took a little longer to "buy in," says Briggs.

"There was another horse that year," he says, "a trotter named Deweycheatumnhowe. He was the rival for attention within the sport."

Boy, was he ever.

"Head to Head!" blazoned the masthead on the cover of the January 2009 issue of *Hoof Beats* magazine. "One Final Battle Looms for Deweycheatumnhowe, Somebeachsomewhere!" The cover image shows the head and shoulders of the two champions running flat-out, as though toward one another, both with nostrils flared, ears pinned, and coats lathered with sweat. The only immediately discernible difference between the two champions—one a pacer, one a trotter, but both bays—was the right front pastern on Dewey, which was white. Both look like they're about to charge over their individual finish lines in first place.

Everyone loves to see two spectacular athletes, whether two- or four-legged, go head-to-head; everyone hates it, too, because the two are beloved in their immediate and wider circles, and everyone wants their baby to win the coveted "best of all" rating.

Briggs understood this tender ground. "Best trotter? Dewey in a landslide. Horse of the Year? The Beach all the way."

Ultimately, "The Beach" was chosen as US Horse of the Year in 2008.

As for Dewey, many honours lay ahead for him. Dewey was and is some horse. He simply wasn't Somebeach, during that magical second year of North American harness racing, in 2008.

"It was a fantastic story," says Briggs.

Even still, he remembers that the same skepticism he had about Beach at two was similar to what the Americans had for him at three.

"The world record helped," says Briggs, "and some of the other performances helped."

Curiously, so did Beach's only loss, at the Meadowlands Pace final.

"His only loss was perhaps his greatest race; that's actually debated," says Briggs. "That's the best performance from a horse in a losing effort that most people had ever seen."

Does Briggs think it was Beach's best race?

"I'll remember it forever," he says.

While Briggs may have teased Brent MacGrath about working as a car salesman and not as a full-time trainer (before he actually became one, at least for one year), he views MacGrath's training and overall treatment of Beach as crucial to Beach's success.

"Essential—because there you have a person with knowledge who has decided, 'I'm going to devote every ounce of my energy to this and my time.' And that's why they made such a big deal about the one-horse stable aspect. There are very few one-horse stables out there. There are a lot of people who have to manage ten or twenty or forty horses; in some cases it's sixty horses and there's a lot of distraction."

MacGrath's single-mindedness about helping to make Beach a superstar was obvious to all in the industry. "Brent's mind was set about what he wanted, and what he wanted to do, and there was nobody telling him any differently," says Briggs. "I think that was critical to the horse's success, too."

This autocratic single-mindedness didn't always go down well, even within Schooner Stables. But trying to stop MacGrath—or his horse—was like trying to stop a locomotive with a full head of steam on it.

"MacGrath certainly had some critics," says Briggs, "but I don't think anybody ever said he did a bad job as a trainer, because the proof was right there."

As a sportswriter, Briggs would have a historical perspective on Beach. Who was Beach as good as—or better than, historically speaking?

"Beach was only really tested once," says Briggs, "in the Meadowlands Pace final. But those are hard comparisons to make, because, historically, it's a totally different set of races. The kind of following that Somebeachsomewhere enjoyed was similar to Cam Fella's.

"But the biggest crowd I've seen at the North America Cup was the one that Somebeachsomewhere was entered in. I wasn't around back in the old days of Greenwood Raceway when it was packed. So, in my time, he drew the biggest crowds and Cam Fella seems to be the comparison."

Briggs says favourites are sometimes generational. For racing fans who are older than him, "there's no arguing with them, Niatross was the greatest horse they've ever seen. And if they were thirtysomethings when Cam Fella was around, there's no arguing with them—Cam Fella was the greatest horse they ever saw, won twenty-eight straight races…. But if you were my age and you saw Beach, you said, 'I didn't experience those horses, so this is my horse.'"

This is my horse, says Dave Briggs—as do so many others who were lucky enough to see Beach blistering down a racetrack.

Chapter 19
CANADA'S BIGGEST STUD

WHEN SOMEBEACHSOMEWHERE WAS TRUCKED FROM THE MARK Ford Training Center in Middletown, New York, to Hanover, Pennsylvania, the first week of December 2008, he would arrive to a whole new green and expansive world, destined to be his forever home. Helping him settle in were the numerous grooms and many staff at the farm, but Beach would primarily be under the sharp eye and in the capable and kind hands of Hanover's chief veterinarian, Dr. Bridgette Jablonsky.

Her first name is pronounced Bridg-ETTE, with the emphasis on the second syllable, which is slightly unusual for the Irish origin name; her surname, of Polish origin, would be pronounced "Yablonsky" in Europe, but Americans apparently prefer to pronounce the J.

At a guess, it is unlikely American-born Jablonsky has ever worried about how people pronounce her names; guessing again, it has probably never crossed her mind. She saves her concerns for the good stuff—a list that starts and ends with the care and specialized breeding of Standardbred horses.

If you've ever seen Bridgette Jablonsky quietly holding court in a fold-out canvas chair at the pavilion at the Harrisburg Selected Yearling Sale, hour after hour, day after day, you'll know how seriously she takes her position as executive vice-president at Hanover Shoe Farms, and how seriously she is taken by the hundreds of buyers who come to sit beside

Dr. Bridgette Jablonsky, executive vice-president of Hanover Shoe Farms, discussing the 2019 crop of yearlings with a prospective client. (AUTHOR PHOTO)

her in the second empty foldout canvas chair, that's waiting there just for them.

Blessed with exceptional recall and deep powers of observation—part training, part lifelong interest in and appreciation of horses—Dr. Jablonsky, DVM, has the answers to what must be the thousands of questions she is asked. And if she doesn't know, out comes her cellphone, and after a few seconds online she'll find out.

Millions of dollars are spent over the week-long sales event, which runs the first week of November each year in Harrisburg, Pennsylvania. Hanover Shoe Farms rents the Harrisburg Farm Show Complex and Expo Center each year to put on the Harrisburg Selected Yearling Sale.

The 2019 sale, in fact, broke the record for average sales per yearling ($48,903 USD), and topped $40 million (USD) in gross sales for only the second time in its seventy-year history. In total, 833 yearlings sold for a gross of $40,736,000 (USD), up 14.6 percent from 2018.

Hanover is the sport's leading consignor. In 2019, the farm offered 233 yearlings for sale, and grossed $14,371,000 (USD), an average of $61,678 per yearling.

Small wonder Brent MacGrath wanted Somebeachsomewhere to stand at stud at Hanover Shoe Farms. There's over a hundred years of knowledge, passion, and success guiding its operations.

Success is an important part of the equation; running an immense, world-class breeding operation doesn't come cheap. Of those dazzling 2019 sales from Harrisburg alone, chairman and vice-president of Hanover,

Russell C. Williams, was quoted in the November 7, 2019, issue of *Harness Racing Update* as saying, "We can buy a lot of fences with that."

The "we" in that statement is the reader's first clue about how many separate farms, all of which need good fences, make up the overall farm.

But first, turn back the clock to the early 1900s in Hanover, Pennsylvania, when a certain enterprising young man by the name of Lawrence B. Sheppard—then a junior partner in the Hanover Shoe Company, owned by his father, Harper Sheppard, and his business partner, Clinton Myers, and which, yes, manufactured sturdy, quality shoes—was dreaming about a full-time life with horses. At that time, horses were only a hobby for the younger Sheppard.

If you dream it, you can do it—isn't that the adage?

With some bold reorganization, luck, and a lot of hard work, the racing and breeding of Standardbred horses became, in time, a more lucrative operation than the shoe business, which ultimately led Lawrence Sheppard to sell the shoe company and focus entirely on developing his stable of horses.

Sheppard then decided to make Hanover one of the biggest names in horse racing—and with more bold buying decisions and more hard work, did that, too. As time went on, Sheppard selected a successful and committed young horseman by the name John Simpson to be his successor at the farm…and on the story gloriously rolled.

Fast forward a hundred years or so, and Hanover's president and CEO is Russell C. Williams, the chairman is James W. Simpson, and the vice-president/human resources is Michael Simpson.

Hanover now boasts the largest Standardbred horse sales in the world.

As an entity, Hanover is a breeding-only operation; it does not participate in racing with its own horses. The farm sells between three hundred and four hundred horses a year, mostly yearlings, which are birthed, raised, handled, socialized, groomed, and cared for on the farm for a full year before being taken to auction. There is much to admire about this business, founded by a horse-lover and run by men and women who continue that fine tradition. But perhaps most admirable is its ethical grounding.

Tar Heel's resting place in the "Graveyard of Champions" at Hanover Shoe Farms.
(AUTHOR PHOTO)

Look no further than the retired broodmare field, where respected dams live out their remaining natural lives in comfort and peace, or look to the farm's "Graveyard of Champions," where magnificent stallions such as Adios, Tar Heel, Star's Pride, Albatross, and many others are buried with simple gravestones. Visitors to the farm can go to the graveyard, take photographs of their favourite stallion's headstone, and spend a quiet moment or two among the best of the best harness racers, both trotters and pacers, who ever raced.

Hanover never forgets its hard-working, brilliant mares, either, and their precious gifts to the world. Rich N Elegant, Armbro Romance, Cathedra, Incredible Margie, Ohyouprettything, Sandlark Hanover, A Gift For You, A Pippin Hanover, Abbie Hall, and All Tucked Up are among the most elite group of broodmares ever to grace a Standardbred breeding farm. Alive or deceased, their names are spoken with reverence at Hanover.

Bridgette Jablonsky was born in Manhasset, New York, but grew up on a farm.

"I was first introduced to horses as a girl," says Jablonsky, who is small in stature, but huge in reputation. Simply stated, she is one of the most influential and knowledgeable horsewomen in North America.

"We had a little farm in Syosset, New York, which was close to a racetrack called Roosevelt Raceway, which was on Long Island, and, unfortunately, closed. It was a beautiful racetrack and I spent a lot of my younger years there. That's how I really grew to love the sport of harness racing and to love Standardbred horses. My uncle was a bettor, actually, and he got the whole family involved. He evolved from being a bettor to buying a few claiming horses and then it took off from there."

As a student in college, Jablonsky had other loves besides horses—even possibly conflicting loves.

"I always liked the Standardbred breed; the only temptation I had was to become a medical doctor—a human doctor versus a veterinarian." She found out the hard way, during a student placement at a trauma centre in a busy emergency room, that she was not cut out to be an MD, so instead, she went into veterinary medicine at the University of Pennsylvania.

The rest, as they say, is history.

"After four years of college, you do four years of veterinary school," she says. "Unlike medical school, unlike becoming an MD, you don't need to do an internship or a residency. Basically, once you get your degree, you can practice."

Incredibly, Hanover was her first and only job.

"I came to Hanover right after graduation in '96. I started out as resident veterinarian, which means one of the veterinarians employed by the farm to [attend] to the good health and care of the horses." In 1999, she was promoted to farm manager while still doing some veterinary work, and in 2018, she was promoted to executive vice-president. "My veterinary duties are very limited now," she says. "I do some of the reproductive work. I really like it. I hope I'm not being immodest by saying that I'm quite good at it. So I keep my hand in the till there, but we have two other veterinarians that do everything else."

Three veterinarians working on one farm? Just how big is this place? And how many horses live there?

Refer back to those three thousand acres, but this time, imagine fourteen yearling fields, twenty-one separate mare and foal farms, and the fairgrounds where farm staff prep the yearlings for sales. At various times in its history, Hanover has been home to as many as 9 to 12 stallions, 336 yearlings, and 500 broodmares.

The farm has what it calls "peak population"—a thousand to eleven hundred horses—when the foals are born, in the spring.

In the autumn of 2019, though, the farm was "a little bit on the north side of one thousand," according to Jablonsky. "We're not at peak right now because we don't have any babies, we just have the mothers and the yearlings. So we're expecting about 360 babies."

Three hundred and sixty babies…

"It's a lot of work, yeah." Jablonsky says they're on a constant look-out for veterinarians, but admits it's not a glamorous job: the hours are long, and it doesn't pay as well as work as a small-animal vet. "You really, really have to love…working on a breeding farm. We're blessed, because our other veterinarian here, Dr. Megan Moschgat, loves it like I love it—she loves the sport; she loves the horses."

Jablonsky is one of about seventy-five employees who take care of the horses and maintain the properties. "I've been here for—let's see—it'll be twenty-four years this year," she says, adding she'd gone through vet school thinking she'd be a racetrack vet. "Then when I got to vet school I figured out I had much more of an affinity for reproduction and babies…I don't think I would've been happy [at a track]. Also, with my career progression, I didn't stay just a veterinarian. Now I'm executive vice-president. That never would've happened for me if I was in a different organization. So things worked out as good as they could've for me."

And all these complex factors considered, Hanover has obviously done well in their choice of Bridgette Jablonsky, too. The promotion has served everyone well.

"We're coming off a fantastic year. We broke our own record for total earnings by a farm of any breed, and we set a sale record for ourselves; we had the best sale [at the Harrisburg Selected Yearling Sale] that we've ever had."

Three-year-old Beach arrived at Hanover in early winter.

"It was on December 12, 2008," says Jablonsky, easily finding the date in her records. "That's the first time I saw him in person. But I'd watched just about every race of his on TV."

Jablonsky was excited the day Beach's trailer came down the long, treed driveway.

"There are a lot of things that go through your mind. You're gearing up for Beach's new career as a stallion, so you're planning; you're thinking, 'When are we going to start training him and what's his life going to be like here? What are his routines going to be, what are we going to do with him tomorrow?' ...There's a lot of responsibility when they hand you over a lead shank, and connected to the lead shank is $10, $12 million dollars' worth of horse flesh."

She pauses, expands the thought well beyond the animal's day-to-day care.

"It's excitement, but it's tempered by the sense of responsibility. This is a big undertaking. He's going to be syndicated, there's going to be shareholders, there will be people who are investing a lot of money. Then there are the original owners, too. It's a lot of money for them. When Brent hands you a lead shank the responsibility [falls on you]. I'm sure Brent felt all of that when he was racing [Beach]. It goes from him to me."

Jablonsky, the staff and owners of Hanover, and Beach's Canadian owners, Schooner Stables, were not the only ones feeling excited and yet sobered and apprehensive, too. A certain 16.2-hand superstar pacing stallion was definitely off his game. (A "hand" is four inches, which made Beach five feet, four inches tall at the withers, or base of the neck.) He was in a new country, at a new barn, with new people—in a whole new world, really.

Perhaps most disorienting to the young horse was that his whole raison d'être had changed—and no one had consulted him. For two years, Beach had raced to the edges of his heart and beyond, and now he was a gentleman stallion of leisure. For a fierce competitor who loved attention, and who was a crowd-bowing ham, the world had taken on a quiet, even boring tilt. Canadian newspaper stories of the time, even Brent MacGrath, referred to Beach as possibly being "depressed."

"I don't know if I would call it depression," says Jablonsky. "I'm not sure a horse can get depressed. But horses are creatures of habit, and when they have a routine, when they have a lifestyle—well, a lot of horses don't very easily adapt to a new routine and lifestyle. Some do and some don't, and Beach didn't."

She agrees that there were many reasons for this.

"Beach was a racehorse. He was used to being doted on—not that he wasn't doted on here—but he was used to being the centre of Brent and Rhonda's world. They were with him all the time…and he was training; he was really a superstar, he was a movie star.

"Then he comes to the farm and yes, he's still a star, but…there are no TV cameras here and he's sharing a handler with multiple other stallions. He's out in his paddock, he's by himself for most of the day, and it's just different for him. He's not getting the same exercise, he's not racing; we're not asking him to be competitive…. I don't think he was unhappy as much as it took him a little longer than most of the stallions to adapt to this new routine."

The veterinarian in Jablonsky considers the subject further.

"The other thing that happens to these athletes is that physically they deflate a little, too. They go from being athletes with muscle—and a horse like him, he was muscular and big and strong—and they kind of shrink up a little bit. I think that added to the perception of him being dejected."

Brent MacGrath offered suggestions to make him happier.

"Brent said he liked to play with a ball, so we hung a ball for him. And I would bring him carrots." She paints a picture for anyone who might not know how a stallion's day might unfold.

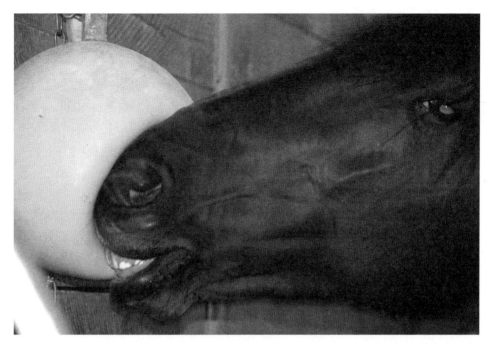

Beach loved his ball and never went anywhere without it. (RHONDA MACGRATH)

"Our stallions are not groomed every day. They're usually only groomed when they go to the breeding shed. We're big believers here in letting the stallions be horses and not over- pampering them. So they basically spend most of their time out in the paddock, and we only bother them, if you will, when they need to go to the breeding shed. Most of them, they like that, they want to be out in their paddock, looking at the mares and grazing. Brent thought that Beach didn't like that, so Brent asked us if we could bring him in every day and groom him, bathe him, and give him extra attention."

Beach also liked to roll in the sand, so they got a few tractor loads of sand and put them in his paddock so he could roll in the sand and scratch his back.

Fortunately, after the first winter, he came around. "They just have to get used to the new home and the new people, and eventually, if you're good to them, they're happy again."

Beach's troubles settling in at Hanover made Schooner Stables uneasy enough that it became a topic of conversation among the group. This may have been prompted by Pam Dean's visit to Hanover, and the very different-looking Beach she found there. She expressed her concerns to the rest of the syndicate. Jamie Bagnell has firm opinions on the matter still.

"Clearly, Beach missed racing," he says. "We thought of doing things like getting a jog cart, and I think they have a racetrack at the farm, but you know, Hanover's been at this now for many years. They have a way of doing things and they don't like to change. So, you know, giving a stallion a jog cart and taking him out every day and jogging him around the racetrack is not something that they would fancy very much.

"But we started to push the envelope some because basically, we own the horse; we own the majority of the horse. We bought him an exerciser, which, again, didn't go over that well at first, but did make a difference to Beach. They don't seem to want to exercise their stallions too much because they're concerned about the risk of them getting hurt, which, of course, can happen."

The exerciser wasn't all.

"We were going to build him a swimming pool," says Bagnell. "That was the next thing Brent wanted to do, because swimming is really good exercise. At this point, Hanover's probably shaking their heads at us."

MacGrath persevered.

"It was Brent who was instrumental in coming up with ideas that made Beach feel better, to get him more exercise so he could eat more—because the horse loved to eat," says Bagnell. "They would put him on a diet because he was getting too fat.... Even with a three-acre paddock to move around in, Beach wasn't getting enough exercise."

The paddock, some people back home in Canada were surprised to learn, had a video camera trained on it.

Bridgette Jablonsky stands, carrots in hand, next to Somebeachsomewhere as a school group from her son's class visits at Hanover Shoe Farms. Stallions can be cranky and aloof, but Jablonsky often took school groups to visit Beach because of his gentle, friendly nature. (HANOVER SHOE FARMS)

"Brent again," says Bagnell, "he put that in. He liked to see how Beach was doing during the day—or even at night, I suppose. The feed came to his cellphone and to his computer screen at work."

Of course it did. Doesn't everyone who cares about their horse who is far away do this? Well, perhaps not. But then again, nothing about Beach's story is ordinary. And few horses have had a more devoted human family.

It is important to understand that Beach was given superb, appropriate care at Hanover Shoe Farms, as is each and every stallion who comes to the farm to stand at stud, or, for that matter, any other horse or foal in their care.

There are many reasons why Hanover is the biggest Standardbred breeding farm in the world, and considered by the majority of horse racing people to be the best.

It's just that most of these stallions aren't, well…pets.

"I think we ascribe a lot of human attributes and emotions to animals that they don't have," Jablonsky says." I'm not sure clinical depression is something that animals do experience…. I think what upset Brent the most was Beach's physical condition, which as I said, was deflated. His hair didn't look great, he got a little potbellied and skinny looking; he just didn't look vibrant."

And so life went on for the sensitive horse, who in spite of life's growing pains, was evolving in his new role as stallion. Jablonsky was with him nearly every step of the way.

"I didn't take care of him daily. He had a groom that would clean his stall, turn him out, bring him in, groom him, but I collected him. And we use the word 'collected' because Standardbreds are bred artificially. They're not breeding the mares. The stallions are collected into an artificial vagina. I believe I collected him just about every time he was collected."

And just how often did Beach do his stud-ly duty?

"Four days a week, and certainly I saw him just about every day," says Jablonsky. "He arrived at the end of 2008, so let's say I collected him from 2009 until 2017, four days a week."

His sperm travelled to some of the best mares in the world.

"The breeding season goes from February to July," says Jablonsky. "We would take the summer off and then I would collect him in the fall for frozen semen to send to Australia and New Zealand."

The price, you ask? That would be $30,000 (USD) a pop or, more correctly, a "straw" of semen.

Of crucial importance, Beach's semen was wonderfully "motile," which is the ideal for impregnating mares. As multiple accounts have noted, however, he was a far less-than-arduous lover. Mounting a "phantom mare"—a man-made creation that has nothing remotely to do with an actual mare, or more to the point, a mare's vagina—didn't stir his passion much. And who could blame him?

Nonetheless, the job needed to get done, done well, and done often. So there are protocols.

First, to get his attention, a mare in heat would be led by Beach's nose. After about ten minutes of teasing, the "tell" of arousal would become obvious, with Beach dancing and snorting. Second, he'd be led to the canvas-covered sawhorse "mare," which awaited his lustful contact. Third, Jablonsky would guide his penis into a custom-fit artificial vagina, which apparently resembles a rubber boot, only bigger, with a pointy end. (Despite the custom fit, it became clear, over time, that Beach preferred it to be loose-fitting.) It was filled with hot water to simulate a mare's temperature.

The process was brief: six thrusts and sixty seconds later, it was over. The end was often accompanied by a triumphant whinny from Beach. Then he'd slip off the phantom mare to return to his spacious paddock, there to enjoy a well-earned snack of whole oats mixed with vitamin-enriched horse pellets.

"Canada's Greatest Stud!" blared the front page headline in the Saturday, July 30, 2016, issue of the *National Post*, accompanied by an adorable, full-page photo of Beach looking over his paddock fence, grass poking out the sides of his mouth, and the upward angle of the shot making him look "all nose," and a punchy and fun article about Beach by Joe O'Connor.

The headline, though, was ironic.

"Beach's libido was never great," admits Jablonsky. "He would breed, but it just had to be perfect. The mare had to be perfect. Even if the mare was perfect, it took him a while…. Some breeding stallions are in and out. It was never like that for him."

Regardless, Beach got the job done, and done well. And one of the most noticeable features of his "get," like their sire himself, was their maturity.

"That was one of the first things we noticed, and that's why they always sold so well—because they were precocious," says Jablonsky. In a field of yearlings, Beach's yearlings would look like two-year-olds and the rest would look like yearlings." Rightly or not, she says, that's what buyers want—a big strong yearling they think is going to be a big strong two-year-old with an advantage over a more slowly maturing one.

"His horses are precocious; they come into their speed early. If anything they're a little bit too precocious, because they can go really fast early…and they would get a little hot, a little aggressive, and you really have to be patient with some of them."

Jablonsky says they have two of his sons and they are so much like him in another very specific way.

"He didn't act like a prima donna. To me he didn't have the look or the personality that you associate with a superstar. He was very humble…. If you walked by his stall, chances are he'd be head-down eating the hay. You wouldn't know you were in the presence of greatness until you knew who he was."

Chapter 20

THE LAND DOWN UNDER

ON JULY 8, 2012, BEACH ENTERED QUARANTINE FOR THREE WEEKS before boarding a flight to Australia. He was going to stand at stud at Empire Stallions, in Avenel, Victoria State. He would fly approximately 16,661 kilometres, or 10,353 miles to do this.

"Their breeding season is opposite ours in North America, so one year, instead of sending his frozen semen, the ownership group wanted to try to send him there," says Bridgette Jablonsky.

Why go to the trouble?

"Frozen semen is harder to use and the conception rate is lower," says Jablonsky. "You can breed more mares if the stallion is there physically. Hanover Shoe Farm is not a great proponent of sending the stallions [abroad]; there's the chance of injury, illness. When he left, I was a little worried."

Nevertheless, it was off to the Antipodes for Beach. No matter what Hanover Shoe Farm thought of the matter, "it certainly wasn't our decision," says Jablonsky. "The [Schooner Stables] syndicate owned the majority of the horse for the life of the horse, and they made all major decisions."

Avenel is a small town in the southwestern state of Victoria, 129 km (80 miles) north of Melbourne, a city of nearly five million. As of 2016, Avenel claimed a population of 1,048. Set between the railway line to

The Empire Stallions grounds in Avenel, Australia—where Beach stood at stud in 2012–2013. (EMPIRE STALLIONS)

Wodonga and the Hume Freeway, the town has forested hilly country to the south, and lands that rise and fall to the north.

Avenel also has a rich horse history. Since 1967, the Goulburn Valley Horse Trials Association has been running the Avenel Horse Trials (also known as an equestrian triathlon, involving dressage, cross-country, and show jumping). This makes it one of the longest continually running horse trials in the country. Even though the event is no longer run out of Avenel, it retains the name and traditions established from the town's earlier glory days.

Empire Stallions, a stallion collection and semen distribution centre, continues Avenel's proud equestrian history. The stunningly beautiful property, with its rolling green pastures, is co-owned, operated, and managed by Canadian-born David James and his partner, American-born Donna Egan.

James's background with horses, like Brent MacGrath's, like Paul MacDonell's—like that of so many horsemen and -women around the world—began in the Standardbred barns near where he grew up.

"My father, Bert V. James, was an automobile dealer in Windsor, Ontario," says James. "He was Chevrolet/Oldsmobile/Cadillac [dealer]. He took in a couple of nice little racehorses to race at Windsor Raceway—took them in as trade on two new vehicles."

Horsepower is horsepower, right? And it all galloped off from there.

"He raced them successfully for a short period of time, decided he liked it, and bought more racehorses and expanded his operation," James continues. "Then he decided he'd like to go into the breeding business and started to buy broodmares." His father leased Bancroft Farm in Avella, Pennsylvania, which was owned at that time by Hall-of-Famer Delvin Miller and his brother Albert.

"We were involved in a breeding operation there, and one of the mares that he bought over the telephone was in foal to Meadow Skipper and had a Meadow Skipper colt at her side. Her name was Voodoo Hanover.... We took the colt to the Harrisburg sale, but he did not sell, did not bring the reserve price of $7,000. That colt turned out to be a horse called Albatross."

That Albatross? The stallion that won fifty-nine of seventy-one starts, including the Cane Pace, Adios Pace, and Messenger Stakes in 1971, and earned $1,201,477? The pacing streak known as Albatross, who, as a three-year-old, set a record for fastest race mile with two races in 1:54.4 at The Red Mile in Lexington? The one and only Albatross who, at the Tattersalls Pace in 1971, set a world record in the opening heat, then an hour later, raced again in the final and equalled that record?

That Albatross, who sired 2,546 sons and daughters, who in turn, won $130,700,280?

Somebeachsomewhere was compared to Albatross's most famous son, Niatross, by numerous horse racing people and sportswriters many times over.

"Albatross was one of the most famous Standardbreds ever—Horse of the Year at two, Horse of the Year at three. He turned out to be a world champion stallion, had a $50,000 service fee at Hanover Shoe Farms many, many years ago." James pauses. "That was my introduction, all those years ago, into the horse business."

James ran Bancroft Farm from a young age.

"Dad had quite a number of broodmares; we were looking at fifty or sixty broodmares breeding for the yearling market. And along came Albatross. He raced Albatross at two himself, syndicated Albatross at the end of his two-year-old season for $1.25 million, keeping 30 percent of him. This new ownership group then sold 100 percent interest in the horse again at the end of his three-year-old season for $2.5 million. Following that, the horse went to Hanover Shoe Farm to stand at stud."

It was indeed one astonishing introduction to harness racing for the kid from Windsor, Ontario.

Breeding Basics

Conception for any mammal isn't always an easy matter. Simply because you buy a "breeding" for your mare doesn't necessarily mean your mare is going to become pregnant and deliver a live foal.

"You hope your mare will have a foal, yes, but there is no guarantee," says David James of Empire Stallions in Avenel, Australia.

And how much semen does that involve? With a single breeding, what kind of chance do you have of impregnation?

"If it's in the United States," says James, "and it's fresh-chilled semen, when your mare is ready to breed you may need to breed two or three times, and on two or three different cycles. A cycle is generally about seven days, and, generally, the best time to breed her is somewhere around the fourth or fifth day. But if she doesn't ovulate, you may have to breed her again two days later and hope she ovulates then," he says. "So you might breed her once or twice in a cycle, and as many as three cycles a year."

That's in the US, where you can't breed more than 140 mares a year to a single stallion. In Australia, you can breed unlimited numbers—a situation which, James says, should be changed.

And it wasn't only an open door to racing, but to the breeding side of the business, as well.

"My background with horses came from the family involvement with Albatross and a large broodmare band that my father accumulated and then sold. All the mares, I think about eighteen of them, were sold to Armstrong Brothers in Toronto in combination with Lana Lobell Farms of Pennsylvania and New Jersey, in a major transaction for more than $1 million back in the early '70s."

The splendid equine business adventures continued.

"In about 1980 I became associated with Woodstock Stud in Monticello, New York," says James, "which was a brokerage company brokering the sale of Standardbreds both privately and at public auction. I'd say that Woodstock was the largest brokerage company of its kind at that particular time. I became a partner in that organization, and I was responsible for the sale of, primarily, pacing stallions to Australia and New Zealand, and several trotting stallions to Europe. So therein lies my connection to Australia and New Zealand."

Life, as it always does, threw a curveball or two at David James.

"My partner, Phil Tully, became ill and died in the mid-'90s," says James. "I started my own brokerage company at that time called David James Blood Stock; it was located not far from the Hall of Fame in New York. Then I decided that rather than selling all the stallion prospects, maybe Donna and I could keep a few of them and stand them at public stud in Australia, and collect service fees and start a breeding operation that way."

Cue Donna Egan, the other amazing half of Empire Stallions, who is pleased to join in.

"Well, actually," she says, "David was doing it a bit before he met me. We've been together twenty-five years now."

And that would be as both business partners and life partners.

"David decided that rather than just take the one-time commission on a sale, that he would go ahead and purchase one of the stallions himself and stand it down here," says Egan. "So he ended up purchasing Albert Albert—who really made everything else possible for us."

James found farms "down under" to which he could lease the stallion. The pair then bought the Abercrombie stallion Jet Lag—world-champion and fastest horse ever on a half-mile track—a record he held for about fifteen years. They also purchased an interest in Beach Towel, a pacing colt who was named 1990 American Harness Horse of the Year, winning eighteen of twenty-three starts, and clocking the fastest race mile of 1:50.

Beach Towel! Wheres The Beach's sire! Beach the stallion's grandsire.

"We were managing the horses remotely from the US at David James Blood Stock, and they were standing under the umbrellas of other farms in Australia," says Egan.

James says the couple started to buy stallions with the idea of standing them in Australia, eventually leasing them to established farms in Australia to attract the customers, breed the mares, and collect the service fees. "We did the advertising and a lot of that type of thing, and the Australian farms to whom we leased the stallions did the actual work attracting customers and breeding the mares here."

They did that for nearly ten years, until, one day, they received a phone call from one of the farms that was leasing four of their stallions. "They said, 'Gee whiz, David, we retired.' And I said, 'When did you retire?' They said, 'Yesterday. What do you want us to do with your stallions?'"

James had to think on his feet—and fast.

"They were lovely horses. I said, 'Well, the breeding season starts in ninety days. What the heck are we going to do now? So we got on a plane, flew to Australia, ended up leasing a farm outside of Shepparton in Victoria, taking the stallions and standing them there ourselves."

It was 2005. Empire Stallions was born.

"We went from managing from afar to actually being on a leased property of 160 acres with the stallions there," says James, "collecting the stallions, breeding mares, doing everything ourselves—which was not part of the original program, but it turned out to be extremely good. And our expertise improved. We got a nice clientele built up and we've added stallions ever since that day."

James and Egan purchased the Avenel property, where they currently reside, in 2010. "Empire Stallions has gone from managing three or four stallions to as many thirteen stallions," says James. "We improved the stallions as we went along, getting better ones. Of course, the very, very best one was Somebeachsomewhere."

There are other collection and semen distribution centres in Australia, but Empire is singular in its operations.

"The one big difference is that Empire is what we call a semen base; we do not have any mares on the farm to be bred," says James. "It is strictly a stallion operation. We have some 'tease-mares,' of course, in order for us to collect the stallions, but only tease-mares."

As such, the property needed to be custom-made for stallions, who have their own robust ways of going through life, quite different from the milder geldings and the generally less-zesty mares.

James explains. "When we purchased the property it was set up for a larger broodmare operation. First thing we did was replace all the fencing. Every inch of it came down and was re-fenced into stallion paddocks or stallion yards of approximately one to two acres, each of which we now have fifteen stallion paddocks. It's all fenced with Kentucky diamond mesh fencing with a top rail and electronic stand-offs. It was all purposely designed for stallions; there are no sharp ninety-degree corners, everything is rounded."

No doubt about it, these stallion paddocks are things of (costly) beauty. As are the flesh and blood stallions. Hence the Cadillac upgrade to the property, putting safety first.

Even still, accidents can happen—because horses are horses: heavy, fast, unpredictable, and in many ways fragile, for all their great strength and endurance.

Somebeachsomewhere's very own sire, Mach Three, died following a "paddock accident," in which he broke his hind leg at Alabar Farms in Waiau Pa, New Zealand, in 2017. He was humanely euthanized at only eighteen years old, which, for a stallion, is relatively young; he could have "worked" for another ten years. Both Mach Three's owners and the farm's owners were devastated by the event, but it was no one's fault, nor was it the exuberant stallion's. As horse people know, horses can break their legs any place, any time, and any way.

"Even just trotting in a straight line," says James. "It's just one of those things that can happen."

Empire Stallions farm also has two lovely homes and a modern barn, along with a collection centre and a large laboratory. James and Egan installed rubber flooring throughout that barn. The box stalls are big, and the roomy barn accommodates seven or eight stallions.

"David was mindful that a lot of the horses would not be ours," says Egan. "We would be responsible to bigger syndicates, bigger farms. We were hoping to attract the very best, and David's number one priority was safety. We always wanted to return the horses in the condition that they came to us in."

The Canadian and the American were on Australian turf, and needed to be aware of the differences.

"The Australian Standardbred industry in particular," continues Egan, "is quite different than what the Standardbred industry is in America. Here, it's more of a hobby. They've done it their whole lives, and their fathers did it and their grandfathers, and it's not as much on the commercial end as it is in America."

For both their own and the stallion owners' peace of mind, James and Egan made it an imperative to care for the stallions exactly as they would be cared for if they were on their farm in America—with the greatest of care and caution.

It was the exact sort of facility—the only sort of facility—that Brent MacGrath and the other members of Schooner Stables, along with Hanover Shoe Farms's Jim Simpson, would consider sending Beach to, from a half a world away.

"David can be a bit on the modest side," says Egan. "He had an impeccable reputation as a bloodstock agent. Sometimes his integrity gets in the way, because he's honest to a fault. Everybody in the business knows David…[and] that he would be trustworthy. We were never going to overbreed horses or take advantage of them. His reputation was really key to all of this."

How did Donna Egan start her life with horses?

"I started in Pony Club; you know, one of the many little girls doing that. I had my horses, but I went back to university in my late twenties and I earned a degree in marketing. To get myself through school I had done a lot of catering, bartending, waiting tables, and so on to pay the bills. One day there was an ad in the paper for a person who knew about horses, who had catering experience, who had a marketing degree, and so on. I can't remember all of it; very odd requirements and not very many people had them wrapped up. And I ended up getting a job at the Harness Racing Hall of Fame."

When Egan and James met at the 1996 Harrisburg Yearling Sale in New York, it was a resonant match, both personally and professionally.

"I had the marketing background," says Egan, "and David had the connections and the horse background."

How does Empire Stallions in New Zealand fit into their business dealings?

"We have a sales manager in New Zealand and we transport the fresh semen via air on a daily basis," says James, adding that they only collect stallions three days a week: Mondays, Wednesdays, and Fridays. On those three days, Egan and James meet their courier by 9:00 A.M. to send the semen throughout Australia for same-day delivery.

"Most times, the semen is in the mares within twelve hours of collection," says James. "Semen shipped to New Zealand arrives very early the next morning, usually within twenty-four hours of collection."

Equine sperm 101: As with humans or other animals, horse sperm needs to be "motile," or speedy, to do the trick. The motility rates for live cover, fresh, fresh-cooled, or frozen semen differ, though some experts believe that non-motile cells (fresh-cooled or frozen) regain their motility after entering the mare's reproductive tract. A lot of complicated factors can affect conception rates using the different types of sperm.

Sperm 101, continued: There are two kinds of semen used for artificial insemination: fresh-cooled (also called fresh-chilled) or frozen.

"I can tell you that frozen semen is equally as good as fresh-chilled," says James, "depending on the veterinarian who's preparing the mare, and/or doing the insemination. Frozen semen is a very viable, excellent product."

The company stores frozen semen at a facility in Christchurch from which it can be shipped frozen to veterinarians for insemination.

Interestingly, Empire Stallions does not employ on-site veterinarians.

"We have a farm veterinarian who lives five, ten minutes max away from the farm," says James, "and she's on call twenty-four hours a day in case of emergencies or injuries or anything that way. As far as collecting the stallions, we do our own. We process all the semen through our own laboratory, just the same way Hanover Shoe Farms does it, or any major operation. We all do our own collections, our own processing, our own packaging, and our shipping arrangements, and away it goes."

The huge amount of work James is airily describing? That would be done by himself and Egan, with very little help from additional staff—although "on collection mornings, we generally have five people in the breeding shed."

"Including us," adds Egan.

"Including us," echoes James. "Donna and I have done the laboratory ourselves for years. We've also used another young lady or two from the US who we hire to come and spend a breeding season with us. So I would say a staff of five or six people, maximum, on breeding mornings. It's a lot of work."

And the days are long.

"Our collection mornings start at 4:00 A.M.," says James, "because we have to get the sperm to the couriers who in turn go to the airport and train stations and bus depots and wherever, and it has to be in their hands by 9:30 in the morning. They're located an hour away from us. On some days we deliver as many forty or fifty semen shippers to them for forwarding to whatever location we're sending it. So four o'clock in the morning and we're generally done by eight. That's doing probably ten or twelve horses a morning."

Seasoned horse handlers need only apply.

"It is really a challenge," David agrees. "It's something to handle these fabulous stallions that we've had over the years and the results of mares in foal with regularity and sending the best possible semen is something that we really, really enjoy."

Job well done, all.

And it's far more complicated than you might first think.

"It's very intense," Egan agrees. "It has to be spot on. You can't make mistakes. If you miss an order or you send the wrong semen or it goes to the wrong place, you missed that mare; the people don't come back. I mean she ovulates, you've missed the cycle, you've put them eighteen to twenty days behind and they're not happy. So that's why I did all the packing. I didn't trust anyone else to do it. That's a big thing, you know, don't touch my shipping boxes."

"You touch Donna's shipping boxes," says James, "you're certain to die sometime soon."

Donna Egan laughs. "Lots of people when I'd walk around the corner and then I'd come back they'd all put their hands up—'Not me, not me, I didn't do it,' because it was very well known you don't touch the boxes."

Egan also does all the paperwork.

"I did the packing," she says, "and later on, I was more involved with the collections. I did collect many of the stallions in the last several years. I can also do the lab as well. But in the beginning, I was just doing all of the packing and the paperwork. The orders could come in as late as midnight the night before and because I'm in the breeding shed I have to have all the paperwork ready with me to go down to the barn at four in the morning. So they were very short nights for me."

And then Beach arrived.

Well, it wasn't quite that sudden. There are protocols for horses to travel internationally, and in this case, to the Antipodes. Somebeachsomewhere left Hanover Shoe Farms in Pennsylvania in early July, and was vanned to Walnridge Farm, a quarantine station in New Jersey. He stayed there for approximately three weeks. During that time he had blood tests and other tests to meet the criteria that Australia demands.

The next step was Kennedy Airport in New York. From there he flew to Auckland, New Zealand—a twenty-five-hour flight—where he spent another four weeks in quarantine. Next, he was flown to Melbourne, Australia, and transported by van to Empire Stallions during the last week of August. Avenel is only an hour away from Melbourne—thank goodness. That had been quite enough quarantine and travelling for Beach.

The trip was coordinated from start to finish by a company from Melbourne called International Racehorse Transport (IRT). "They're owned in Melbourne. They might be the best company in the world to transport horses of any kind and lots of other animals, too," says James.

Egan agrees. "They're exceptional. They do all the Olympic horses, all the horses that compete in international jumping, Grand Prix shows and such. That's all they do, is transport horses."

"They have a groom on board each plane," James says, "feeding them and checking their water intake and just generally looking after them during the flight."

The horses are not medicated.

"Medication tends to dehydrate horses," says James, "and that is avoided unless there's an extremely unruly horse. I've only heard of one in the last fifteen or twenty years."

But how are they positioned on the airplane?

"They're on pallets three horses wide," says James, "and they're a stall-and-a-half each. So there's plenty of room for them while they're standing. They can't turn and walk around; they're standing next to each other, but there's plenty of room on there.... There is a terrific certified veterinarian on every flight as well."

Beach took the trip like a champ. "He jumped off the truck and said, 'I'm here!'" says James. "He whinnied, called out, took one look around, and was led inside in his big box. He had a double foaling stall, very roomy and lovely, started to eat hay, and settled in nicely. He was energetic and a happy horse the entire time he was with us."

Bugling and keen to start life, just like the day he was born, Stephanie Smith-Rothaug would say.

"Beach was the perfect gentleman," says Egan. "You couldn't ask for a nicer horse."

Beach was eight years old at this time. His Canadian family anxiously awaited word about his safe arrival.

"I called Brent MacGrath and Hanover Shoe Farms the moment Beach landed here. Brent and Hanover Shoe Farms—we kept in touch equally with both, regardless what time of the day or night it was."

How had David James become aware of Somebeachsomewhere in the first place, and how had he convinced Schooner Stables to let Beach come to Australia?

"I watched Beach race at two, I saw him race at three, I saw him when he was syndicated and retired at Hanover Shoe Farms," says James, "and boy, if there was a horse that I really, really wanted, it would have to be Somebeach."

He hadn't yet met Brent MacGrath, but he did know someone who knew him.

"I'm a good friend with another Canadian by the name of Harold Howe," says James. "Harold was the editor of *Trot* magazine. He also owned the website *The Harness Edge*. Harold lives in Brantford, Ontario. We've been friends for a long time. Harold, at my request, called Brent and introduced me over the phone and said, 'You two should get along! David's an ex-car dealer, and Brent, you're in the car business—a match made in heaven.'"

In April 2012, James called Brent to discuss the possibility of Somebeach coming to Australia. Eventually James, MacGrath, and Jim Simpson at Hanover Shoe Farms put together an agreement.

It couldn't have turned out better, in anyone's estimation.

"It just came together beautifully," says James. "Everybody seemed to be on the same wavelength. There were no objections; everything kind of just went one, two, three."

At Empire Stallions, however, there was no video camera to reassure Brent MacGrath.

"By the time we got around to discussing that, it was halfway through his season here," says James. "If he'd come back the next season we would've had it in operation. But we kept in constant contact and our vet was here on a regular basis—checking, checking, checking, just as a precaution. Beach was in absolutely terrific health the whole time he was here."

While James is the first to admit that Bridgette Jablonsky and the now-chairman of the board at Hanover, Jim Simpson, are not in favour of "shuttling horses," as James terms it, "it worked out extremely well with Beach," he says.

"Beach went back looking absolutely sensational," says James. "He's a horse that can overeat; he loves to eat, so you've got to keep him on a diet, and we even had an exercise program. We put him on a lunge line and lunged three or four days a week…just to keep him in nice trim condition, which is the way we received him. He looked great when he got here from the quarantines. He went back looking exactly the same way."

Well, perhaps a tad plumper, according to Dr. Jablonsky, but indisputably happy and healthy.

Not long after Beach arrived at Empire, he was put to work making babies.

"We had roughly three to four weeks of no collections," says James. "We did collect him the last week of September so he had a good three, three and a half weeks of just being turned out in his paddock, eating grass, and coming in for a bath," says James. "So he relaxed for three weeks before we started collecting him."

Beach had two main caretakers. "We had a fellow who led him in the breeding shed on collection mornings, Ray Jessop. He's a local chap, been around horses all his life and got along with everybody very well," says James.

"He's been with us for twelve years now," says Egan.

The second caretaker was an American by the name of Jessica Gratien, a graduate of the SUNY Morrisville program in New York who was also working for Carter Duer at Peninsula Farm in Lexington, Kentucky.

Beach enjoyed having two human friends spoiling him again; it wasn't the whole MacGrath family, but he was comfortable and content, James and Egan agree.

"We followed the same routine he had at Hanover Shoe Farms. We tried to emulate everything exactly the same: the collection methods, the extender in the semen [this liquid diluent contains protective ingredients that permit survival of spermatozoa outside the reproductive tract], his daily routine, when he was fed, that type of thing. We tried to match everything in the US, because we know four months from now he's going to have to go back to that same routine."

This duplication of routine extended right down to the feed. Few things can throw off a horse faster than an abrupt change of feed.

"We got a list of what he was fed at Hanover Shoe Farms—what kind of hay and all that kind of thing. So we tried to match up everything that he'd had for the past year or two. Typically, stallions don't like change; in fact, most horses don't, but especially stallions. So we really followed the example that Hanover was using with him."

Egan points out that, because the farm is custom-made for stallions, the paddocks are set up in such a way that horses are separated, but still get the company of the horses next to them. "David really was very masterful at putting horses next to each other who liked each other," she says.

As horse people will tell you, this takes a thoughtful and caring eye. The end results also make for a quiet farm.

"You could drive onto the property at any point and we would have fourteen stallions here and you would never hear anything," says Egan. "There was none of that ruckus or commotion or running around or carrying on, or the screaming and hollering and trying to prove 'I'm bigger than you'...there's none of that challenging. They were all comfortable. This farm is very quiet; it's in a beautiful setting, surrounded by hills. They just put their heads down, ate grass, and did their business when they were supposed to. They were all very well settled and that's a credit to David."

The "tease-mares," meanwhile, were tucked away in back where the stallions couldn't see—or more to the point, smell—them.

Over a four-and-a-half-month period, Beach was "collected" three times a week for eleven weeks, for a total of thirty-three to thirty-five collections.

And apart from that, "Beach pretty much did his own thing," says James.

That is, when he wasn't waving or perhaps bowing to the crowds.

"Australia's a little bit different than North America," says James. "People here like to come and look at the stallions. I would say that Beach had attracted several hundred people to come out and look at him. We even, the week before breeding season, we even hosted a—"

A Beach Party! Well, not quite, because North American Beach Parties were held at the tracks where Beach ran, or at venues where they showed the simulcast races, but it was a party, was it?

"—an event for him," finishes James. "The Minister of Racing for Victoria is the minister of all the codes—greyhounds, Thoroughbred, and harness racing, and he'd never been to a Standardbred farm before. At the time, not to take anything away from Beach, but we also were standing RocknRoll Hanover, and the two of them were probably the two best sires in the country, and two of the most prolific stallions ever in my lifetime. I don't think there's ever been another farm in history that can say that they had the privilege of standing two stallions of that calibre simultaneously.... Those are the horses of a lifetime."

Horse of a lifetime... Beach had heard that phrase before.

"The minister of racing realized that we had a big coup here and that this would probably never happen in Australian history again," says Egan. "There were some things happening in the government, they were trying to pass some legislation, so he set up his whole entourage to come here. We had a marquee set out, and guests and the press were here, and they took photos and it was all very heavily publicized. Beach was a very big part of that."

Beach the Ham was in his element. And he was popular with more than just elected officials.

"People came here seven days a week to see the horse," says James. "We never turned a person down and did the very best we could. He was always cleaned up, so it was not a big deal to show him at any hour. Occasionally we had people come here near dark and we'd have to show him inside the barn."

"I remember people turned up when we were having an American Thanksgiving," says Egan. "I was going to town to get sweet potatoes. I went down to the front gate and it was locked, and there was a car sitting there and I said to the man, 'I'm sorry, can I help you?' And he said, 'Yeah, we were hoping to come and see Somebeach.' I said, 'How long have you been sitting here?' 'An hour,' he said. 'We were waiting for someone to come through.' Even though the phone number was at the gate! So I let him in and showed him Beach."

These visitors had come from the other side of Melbourne, about a two-hour drive.

"Beach was a destination stop," says Egan.

People came to visit, in fact, from all over Australia.

"People from Perth—five thousand miles away—if they were in Melbourne on business, or went to the races at the big racetrack in Melton, they'd call and say, 'Listen, I've got a couple hours. I'd like to stop up and see Beach….' I said, 'Just come on up at eleven o'clock.' …I have a feeling why most people called was because they heard that Donna was a good cook and baker," James laughs.

"I gained so much weight I can't even lose it now," says James. "Anyway, they came from everywhere to see Beach and if they had a chance they stopped in, if it was ten minutes or an hour and they'd bring the family. We had hundreds and hundreds of people stop to see Beach."

And, like a family dog who is friendly with everyone, so was Beach.

"He was a kind, gentle horse," says James. "If a little child came by, he would bend down and nuzzle him."

Beach was kind to all his caretakers as well.

David James and his partner, Donna Egan, of Empire Stallions, with Denis Napthine, minister for racing and premier of Victoria, Australia.
(EMPIRE STALLIONS)

"Whenever we turned him out in his paddock," says James, "we put bell boots [rubber boots that cover the front heels] on him, just as a precautionary thing, and whoever was putting the bell boots on, generally Jessica or Ray, Beach would check every pocket in their jeans, in the jacket, in their shirt, because he knew that somewhere there was a carrot. He would go all over them. He would stand and let you put the bell boots on, but in the end you had to give him the bloody carrot."

They bought carrots at the local grocery store—25 kilos (55 pounds) at a time.

"He'd go through that like nothing," says James.

"I'm surprised he didn't go home orange," laughs Egan.

Beach's influence on the Australia and New Zealand Standardbred racing world has been huge.

"Basically it's playing out now, in the 2020s," says James. "The year that he stood here, he bred a large number of mares with fresh-chilled semen and did an extremely good job; it was a wonderful crop, and many of them are still racing." Beach's first crop included Breeders Crown winners, and his offspring have included major grand circuit participants every year since then.

Daddy Beach was indeed prolific. In 2013, he bred 166 mares in Australia and ended up with about 120 foals. He also bred 75 mares in New Zealand that year, for a total of 241 that year.

Saying goodbye to Beach when he had to return to the United States was not easy for either James or Egan.

"It was over so quickly, and it was much too short," says James. "We'd love to have had him forever…"

Still, James and Egan were grateful for the opportunity to host Beach.

"It may be the highlight of our entire horse breeding career that we were afforded the opportunity to have this horse," says James. "And I do not mean only from a monetary standpoint—but from every standpoint."

Syndication

How does syndication work when a harness racer retires and begins his second career as a stallion?

At the time he went to Australia, Beach was owned by the Somebeachsomewhere syndicate, which included Schooner Stables, Hanover Shoe Farms, and several other people who owned shares. "So Beach had an ownership...of probably, I don't know, eight or ten or a dozen or more people," says David James of Empire Stallions in Avenel, Australia.

"When you syndicate a horse," he continues, "you divide him into, let's say, 120 shares, and [each share] entitles you to one breeding each year for the lifetime of the horse." That means that if you want to breed three mares to your horse, you have to buy three shares. If you don't use your shares to breed, you can sell them each year for the advertised stud fee, or for what you paid. "It's yours to use, sell, trade, buy—whatever you choose to do with it within the guidelines of the syndicate agreement."

"Hanover Shoe Farms is the syndicate manager for Beach," says James's partner, Donna Egan. "So all the decisions were put through them first, and then they would take them to the syndicate members; whoever had the majority—which I would assume would be Schooner Stables—had authority interest."

So together, Schooner Stables and Hanover Shoe Farms had final say in any decisions pertaining to Beach's care and...work schedule?

"Yes," says David. "When Beach came down here to stand at stud we dealt with strictly the Somebeachsomewhere syndicate, which was basically made up in the majority by the Schooner Stables and Hanover Shoe Farms. We didn't deal with anybody but those two entities."

"But," says Egan, "the syndicate didn't breed mares here, so we were open to sell breedings here."

And how does the lolly sharing work?

"So when a horse such as Beach comes down here he's placed into our hands," says David. "We will breed a reasonable number of mares or a number agreed to by the syndicate, get them pregnant, collect the stud fees and remit the money to the syndicate manager. They take the money that they get from us—we have our share that we keep and we have expenses, etcetera—but the money that Hanover gets on behalf of the syndicate members is then divided up among the syndicate shares. So everybody who owns a share in the US does get some portion of money that's earned down here in Australia. They can't use their breedings here, but they are going to get an income. To send a syndicated horse to Australia is an income opportunity for the syndicate, the owners."

The summation of a complicated business is coming.

"When you buy a share in a top stallion," says James, "two really good things can happen. First of all you get a breeding for your mare or you can sell that annual breeding, which is worth in the case of Somebeach $25,000, $30,000. His yearlings averaged $100,000 at public auction. So if you had a yearling by Somebeach in the United States and you got lucky and sold at a good price, you could be looking at a $100,000 return on your investment," says James.

"Down here I can sell all of the breedings—let's say there was 150 or 200—and make as much money as we possibly can for the syndicate, and then send the syndicate the funds at the end of the season. The syndicate then takes that money and presents it to all of the shareholders in the US. So you have two income streams, one in the US, and one here."

It is a credit to Empire Stallions that Hanover Shoe Farms doesn't stand stallions with any other farm in the southern hemisphere but them.

Chapter 21

HORSE OF A LIFETIME

NINE YEARS HAD PASSED SINCE SOMEBEACHSOMEWHERE HAD begun his career as a stallion at Hanover Shoe Farms. He'd travelled to Australia in July 2012, had a triumphant experience there, and returned to Hanover, Pennsylvania, in January 2013. For the next four years, he did all that he was asked to do in the breeding shed, and otherwise lived a life of ease, mostly outside, in his three-acre paddock.

Then some dark clouds rolled in.

"It was that winter of '17; I think it was February," says Dr. Bridgette Jablonsky. "It was a Saturday. I got a text from one of the vets saying 'Beach didn't eat this morning,' and that was weird. Any time the stallions look at us the wrong way, we completely go overboard with diagnostics and treating because they're very valuable. So if it was another horse, we might not have gone into full flight, full treatment mode; we probably wouldn't have been as aggressive as we were."

As with other mammals, humans included, not eating can be sign of illness or disease. With horses, not eating is a serious matter and often indicates "colic," which presents as abdominal pain, and can mean many different gastrointestinal troubles, some of which can lead to death. Jablonsky's heart must have skipped several times over.

"We put him on GastroGard, which is an anti-ulcer medication. I believe we had put him on GastroGard when he got here, thinking maybe he had an ulcer and that's why he was looking poorly. Oftentimes when a horse doesn't eat, they don't drink [either].... When they don't drink, you worry that they're going to get an impaction. So I said to the vet, 'Pull some blood on him. We'll send it out and make sure white blood count is okay. But also, let's do an in-house hematocrit and total protein to see if he's dehydrated, because we could tube him with some water.'" Jablonsky explains that if a horse is dehydrated, his proteins and hematocrit will be increased. The vet who called her back said Beach's protein was actually really low.

"It was like three in the afternoon. I said, 'That's impossible; do it again.' She did again. She called me back. She said the rate and then we said, 'We have a problem here,' because a horse's normal protein should be around 6—between 5.5 and 7.5, but most are in the 6 range."

Jablonsky was unsettled, but she was determined to figure out what was going on.

"Most commonly in a horse, there are reasons for low protein, but most commonly in an adult horse, they're losing protein...through their kidneys. So we did a chemistry on him."

Beach's kidneys were fine; the next step was a urinalysis, which showed that there was no protein in his urine; he wasn't losing it that way.

"So if he's not losing it from his kidneys, he's losing it from his gut."

And that was not good.

"There are two main diagnoses in horses that would cause them to lose protein through their gut," explains Jablonsky. "One would just be inflammatory bowel disease, and that would be non-neoplastic, non-cancerous. The other is cancer. That first week or two, cancer was on our brain, but it's a differential. We treated him systematically. He started eating again within a few days, but his protein was never really coming up. We made the presumptive diagnosis of IBD [Irritable Bowel Disease] and he was spiking some fevers, so we were treating him with some drugs such as antihistamine...and a couple of other drugs, to just quiet the gut down.

Then we started him on prednisolone [powerful anti-inflammatory drug] in March and that made a huge difference; that really helped him."

But no one was resting easy. Somebeachsomewhere was too valuable and too beloved.

"We did a few diagnostics," Jablonsky continues. "There's a blood test you can do that's kind of a marker for cancer. It's still kind of being worked out in a horse. It's hard to diagnose cancer in a horse, in the gut of a horse. Their bowel is so long you can't just get a biopsy from whatever section of the bowel you want. You'd have to open him up, and we're not going put this horse under anaesthesia and open him up to get a biopsy."

So they did what they could do. A blood test came back with a reading that suggested cancer was unlikely. They did two biopsies: a rectal biopsy, and a scope down his esophagus, through his stomach, and into his small intestine. The biopsies showed inflammatory bowel disease so for all of 2017 he was treated for that.

"He was very responsive to the prednisolone; we would try to wean him off it, but we couldn't quite get him off of it," says Jablonsky. "We would wean him, and if we got him too low, he'd kind of get a little miserable again on us."

Everyone at Hanover Shoe Farms remained vigilant.

"Beach was doing okay until October, and then he just crashed on us, which means he lost the ability to know where his feet were. He wasn't tracking right. He lost his ability to put his feet down in the right place; he was wobbly. He started getting blood clots in his veins, so we shipped him to the Mid-Atlantic Equine Center. He left here on October 6, 2017."

They were pulling out all the stops for Beach. The Mid-Atlantic Equine Medical Center in Ringoes, New Jersey, has a reputation as one of the finest equine veterinary hospitals in the US. It has staff of forty, including board-certified specialists in surgery, internal medicine, sports medicine and rehabilitation, and cardiology.

Jablonsky was eager to confer with the specialists.

"Beach always had this interesting finding on ultrasound, which we did here at Hanover," she remembers. "While he was there at the centre, he had several ultrasounds. We were trying to find masses…and he always had this finding where you couldn't see his kidneys, because he had colon between the body wall and the kidney, up over his spleen. And that's called a nephrosplenic entrapment. Some horses can live like that. It causes some horses to colic, but Beach always had that finding." (Again, colic in horses is severe abdominal pain, typically related to problems with the gastrointestinal tract.)

"He did colic here [at Hanover] a few times but he would work out of it; he never required surgery," says Jablonsky. "He colicked there [at the Mid-Atlantic Equine Medical Center] once and worked out of it. I believe the second time he colicked, the decision was made to take him to surgery. That was in November 2017; the Harrisburg sale was going on. The vet there said, 'You know, we should probably fix this; maybe the fact that he's chronically displaced is causing the inflammatory bowel disease.'"

Jablonsky explains that the GI tract is like a big hose; everything has to flow right. If you have a kink in the hose, anything before the kink is going to get backed up. The theory was that, if the backup was causing Beach's inflammation, relieving that kink would give him a chance to heal.

"He wasn't doing well; we had to do something," Jablonsky says. "So we made the decision to do surgery on him." The surgery relieved the backup, but the surgeons also found a small nodule. It was the size of a grape.

"They called me. It was before the Harrisburg sale, in October. They called me and said, 'Surgery went well; he's fine, he's good.' Just as an aside they said, 'We found this little nodule on his intestine, in the wall of his intestine.' It looked like a lipoma, which is a non-malignant fatty tumour, but they said, 'We're going to send it for biopsy.'"

Jablonsky got a call during the Harrisburg sale. "They said, 'You're not going to believe this.' And I said, 'What?' And they said, 'That nodule we sent is lymphosarcoma. He has cancer.' And that's when we had our diagnosis."

Somebeachsomewhere, the fastest three-year-old pacer in the world had cancer—and he couldn't run from it.

"It was November and we had our diagnosis. It wasn't non-malignant inflammatory bowel disease; it was cancerous. It's very, very rare in horses. Less than 1 percent of horses get lymphosarcoma of the GI tract. That's how unlucky and unfortunate he was—not only him, but the two businesses to lose him to that," she says, referring to the original Schooner Stables and the secondary members of the expanded syndicate who came on board when Beach went to stud.

"The number is so small it's almost like a horse being struck by lightning; it's because they don't usually live long enough to get cancer. I've seen lymphosarcoma, but I've seen it in young horses. In my experience, we'll have a weanling or a yearling maybe once every five or six years that all of a sudden stops eating, gets really sad looking. You pull their protein and it is low, but you see huge masses when you ultrasound them and you have your diagnosis. They die very, very quickly."

With Beach it had been a markedly different story.

"Everyone was astonished that the steroids had kept him alive for eleven months," says Jablonsky. "We were thinking hey, maybe it's not so aggressive. We were able to keep him going so long with just the steroids, it's worth trying to treat him.

"So we tried chemotherapy, and while all this is going on, we're talking to experts. I even talked to oncologists from the Mayo Clinic. There's a man that owns Standardbreds; he's on the board of the Mayo Clinic, and he had two of their best oncologists call just to talk about this horse. I was talking to experts not only in veterinary medicine, but human medicine, and at the end of the day, we made the decision that we were going to try chemo on him."

Only a small number of small animals get chemo; it's a much, much smaller percentage in large animals, says Jablonsky.

"I don't know many horses that are getting chemotherapy. I would venture to say it's hardly any. So Beach is still at Mid-Atlantic; we have a veterinary oncologist coming, giving him chemotherapy. He seemed to handle the first few okay and then he just…we don't know, and we never will know if…the cancer was killing him at that point, or if he couldn't handle the chemo. Between November and January, though, he just went downhill."

Jablonsky's voice is soft. "I went to go see him—I'm going to say the end of November, maybe the beginning of December—and he was out in his paddock. He looked bad, but he was grazing. I brought him carrots; he ate them.

"The Friday before he died he started to go into distress. He went down; he couldn't get up. We put him in a sling, and he was no better on Saturday, and on Sunday, Dr. [Rodney] Belgrave from Mid-Atlantic called me and said, 'What do you want to do here?' And I said, 'He's not going to make it right?' He said, 'No, he's dying.'"

And that meant one scenario to Jablonsky.

"In veterinary medicine we have a huge advantage because we have the ability to euthanize," she says. "I believe people should have that option, too. But we don't have to let animals suffer any longer than they need to."

She called Brent MacGrath, who she says was emotional and couldn't talk. "I said, 'Okay, take your time.' Beach was sedated. He wasn't suffering; they were keeping him comfortable.

"Brent called me back in thirty minutes. He said, 'I spoke to everyone and we want to put him down.'"

Beach died at the Mid-Atlantic Equine Medical Center on Sunday, January 14, 2018.

Almost three years later, the pain of loss is fresh.

"We had to do it," says Jablonsky. "You always go back and you question yourself. Did we try too hard? We were trying to save his life, but maybe we shouldn't have done the chemotherapy."

Dollar bills were not a part of this equation—not at all.

Beach's final resting place in the "Graveyard of Champions" at Hanover Shoe Farms. (AUTHOR PHOTO)

"We weren't doing it out of greed," Jablonsky says. "We never thought he'd breed another mare.... We just wanted to give him maybe another spring out in his paddock. I think what we really wanted was to have him die at home.

"It really, really was sad to us and upsetting to us that he died at the hospital. And I think the whole goal was just to get him home, to get him well enough [to travel]. We were all set to do the chemotherapy here. We were already making plans and we were learning how to do the chemotherapy here. The plan was to bring him home. We weren't naïve enough to think that this horse would ever be a breeding stallion again...but we just didn't want him to die away from home."

It was not to be.

"He really went downhill. We never got to the point [where it was feasible].... He got cremated and his ashes are here buried in our cemetery. So he's home, but it's sad that he never got to come back to his stall; he never got to come back to his paddock."

Beloved by so many, Beach slipped away without his closest human family, either. But he created love and caring wherever he went.

"He had been at Mid-Atlantic since October," says Jablonsky. "He was there for three months, so he had gotten to know those people. He had friendly faces around him when he was euthanized."

In January 2018, Dr. Bridgette Jablonsky took out a full-page advertisement in the *Harness Racing Update*. She accompanied the letter of goodbye with a sweet photo of Beach, his head dipped over in the paddock fence at Hanover Shoe Farms, a crowd of awestruck children on the other side, looking up at him.

> *Beach,*
> Quite simply, you were the best.
> It was an honour to be a part of your life and I
> thank your owners for giving me that privilege.
> Your shoes will never be filled.
> Although my heart is broken, I take comfort in
> knowing that you are at peace now.
> I will treasure the memories I have of you forever.
>
> *Bridgette*

Chapter 22

A STAR THAT SHOT
ACROSS THE UNIVERSE

SOMEBEACHSOMEWHERE LEFT A LEGACY THAT DEFIES SUMMA-
tion. He had an indelible impact on the lives of the people around him
and on the harness racing industry as a whole, and he left progeny that
are changing the face of the Standardbred breed even today.

Paul MacDonell is one of those whose life changed dramatically when
Beach came along. And while it's tempting to freeze MacDonell in time as
Beach's career driver, the popular competitor from Guelph, Ontario, has
done mountains more than that. In fact, MacDonell has driven enough
superstars to surpass earnings of $1 million for thirty-three consecutive
years; those same horses have won in excess of $122 million in purse
earnings.

He even has his own stable of horses now. "I've had probably a hundred starts out of my own stable," he says.

Are there any Beach babies in there?

"Yes, we have a Beach filly. Actually, Brent owns her and I trained her
for him. Her name is Martinique Beach. She's good. She won two races
and she's just a two-year-old. She's done now for [2019]. She'll go back to

Florida and train with Brent when he goes down there after Christmas." In general, says MacDonell, Beach has had "really nice fillies."

On a personal basis, life has been good, too. MacDonell is married to Lynn MacDonell and the couple have three daughters, Jenna, Lauren, and Shelby.

In the autumn of 2019, MacDonell was thinking about the years ahead of him in the horse business.

"I'm fifty-seven now," he says. "I'm kind of over the hump a little bit as far as catch driving—driving for other people. I did some in 2019, probably six hundred to seven hundred, something like that."

By now, MacDonell has over fifty-six hundred wins to his credit. But he remains humble about his career.

"Sure, it's a lot of wins, but to put it in perspective, there are people with fourteen thousand, even fifteen thousand." He tips his hat to all drivers in the sport, with an especial acknowledgement of Clare MacDonald, from Antigonish, Nova Scotia. "She's one of the best drivers in the world."

Others might say that the real gauge is the money MacDonell has made as a winning driver. He's in the top twenty of all time. And the biggest paycheque he ever received for one race?

"It would've been Beach's win in the North America Cup. The race went for $1.5 million, so he picked up $750,000 and I got 5 percent."

Not bad for one minute and forty-nine seconds' work.

MacDonell acknowledges that, as a driver, his name will always be linked with Somebeachsomewhere.

"I'm not complaining one bit, because most people that have gone through their careers never had anything like Beach—not even close. So bring it on! I don't care if they want to associate me with Beach, that's fine."

But is there anything else he'd like to be remembered for during his career?

"Well, maybe that I was an all-around driver? You know, that I could handle trotters, pacers, young, older, just all kinds of different horses. I think I probably will be remembered in those terms."

On April 12, 2020, Paul MacDonell was inducted into the Canadian Horse Racing Hall of Fame. Brent MacGrath, his long-time fellow horseman and friend, had nominated him.

They'd both come a long, long way since the early days at Greenwood Raceway.

SCHOONER STABLES

The original Schooner Stables folded after the deal was made with Hanover Shoe Farms and the syndicate expanded. In 2011, Schooner Stables II was born. Members are Brent and Rhonda MacGrath, Stu Rath, Jamie Bagnell, and Garry Pye. As mentioned earlier, Petitpas remains active as a horseman specializing in harness racing Standardbreds, and Pam Dean remains an active rider and harness racing fan.

All members of the original Schooner Stables are optimistic about their ongoing futures with horses, and are grateful for their unexpected and exceptional past with Somebeachsomewhere.

Stu Rath, the least horse-connected person in the group, would never put himself forward as a spokesperson for Schooner Stables, and yet his words of summation ring true for all.

"I wish the story of Beach hadn't been such a relatively short and tragic one," he says. "And yet that's part of what makes it so memorable, too," he says. "It's all heart. He was such a pet."

And no matter what happens next, Rath will always be grateful to a big bay stallion named Beach, who helped heal his heart when it was shattered.

"We aren't meant to be alone," Rath had said, of the human walk through life.

Nor without magic and dreams, others might add.

Beach's son Captaintreacherous now stands stud at Hanover Shoe Farms. (AUTHOR PHOTO)

BRIDGETTE JABLONSKY

A legacy for an individual person is often formed by their life work, and by the children they leave behind.

It is no different for high-performance horses.

"Beach's legacy goes on," says the calm and capable Dr. Bridgette Jablonsky. "He has sired 1,069 foals in the United States. Many more, of course, around the world."

Beach stood at stud at Hanover for nine years. Captaintreacherous and Stay Hungry, two of Beach's spectacular sons, stand at stud there now.

In 2017, Beach's progeny earned $23.7 million dollars. This is a single-season record for a Standardbred stallion. Like everything else about Somebeachsomewhere, the records tend to stand as tall and unchanging as he did.

Interestingly, Beach's sons share other attributes of his, unrelated to appearance.

"I think they're very, very similar to Beach," says Jablonsky. "I think Captain looks a lot like Beach, and he sounds like Beach—he has the same voice.... When Captain comes in the breeding shed and he starts calling for the mare it makes me sad, because it sounds like Beach.... And they act the same in the breeding shed. For a breeding stallion, Captain has impeccable manners."

Jablonsky reconsiders. "He's a little more nippy than Beach. Beach wasn't much of a biter. Captain's a biter.... All three—Beach, Captain and Stay Hungry—they all have that laid-back attitude."

Beach has passed on other elements of his temperament.

"His fillies on the racetrack, and even here at Hanover, can be a little hot and a little temperamental. I don't know what his colts are like when they're training now, but I know him and those two horses [sons] are very pleasant horses."

Amusingly, Beach's sons are no Lotharios, either.

"These two guys are the same way," says Jablonsky. "If you don't have the right mare, if not everything is perfect, they're going to make you work for it."

It's obvious that Beach's genetics are very strong.

"He's a sire that stamps his offspring in so many ways," says Jablonsky. "In looks, in voice, temperament; I see them do the same actions. You'll get some stallions that their foals look different, act different, and they tend to take after their mothers, but his genetics came through so strong in his foals."

When horse racing people speak of Beach's son, they often speak of Captaintreacherous, who was among his dad's first offspring.

"Captaintreacherous has done a remarkable job of trying to fill [Beach's] shoes. It's amazing how he has stepped up to become the dominant pacing sire that his father was. Captaintreacherous is the best pacing stallion in the business."

And for fillies?

"I would say for mares, for fillies, it's a filly called Pure Country. She made $2.4 million to the mark of 1:48 [for the mile]. She was a great, great mare; retired now. She belongs to a farm called Diamond Creek Farm."

Captaintreacherous, at ten years old, should have many happy and healthy years ahead of him.

"We hope so," says Jablonsky. "We thought Beach had years ahead of him, and—you know. That was always Brent's favourite question: 'How many years do you think Beach can breed?' And I would tell him, 'Oh, we've had stallions breed until they're thirty, surely he'll make it to his early twenties.' Most stallions breed until their early twenties."

Would it be fair to say that Beach has basically changed the future of Standardbred racing with his presence and his progeny?

"Absolutely," says Jablonsky. "I don't know where we would be without him…. It used to be that with the trotters there was just a couple of sire lines that you had, and it was really hard to select matings. It seemed like they were all kind of bred the same, and with the trotters, we were breeding ourselves into a corner. And then it happened that a good trotter came along with the different bloodlines, and then another one, and now there are many different selections of trotters you can breed to.

"Now we're seeing it with pacers. But Beach was *the* horse. He was the horse that we needed, because we were getting so inundated with blood from the Western Hanover line and Artsplace line and the Cam Fella line, and when Beach came along it was like—wow, we can breed all of these mares by these stallions to Beach. He's such an outcross; he's such a hybrid, you know? He has so dominated things that now, if you want to breed a top horse, it's hard because they all have Beach blood in them. He's completely taken over. He was the one we were looking to, to be our outcross stallion, and he has become the main gig."

Jablonsky says we are just seeing the beginning of Beach's legacy. "We'll be talking about Somebeachsomewhere in twenty to twenty-five years. You'll see his name in pedigrees for years and years to come."

And the miracle of it all was that Beach was so unexpected, as all horses-of-a-century truly are, no matter how careful the breeding, and how high the breeder's hopes.

"Beach's sire, Mach Three, he's a good sire, but he was not a superstar stallion. When you say a sire line starts here, you say it starts with the great one…the Somebeachsomewhere line."

Horse racing people and laymen alike puzzle over the dazzling appearance of Beach in their midst. It is such a human quality to be fascinated by excellence.

Jablonsky has seen many brilliant pacers in her life, even as a very young girl, that great Niatross, who died in 1977, aged twenty-two.

"But I would say Beach was the best pacer I've ever seen. He was an unbelievable horse."

There's no denying that Beach bolstered the harness racing industry in Canada.

"It was much healthier then than it is now," says Briggs, "but it's not bad now."

But even with creations such as the "Mohawk Million" at Woodbine Mohawk Park, the harness racing industry still needs to get those backsides in the bleachers.

"Take this idea all the way back to Beach," says Briggs. "That's what people found so compelling about his story. It was Maritime people, and there's a sort of myth in the industry that Schooner Stables were just some common Joes who have regular jobs and kind of went out and bought a horse together. No, they're all fairly wealthy people; I get all that.

"It's that they shared the horse with the people. That was the compelling part. It's Brent taking the horse back home to Nova Scotia at the end of the two-year-old year and training him over the winter at Truro. No one would ever do that! If anybody had a talented two-year-old here now, doesn't matter where their home base is or where they're from, they would go the traditional route and it would be, 'We're going to take the horse to Florida,' or 'We're going to keep the horse in Ontario and train it for the winter.' Why would we take it out east where your weather conditions are not going to be that favourable to keeping the horse healthy and training well?

"But Brent didn't care. He said, 'This is where my home is and these are my people,' and that's when I think they took to it, too. And all the Beach Parties held at Truro Raceway when he raced where people watched and had fun joining in, one of their own. That's always the way. We cheer on Olympic athletes in that way, don't we?"

Would there have been a Somebeachsomewhere without Brent MacGrath?

"Well, it's funny because I know many people, and they're not just saying it for attention—they say, 'I was the under-bidder on that horse.'

"But I know for a fact there were a number of talented people who wanted to buy that horse and circumstances that day prevented that. Would it have turned out exactly the same with somebody else? I would say no. I think all this had to come together to make this horse as successful as he was; just the simple fact of Brent being able to devote all his time to him. Who knows how many races he won because of that?

"It just seems like this one horse was meant to be with that man and that's what made him."

DAVID JAMES AND DONNA EGAN

If David James and Donna Egan thought their goodbye to Beach in 2013 was difficult, the final goodbye in 2018 hit them doubly hard. The couple, who had cared for Beach so carefully and lovingly, was deeply shocked to learn of the cancer diagnosis, and ultimately, of Beach's premature death.

"Unbelievable, incredible," says James. "It never crossed our minds, because generally, horses don't die of cancer; it's not diagnosed."

And while Beach only stood as a stallion on two continents for the relatively short period of nine years, James is the first to say how much the stallion changed Standardbred history.

"I would say that he's had a major impact on both the breeding and racing scene in Australia and New Zealand," says James. "He may be the best stallion that's ever come along."

In particular, what about his legacy in Australia and New Zealand?

"He's going to live on forever here through his fillies and mares who will be breeding," says James. "Most of them are too young to breed at the moment, but he's going to leave a lasting impression on daughters being bred to other sires and leading winners."

Beach is never far from Egan's thoughts, either.

"I still have the image in my head," she says, "of looking out my window from the office and seeing him with his head down just grazing.... The look of excitement on people's faces when they got to see him was so satisfying.... He didn't let them down. It was like he was everything they thought he would be, everything they expected him to be, and then much more."

STEPHANIE SMITH-ROTHAUG

Stephanie Smith-Rothaug says Beach's progeny continue to dominate. She is excited about the fourteen Beach babies coming to the Harrisburg auction in 2020. "That's the last of the last of the last. Brent and Schooner Stables want to buy one."

Some might think of such a time as bittersweet, but not Smith-Rothaug. "I think of him as a star that shot across the universe. He wasn't supposed to stay in this universe. He was this brilliant living magic horse that had to go on."

THE CURRENT WORLD RECORD TIME FOR A MILE FOR THREE-YEAR-OLD PACERS

On Sunday, October 4, 2020, at The Red Mile in Lexington, Kentucky, a certain colt did something only one other three-year-old colt has ever done: he paced a mile in 1:46.4. Appropriately, it was none other than Cattlewash, the Somebeachsomewhere–Road Bet colt, who matched his sire's world record time, which was set in 2008, also at The Red Mile. With that scorching time, Cattlewash handily won the opening division of the Captain Treacherous Bluegrass three-year-old Colt and Gelding Pace. He also sliced off a full four seconds from his previous lifetime best.

Cattlewash is bred and owned by Bill Donovan, and trained by Ron Burke.

Papa Beach would have been proud.

Chapter 23

MAYBE HE'LL BUY A HORSE

IT'S BEEN OVER FOUR YEARS SINCE THE PASSING OF THE legendary Somebeachsomewhere, who, to the MacGraths, was more simply a member of the family who truly loved his carrots, having his back scratched with a wooden rake, and going for halter walks with his humans so he could graze on choice grass.

In his home community of Truro, is Brent MacGrath back to being known as a car dealer, or is he still known as the owner of Beach?

"I think probably both," he says. "Obviously, with people who loved horse racing it was the Beach connection; I was always a horse person to those people. And, of course, with the news media it was certainly Beach. The people I sold vehicles to, most of them followed the story. The town, the whole community, they all just jumped right on board."

The day Dr. Bridgette Jablonsky had phoned MacGrath long-distance from Pennsylvania, he knew the news wouldn't be good. Ordinarily, she would simply text him with any news she had about Beach.

"Yeah, I was pretty sure it wasn't a good call," he says. "But really, there wasn't any decision that had to be made. It was done; Beach made the decision."

Jablonsky, though, did what all good veterinarians do—she made MacGrath feel slightly less awful about the looming euthanasia.

"She told me that when horses can't get up on their feet by themselves, they're like any wild animal; they become scared. They know what's in store for them when they're in the wild, they're injured, and they can't get up. They're not stupid. That put it in perspective for me, made the decision easy. It was living without him that was harder to get our head around."

MacGrath told Jablonsky he'd call her right back; then he made the calls to the five other co-owners. The phone calls, he says, "lasted seconds." Obviously no one could bear the idea that Beach was in pain and feeling scared, and readily agreed to the euthanasia. Within minutes, MacGrath had made the return call to Jablonsky.

"It's hard to imagine the whole ride he took us on," says MacGrath, "but the fact of the matter is that he opened so many doors for us and introduced us to so many people that it's really, really hard to pick a favourite memory. I loved training him in Truro; I loved the fact that when he came back between two and three, I knew all the horse people in Truro [would support him].

"Typically, horse people are a big family who fight and get along all at the same time, just like families do; that's just how it is," he says. "But what they did, what the horsemen did for Beach—like...me opening up the barn and letting the air flow through, and these guys working in that cold all day while I'm sitting warm at the car dealership, but because I wanted the windows open for Beach to have fresh air and not dusty snow—not a word said.

"And it wasn't me they were doing that for; it was Beach. Whatever he needed, whatever was available for him, it didn't matter to anybody else how much of an inconvenience it might be for them—he came first."

It wasn't just fellow Canadian horsemen and -women who went out of their way to support Beach.

"I was down in Lexington, the fastest, the greatest, most historic racetrack in the world. The track men there are Dan and Greg Coon and father Chuck—the best track men in North America. Dan comes to me before the midweek training, and says, 'What day are you going to train on? How do you like the track?' I told him, and lo and behold, he had that track absolutely perfect. And when I'm jogging Beach around, ready to turn—what we call 'turn' means to go the right way, the racing way, which means I'm going to go a fast mile with him—the track man's not letting any of the other horses turn at the same time. 'You can't turn until after Somebeach goes.'

"So if you're a skier, you know what it's like to go over a groomed trail that nobody's been on before, or a snowmobile, well, it's like being on carpet for a horse and he was letting nobody go on the racetrack, on the inside of the racetrack where I was going to be training. Nobody could do that until after I had finished my mile. And here we are at the best racetrack in the world; all the great horses went over that racetrack, and here they're holding up everybody for Beach. I'm the one training him, so those things you never, ever forget."

It's one story of many that MacGrath has about the courtesies extended and homage paid to Beach.

"It's kind of like Wayne Gretzky," says MacGrath. "Protecting him a little bit in the hockey games; you know, don't hit him too hard. It was in no one's best interest that Wayne Gretzky got hurt, and it was in no one's best interest that Beach didn't race to his full-on best, even if you were in the race, because of what Beach was doing for the industry, the attention he was bringing to it."

While MacGrath is the first to say that horse people are known for how they will help other horse people, he was still shocked by how generous they were to Beach. "Whatever he needed, he got it, and whoever had the help to contribute helped."

There is something singular, exhilarating about being around greatness.

"Exactly, that's the whole point, I guess. They wanted to be a part of it."

Does MacGrath think lightning could strike twice? Is it possible you could have, if not a Beach, then a really spectacular Beach baby come along in the next few years?

"Do I think that it's possible that lightning could strike twice? Yes, sure I do. I have to—that's the dream. Do I put a lot of pressure on myself to do it? No. Am I going to? No. Am I going to be okay if I never have another good horse? Yes. I love the horses, and I like breaking them and training them and educating and teaching them what they're supposed to do. If they don't have the talent to do exactly what it is we would like them to do, then I find a home for them or I move them on. But they'll have been fun, and that's how I have to look at it."

Interestingly, MacGrath did do some thinking about the other direction—how to move forward when Beach retired, and, of course, after Beach died.

"I had a bit of a road map laid out for me about what most trainers had done when they had a great horse in the past," he says. "They took all the phone calls from owners and potential owners, and bought as many horses as they possibly could buy, chasing the dream—and that just wasn't going to happen with me.... I've had the dream, and I wasn't chasing the dream when it happened. I was trying to buy a nice horse and we ended up with the dream.

He never worried about what he was going to do when it was over. "I knew the phone was going to stop ringing. I knew the microphones and the cameras were going to stop being shoved in my face, and I was ready for that. I was fine with it. Sure, I enjoyed the cameras; I enjoyed the interviews, the phone calls. I have said on more than one occasion Beach loved to win, and I loved to talk about him winning."

Good quote; may even be in the book.

"It should be, because it's the truth. That quote and the one they threw in my face in Toronto, about the pressure of all the interviews, the media attention about Beach, and my response being, 'You call that pressure? Pressure is when you can't feed your kids or make your house payment. This isn't pressure, it's fun.' Those two statements that I made were me."

So would you say Beach changed your life completely—and not at all?

"Well, it's funny that you say that, because it's pretty much true. Rhonda and I were doing well before Beach came along. Were we financially where we are today? No, but we were chugging along quite nicely, and doing exactly what we wanted to do. We had gotten into a couple of new businesses. What Beach did really was pay off our debts," says MacGrath.

"So, did Beach take the pressure off? For sure, but there wasn't very much pressure there to begin with, and it's not like he took us from rags to riches. We were on our way to doing quite well and he just sped it up." MacGrath admits they wouldn't have met some of the people they now know, and they might not have been welcomed with open arms they way they are now—ten years after Beach left the racing scene.

"But would we have got by fine? Yeah."

One in Beach's first crop of sons, Melmerby Beach—a good, if not brilliant, pacer like his sire, had "come and gone" by 2018. Schooner Stables II also owns a full sister to Melmerby Beach, a filly named Martinique Beach, who is out of the Art Major mare DB Blue Chip.

"We also had a couple of mares that we were breeding," says MacGrath, "I'm With Her being one of them."

I'm With Her was a $100,000-plus purchase for Schooner Stables II. Thanks to frozen sperm, says MacGrath, the mare now has a "gorgeous colt" by Beach, who is just being weaned. The colt's name is Beach Glass.

During the post-Beach days, MacGrath and Schooner Stables II were "going along," he says. "I wasn't overly concerned. We had a mare that … was throwing out not bad horses, so we were in the game. We weren't paying great big money for them like some people were, and we were competing. So I was running the car business and enjoying the horses as they were meant to be—as a hobby…. I'm happy right where we are today; very happy."

Happy, but curious, too, about what comes next.

"Yes, I want to get ready for the new wave," says MacGrath.

Brent MacGrath at the 2019 Harrisburg Yearling Sales. (AUTHOR PHOTO)

Lately, he has been focusing more on the last-of-the-last Beach babies who will go up for auction at Harrisburg in November 2020. Schooner Stables II already owns a half-interest in the twelve yearlings. MacGrath plans on buying a daughter and a son from Beach's last crop at the sale.

The complete plan includes Brent and Rhonda going to Hanover Shoe Farms to look over all the Beach babies a couple of weeks before the sale at Harrisburg. "We're unable to attend the sale in 2020," explains MacGrath, "but I intend to buy online."

Is it as much fun as attending in person?

"Oh, yeah," says MacGrath. "I mean, what's fun is getting the one you want."

That, of course, is how the whole adventure with Beach began: wanting that big, handsome bay colt badly—and against all odds, getting him and, along with the five other members of Schooner Stables, sharing a life with him for thirteen astonishing years.

Maybe Brent MacGrath will buy a horse; maybe he'll buy two. It could be his lucky day.

SOMEBEACHSOMEWHERE'S

CAREER RACES

$\overline{}$

QUALIFIERS, 2007

Truro Raceway, June 24, 2007. Two-year-old qualifier. Purse: $0. Finish:
1. Times: 0:32; 1:03.2; 1:33.4; 2:04.3.

Truro Raceway, July 1, 2007. Two-year-old qualifier. Purse: $0. Finish: 1.
Times: 0:30.4; 1:01.4; 1:33.1; 2:02.1.

Truro Raceway, July 8, 2007. Two-year-old qualifier. Purse: $0. Finish: 1.
Times: 0:31; 1:01.2; 1:31.4; 2:00.1.

Driver for first three qualifying races: Brent MacGrath
Career Driver: Paul MacDonell

STAKES RACES, 2007

Grand River Raceway, July 30, 2007. *Battle of Waterloo – Elimination.*
Purse: $24,000. Finish: 1.

Grand River Raceway, August 6, 2007. *Battle of Waterloo – Final.* Purse:
$300,000. Finish: 1.

Mohawk Racetrack, August 25, 2007. *The Metro Pace – Elimination.* Purse: $40,000. Finish: 1.

Mohawk Racetrack, September 1, 2007. *The Metro Pace – Final.* Purse: $1 million. Finish: 1. Fastest mile by a two-year-old: 1:49.3.

Mohawk Racetrack, September 8, 2007. *The Champlain Stakes.* Purse: $115,884. Finish: 1.

Mohawk Racetrack, September 15, 2007. *The Nassagaweya Stakes.* Purse: $145,300. Finish: 1.

QUALIFYING RACES, 2008

Mohawk Racetrack, May 5, 2008. Purse: 0. Finish: 1.

STAKES RACES, 2008

Mohawk Racetrack, May 31, 2008. *Burlington Stakes.* Purse: $100,000. Finish: 1.

Mohawk Racetrack, June 7, 2008. *Pepsi North America Cup – Elimination.* Purse: $50,000. Finish: 1.

Mohawk Racetrack, June 14, 2008. *Pepsi North America Cup – Final.* Purse: $1.5 million. Finish: 1.

The Meadowlands, July 12, 2008. *The Meadowlands Pace – Elimination.* Purse: $50,000. (USD) Finish: 1.

The Meadowlands, July 19, 2008. *The Meadowlands Pace – Final.* Purse: $1.1 million. (USD) Finish: 2.

Mohawk Racetrack, August 3, 2008. *Three-Year-Old Open.* Purse: $50,000. Finish: 1.

Mohawk Racetrack, August 10, 2008. *Ontario Sires Stakes – Gold Final, Three-Year-Old Colts and Geldings.* Purse: $180,000. Finish: 1.

Flamboro Downs, August 17, 2008. *Confederation Cup – Heat*. Purse: $50,000. Finish: 1.

Flamboro Downs, August 17, 2008. *Confederation Cup – Final*. Purse: $493,000. Finish: 1. Fastest mile set by a three-year-old on a half-mile track: 1:49:2.

Mohawk Racetrack, September 6, 2008. Simcoe Stakes. Purse: $132,326. Finish: 1.

The Red Mile, September 27, 2008. *Bluegrass Stakes, Three-Year-Old Colts and Geldings*. Purse: $134,000 (USD). Finish: 1.

- Finish time: 1:46.4 = world record for a three-year-old pacer.
- Fastest race mile in history, tied with the race mile recorded by five-year-old Holborn Hanover (August 5, 2006).

The Red Mile, October 4, 2008. *The Lis Mara* (a division of the Tattersalls Pace). Purse: $293,000 (USD). Finish: 1.

Yonkers Raceway, October 25, 2008. *The Messenger – Final*. Purse: $650,000 (USD). Finish: 1.

Woodbine Racetrack, November 15, 2008. *Ontario Sires Stakes Super Final, Three-Year-Old Colts and Geldings*. Purse: $300,000. Finish: 1.

The Meadowlands, November 29, 2008. *Breeders Crown – Final, Three-Year-Old Colts and Geldings*. Purse: $500,000 (USD). Finish: 1.

BEACH AT A GLANCE

Breed	*Standardbred*
Sire	*Mach Three*
Grandsire	*Matts Scooter*
Dam	*Wheres The Beach*
Dam Sire	*Beach Towel*
Foaled	*May 25, 2005*
Colour	*Bay*
Breeder	*Stephanie Smith-Rothaug*
Owner	*Schooner Stables*
Trainer of record, 2YO Year	*Jean Louis Arsenault*
Lifetime Trainer	*Brent MacGrath*
Lifetime Driver	*Paul MacDonell*
Earnings	*$3,328,755*

MAJOR WINS

Metro Pace (2007)

North America Cup (2008)

Breeders Crown (2008)

WORLD RECORDS

Fastest mile by a two-year-old – 1:49.3, set winning the $1 million Metro Pace on September 1, 2007, at Mohawk Racetrack.

Fastest mile by a three-year-old on a half-mile track – 1:49.2, set in the second and deciding heat of the $493,000 Confederation Cup on August 17, 2008, at Flamboro Downs.

Fastest mile by a three-year-old – 1:46.4, set in the $134,000 Bluegrass on September 27, 2008, at The Red Mile.

Fastest race mile in history – 1:46.4 (equalled the race mile recorded by five-year-old Holborn Hanover in the $195,000 (USD) Pacing Championship on August 5, 2006, at the Meadowlands).

MAJOR AWARDS
2007

Canadian O'Brien Award – Horse of the Year (tied with Tell All)
Canadian O'Brien Award – Two-Year-Old Pacing Colt of the Year
US Dan Patch Award – Two-Year-Old Pacing Colt of the Year
US Nova Award – Two-Year-Old Pacing Colt of the Year (HTA)

2008

US Dan Patch Award – Horse of the Year
Canadian O'Brien Award – Horse of the Year (unanimous choice)
Cam Fella Award (honouring meritorious service to harness racing in Canada)
CBC Nova Scotia Newsmaker of the Year
Canadian O'Brien Award – Three-Year-Old Pacing Colt of the Year
US Dan Patch Award – Pacer of the Year
US Dan Patch Award – Three-Year-Old Pacing Colt of the Year
US Nova Award – Three-Year-Old Pacing Colt of the Year (HTA)

Halifax *Chronicle Herald* Sports Story of the Year
Truro *Daily News* Newsmaker of the Year
Canadian Sportsman Readers' Choice Horse of the Year
Canadian Sportsman Newsmaker of the Year
2017 Horse of the Year Award—The Hickstead Trophy. (Created in 2011, there have only been four other recipients of the award: Hickstead; Northern Dancer; Big Ben; and Fine Lady 5.)

HONOURS

Canadian Horse Racing Hall of Fame (2009)
United States Harness Racing Hall of Fame (2015)

THE ART OF NAMING HORSES

WHEN ALL'S SAID AND DONE, SERIOUS HORSE PEOPLE FROM ALL disciplines and sports like to laugh and kick up their own heels. They work hard, compete hard, and sometimes, deal with hard, even tragic, circumstances, the way Schooner Stables did when they unexpectedly lost Beach at only thirteen years of age. Even long-lived horses only live about twenty-five to thirty years, so the humans who cherish them are a determinedly forward-looking bunch, knowing that each spring brings new life and joy to country barns and fields.

Each and every one of those new baby horses needs a name. Bring on the puns, let loose with the tongue twisters. Invoke the beauty, speed, and intimidation.

Dollars And Spence. Mabou Ridge. East Coast Invader. Maple Leaf Dare. Century Farroh. Ramblinglily. Tall Dark Stranger. Party Girl Hill. Admirals Express. Amor Angus. McWicked. Chancey Lady. Love A Good Story. BC Count. Scardy Cat. Yoga Pants. Tiger Tara. Custard the Dragon. Major Custard. Custard Smoothie. Im Themightyquinn. Aspoonfulofsugar. Hot and Treacherous. King of Swing.

Go on, enjoy yourself!

And if you're superstitious (like so many in the sports world, many horse people are!), well then, name your foal to bring some luck his way.

A General Guide to Naming Horses

When naming a registered Standardbred you can't:

- Use more than four words
- Exceed a total of eighteen letters and spaces in the name
- Copy the spelling and pronunciation of another horse's name
- Reuse a shining name from horse history
- Mislead as to family, origin, relationship, or sex
- Be offensive or vulgar
- Use, in whole or in part, the name of a famous or outstanding horse, unless that horse is the sire, dam, grandsire, or grandam of the horse to be registered
- Use, in whole or in part, the name of a living person, unless you have written permission from them
- Choose the name of a famous or notorious person

Others can't resist alliteration—Turn the Tide, a Thoroughbred gelding from Australia—or just plain silliness—Doremifasolatido, an American Thoroughbred filly.

But owner beware; when it comes to naming registered racehorses of any kind, Thoroughbreds, Quarter Horses, or Standardbreds, both trotters and pacers, you are allowed to have some fun, but you will also have to follow the rules set down by *Standardbred Canada* in By-law #2, Article 4, which you can find online.

Somebeachsomewhere was registered as one word because yes, count 'em, that configuration is eighteen letters. With spaces between the words, it wouldn't have worked. The name itself is a reference to a country and western tune, "Some Beach," written by Rory Feek and Paul Overstreet, and recorded by American country music artist Blake Shelton.

Remember: Stephanie Smith-Rothaug loved country and western music.

Then there was the strange and lovely fact that the Beach-related foals Smith-Rothaug brought into the world often arrived on family birthdays. No less than three foals in a row, all coming after Beach, were born on family birthdays.

"We had a handsome colt who was born on my dad's birthday," laughs Smith-Rothaug, "so we named him Roger Mach Em, after my dad, Roger, because he said only a handsome colt would do for a namesake! The colt looked like Beach."

The colt was the product of Mach Three and Beach's half-sister, Remis Rocket.

"The next year," Smith-Rothaug continues, "we had a filly, born on my mum's birthday. We named her NicknackPattyMach, for my mum, Patricia."

Again, the filly's sire was Mach Three, and the dam was Remis Rocket.

"Then finally we had another colt, born on my brother Scott's birthday," concludes Smith-Rothaug." We named him RockStockScott."

Same busy dam, but this time, the sire was RockinAmadeus. And yes, all three horses in that Beach line did well on the racetrack.

In 2009, Smith-Rothaug was proud to welcome a full sibling to Somebeachsomewhere (same sire and dam), and just as proud of the name she gave the gorgeous little filly.

"I called her 'Someheartsomewhere' because she had a perfect little white heart on her forehead," she says.

As mentioned, horse people love a good laugh.

"Members get very creative and humorous with their name choices," says Barb Wilson, of Member Services at *Standardbred Canada* in Mississauga, Ontario, by email. "They usually try to combine parts of the sires' and dams' names when they name their foal. Somebeachsomewhere has several offspring with the same slant on their names: Outtheresomewhere, Someangelsomewhere, Somesurfsomewhere."

Of course, there are themes.

"We have a sire called Betterthancheddar," affirms Wilson. "Some of his foals are Gooderthangouda, Who Cut The Cheese, Aged Cheddar, and Say Cheese Please."

The stunning, record-setting Betterthancheddar himself is now owned by Winbak Farm in Chesapeake City, Maryland.

Because they're irresistible, Wilson circles back to themes. "Years ago there was a mare called Smell Me. One of her foals was Little Stinker, and she had Hold Your Nose. A mare called Armbro Ochita had foals who were named after condiments: Mayonnaise, Mustard, Relish, Catch Up M, Hold the Pickle M, Chili Pepper M and Onion Rings M."

As many are, Brent MacGrath was inspired by geography—in his case, his ruggedly beautiful home province of Nova Scotia, and, in particular, beachscapes.

"We had a bunch of Beach babies with Maritime place names," MacGrath confirms. "Martinique Beach, Melmerby Beach, Lawrencetown Beach, Queensland Beach, Caribou Beach."

Or the Beach part came first.

"That's right. Beach Meadows, Beach Glass..."

MacGrath says there is "no template" for how to come up with a good name for a horse. "But," he says, "I'm not keen on the crazy names. You know, 'Kiss My Flaps,' or some such. That's not right. I like the lower-profile names."

And if you think coming up with one bell-ringer is a challenge, try coming up with three hundred new names each and every year, as Hanover Shoe Farm does. But then, the farm is smart about this. It actually has a page on its website for the general public to suggest names for them.

Give it a try!

Appendix D

AFTER THE RACES ARE OVER

NOT EVERYONE IS A FAN OF HARNESS RACING—OR OF RACING horses or animals of any kind, in any way. Not only is there a risk of the animal being hurt, or even killed, on the racetrack, but many would argue the animal is not living any sort of natural life (not that many domesticated animals do). More tragically, when money and animals come together, money often trumps the best care of the animals, who, at the end of the day, may be regarded as disposable if they don't live up to human-made measures of success.

Not every Standardbred harness horse retires to the luxury of Hanover Shoe Farms, where Beach himself had an ultra-comfortable double stall—a corner suite, if you please—so he could see out the barn door and up the broad driveway, which is bracketed by tall oak trees that in turn cast shade into the stallion paddocks, some of which, like Beach's, were three acres in size.

Nor does every retired Standardbred harness racer retire to a relentless life as a carriage horse for an Amish family, though some do and, heartbreakingly, become known as "pavement pounders." (Sadly, abuse of horses exists in every horse community under the sun. Recognition of the highest order must go to the many men and women who devote their working lives to the prevention of cruelty to all animals, not just horses.)

No one denies that many breeds of horses have abrupt, brutal ends at the abattoir. We eat horsemeat, we use it in dog food, we take on horses we can't afford, and they suffer for it, or we lose interest in them when they become too old or cannot be ridden or worked. We must do better in all these areas and, especially, we must strive for more humane ends for the horses that give us so much—all of us.

But there is good news, too. Some of these remarkably versatile, smart, and amiable Standardbred horses are "rehomed" as saddle horses, engaged in myriad new disciplines. Sometimes their new job is to be a companion horse for another lonely horse or pony or human, and sometimes they take up the equally noble work of being therapy horses for those who need their gifts of gentleness and loving intuition most of all.

Schooner Stables (Beach's original six co-owners) and Schooner Stables II (formed in 2011), and many other individuals and businesses in Canada connected to harness racing around the world, support rehoming of retired Standardbreds. They do so because they love the breed, respect how they have served on a racetrack, and know how much joy they can bring to new families and new people. They also understand the revived sense of purpose and pride the horses feel when they learn or master additional skills and develop new partnerships with their human caretakers.

And unlike in a horse race, everyone wins.

SPRING 2020

Joanne Colville can't remember a time when she wasn't surrounded by Standardbred horses.

"I've been in Standardbreds my whole life," says the Toronto-born horsewoman, now a farm owner in Milton. "My dad trained horses as a hobby and it was just something that I grew to love."

As a child, Colville, now forty-eight, lived close to the old Greenwood Raceway. "We lived around the corner from Greenwood, really," she says.

"So that was my weekends and my winters. When I was old enough to drive [the horses], I got a job at *Standardbred Canada* and started coming out to Mohawk, and then I moved out this way, to Milton."

Colville is the founder and president of High Stakes Farm. Along with her partner, Jack Moiseyev, a seasoned driver, Colville runs a breeding operation and a racing barn. She also retrains and rehomes retired harness racers.

The breeding farm employs two full-time and three part-time employees to look after fourteen farm-owned broodmares, who are both pacers and trotters.

"[Counting] horses of all ages, we'd be near the forty-five mark with this year's newborns arriving," says Colville. "I generally breed between thirty-five and forty mares each year at the farm or close by, and deliver twenty to thirty foals a year."

At a nearby training centre, where the couple stable their racehorses, Moiseyev and two other full-time trainers work with the young pacers and trotters. They are currently training seventeen horses.

But it is Colville's work as the manager and events coordinator for the Ontario Standardbred Adoption Society (OSAS), finding "forever homes"—mostly for retired harness racers—which brings her a particular satisfaction and joy.

Schooner Stables donated a percentage of Beach's career earnings, totalling $6,000, to OSAS. This idea was initiated by Rhonda MacGrath.

Founded in 1996, OSAS is an approved charitable organization that assists in the adoption and relocation of retired and non-racing Standardbred horses in Ontario. It is funded through fundraising, contributions from racetracks, horse industry organizations, and private donations.

Although Colville's position at OSAS is labour-intensive, she loves it. The important thing is to match the right owner with the right horse so they can begin successful new lives together. In fact, for Colville, any opportunity to tell the world just how multi-talented, intelligent, and kindly Standardbreds are is time well spent. Colville is also proud of OSAS's role in the fostering aspect of rehoming.

"We have foster farms throughout the province of Ontario who have been with us quite some time," she says. "I currently have nine OSAS horses here at High Stakes. If they're close enough to me, I like to get them in to my place so that I can assess them first before we move them on to foster care—so I know a little bit about them and I can answer some questions when the applications come in."

Ordinarily, the farm wouldn't have that many OSAS horses all at once.

"But, of course, we were the winners of the Breeders Crown charity challenge [in October 2019] and we wanted to take in some more horses," says Colville.

Launched in June 2019, the Breeders Crown Charity Challenge featured four teams consisting of a celebrity, a charity of their choosing, and an award-winning three-year-old Standardbred. Each charity received 1 percent of their horse's earnings from June through October.

"The win enabled us to take in probably double our capacity," says Colville. "So we started bringing them in and working with them."

People often ask Colville how the horses come to be at the farm.

"Sometimes, people will donate the horses to us. They'll email me, or I'll see them at the track, because I work at Mohawk at night."

Incredibly, Colville has yet another job, as a parade marshal at Woodbine Mohawk Park. "I ensure the post parades are in the correct order and do equipment checks to make sure nothing is undone or out of place. I take rambunctious horses to the gate and help ones turn that don't maybe turn on the track. I have a radio so I can speak with the starter and the judges and let them know what's going on if someone needs to go back to the paddock or needs something done."

On big race nights they carry flags and do it up with some pomp and pageantry. "Generally my daughter, Emma Christoforou, and Debi O'Brien-Moran will ride with me on those nights. I do all that, set it up, design our outfits or purchase our outfits."

Moiseyev, Colville, and her daughter, Emma, move in a wide range of circles.

Joanne Colville parading at Woodbine Mohawk Park aboard Reverend Hanover for the Breeders Crown, October 2020. (GERRY DEBRESSER COLVILLE)

"I see quite a few people," Colville agrees, "and we race at different tracks, too. They [the racing community] all know my daughter, so they call or they email or I see them in person and we take in the horses. I've got one here that is doing some rehabilitation work. [As I say], it's easier to keep them closer to home here so I can monitor them and get to know them a little bit before they go to foster."

Re-homing, in the best-case scenario, is a three-part deal: the horses come to Colville and other experienced horse people first; they then make sure that the horses are able to go on to a foster home; and then comes the permanent adoption.

Those permanent adoptions are not given out easily; there are rules.

"Yes, there are," confirms Colville. "We always ask potential adopters what discipline they are interested in," she says, referring to things like Western or English riding, jumping, or Three-Day Eventing. "We need the horses to be able to go on to a second career. We only have so many what we call companion-only spots. The companions and the older horses don't move as well. People want horses that are usable. We currently have ten or eleven horses on the website, so those spots don't become available as often. We're sponsored heavily by Purina and they supply food for horses that can be retrained, and we have to be cognizant of the fact that, obviously, they want to spread the wealth of the food. So, for example, we can't take in forty horses and have the same forty horses in foster care for twenty years."

This means Colville and others need to carefully select the horses to be rehomed. "We try to take horses under the age of fifteen." Colville pauses, and while the next words may seem contradictory, they will not surprise any horse person on Earth: "There are exceptions to every rule."

Because, any one of these people might tell you, that fifteen-year-old mare you perhaps shouldn't take on is sound as a dollar and one of the calmest horses imaginable, perfect for a young person's saddle horse. Besides, she's precious, and deserves a forever home.

They all do. This is why OSAS is so busy—and so broad in scope when it comes to its selections.

"A horse that might not be riding sound could be therapy sound," says Colville. "We have a few that go to therapy homes. So it just depends on what's going on."

Therapy horses are used to enhance and enrich the lives of so many children, young adults, or adults who are on the autism spectrum or who live with attention deficit hyperactivity disorder, anxiety, cerebral palsy, dementia, depression, or post-traumatic stress disorder.

For this work, it does not matter if the horse is "riding sound." She or he may have a tad of arthritis or be unsound due to an old injury and move slowly, but most importantly, the mind is clear and the heart is generous.

And then there are companion-only spots within OSAS.

"I would say we have ten companion-only spots," says Colville. "Those are the horses that for one reason or another are not rideable. And then we keep about twenty-four spots open for the other horses. Two of the horses are OSAS ambassadors—Reverend Hanover and Ruff Me Up."

Ambassadors?

"Reverend Hanover is a graduate of the Ontario Sires Stakes; he's the fastest gelded son of Sportswriter," says Colville. "We use him at public events for people to meet and greet; we use him to post parade, like the Sires Stakes."

The handsome and gentle Reverend Hanover retired in 2017 and became an ambassador at OSAS in September 2019. With career winnings of $550,000, Reverend Hanover was owned throughout his career by Coleman's West Win Stable, Steve Calhoun, and Anthony Beaton.

Ambassadors also get to travel.

"We take him off-property to different events like maybe a fox hunt or we do a Hooves for Hospice trail ride; we do hunter paces," says Colville. "We keep a couple of those horses on hand to take to public events at racetracks where we know they're sound and can take the people and the traffic and the noise and all of that."

Sometimes the horses are "under saddle" (have a rider aboard), and sometimes not.

"We also use them in harness for the Drive With Us program," says Colville, "where a fan gets to go once around the track in a double-seater jog cart." People love doing that, says Colville.

Standardbreds literally "do it all," she says. Another one of their ambassadors, a registered Standardbred named The Painted Pony, shows Open Jumper, does barrel races, does fox hunting and Western Pleasure.

A Standardbred—a gaited horse—and he does all that?

"Oh, yes."

And this is why Standardbreds can be rehomed: because so many love a new challenge. And with those big old Standie hearts and brains, they succeed at almost anything they try—including losing the "gait," or pace, to trot, canter, and gallop, or, for the trotters, learning there is life beyond an immense, ground-eating trot.

Of course it takes time to get beyond the transitional "tranter" (four-beat trot plus three-beat canter equals many-beated tranter), but Standardbreds seem more willing to learn and to please than some other breeds. One really can generalize and say they are as honest as they are hard-working.

Colville is pleased to say that the adoption program is "in demand," though she believes it could be even more so.

"Standardbreds are always behind Thoroughbreds and Quarter Horses in people wanting them," she says. "Standardbreds can do anything you want. Obviously, they take a little bit more training, because the pace is not something people want. So there's a little bit of stigma attached to the Standardbreds."

There are also some old prejudices against the breed, which include calling them "jugheads" due to their once-prominent Roman noses, now rarely seen, and for the pacers, "sidewheelers," as the unilateral gait can make them appear to roll from side to side. Sometimes, as well, Standardbred ears are on the generous side of large, a look not everyone likes.

But the horsewoman with at least three jobs is optimistic by nature.

"I think in the last two years we've done a tremendous job with the help of everybody showcasing these horses to let people know that they can do dressage, they can do open jumping, they can do anything you ask of them."

Level-headed Standardbreds are also well-suited to "green," or new, riders or returning older riders.

"Our horses are used to the vehicular traffic," says Colville. "They load and they unload going to the racetrack and they're handled so much more that they're quiet for a first-timer. Those things are all great attributes to our horses."

No one would deny that track life is intense. Or how much a competitive horse like Somebeachsomewhere enjoyed every second of it.

When a person adopts a Standardbred from OSAS, they are adopting a horse that has had many hours of fine and loving care and retraining—literally from the ground up.

All of this takes a good bit of coin to sustain.

"We have a very good group of industry individuals that always have supported us and continue to support us," says Colville. "Our biggest yearly fundraiser is our stallion auction, an online stallion auction."

In support of OSAS, a changing group of stallion owners generously donate stallion services to this annual fundraiser. Among the 2020 stallions are Beach's old friend Dali, and many other outstanding studs, seventeen in number.

"So that's the breeding farms supporting the cause," continues Colville. "We usually get anywhere from $18,000 to $35,000 every year out of the stallion auction. Obviously, it's very dependent on the mares catching and carrying to term. So we never count our chickens before they hatch because breeding is a very humbling experience. Sometimes everything works right and other times everything goes wrong. We also have a golf tournament every year that I organize; we usually make about $20,000 from that. Our racetracks in Ontario donate 15 percent of 1 percent of the total purses, the gross purses."

In addition to the "tremendous industry support," says Colville, the adoption society offers popular items for sale. "We have a clothing line of T-shirts, hooded sweatshirts, full-zip sweatshirts, toques, and ball caps."

But most of all, she says, "Our industry is phenomenal when it comes to supporting us and I can't thank them enough. Year after year they always come to the plate for us."

So how would Colville respond to that potential adopter who says to her, 'I was thinking more about a Quarter Horse or a Thoroughbred or a warmblood?'

"You know what?" asks Colville. "Once they ride behind us for a while and they see that our horses are willing and versatile and calm and level-headed, the horses end up selling themselves."

Colville will always remember Beach, and says she could pick him out of a field of horses in a heartbeat. "There was a definite presence about him that I haven't seen in many other horses. I can't pinpoint it but he had a menacing way about him, too. He was regal but he had a menacing presence at the same time. And he was all business on the racetrack. I'm glad I didn't have to race against him."

There are other Standardbred rehoming and rescue programs in Canada, among them British Columbia's Greener Pastures; Performance

Standardbreds in Alberta; Standardbred Québec Adoption in Saint-Just-de-Bretenières, Quebec; Galahad, also in Quebec; Morningstar Acres in New Brunswick; and Sadie's Place in Prince Edward Island.

And of course, there are many other programs in the United Kingdom, Europe, the Antipodes, and the United States, wherever Standardbreds are raced and revered.

Standardbred folk love their Standies; given time, it seems certain that the rest of the world will see just how astonishing these horses are, on the racetrack, and off.

For Colville, every time she rehomes a harness racer she dances the proverbial jig.

"The satisfaction of being able to sit back and watch these horses transition into a second career, it's a personal satisfaction unlike any other," says Colville. "Watching them with the therapy programs, there's no better feeling than watching the smiles on the faces of the ones that you're helping. That in itself is reward enough for me."

It's a satisfying feeling of teamwork, too, she says, commending the "ten to twelve diehard volunteers who never ever let me down."

As well, Colville is grateful to her "phenomenal board."

"We have two Hall-of-Famers in it: Bill O'Donnell, a harness driver, and Ian Fleming, race secretary. We've got President Jim Evans who's a lawyer, horseman, and trainer; secretary/treasurer in Heather MacKay-Roberts; and Kelly Spencer from Grand River Raceway who used to be publicity and promotions. They are awesome people."

And of course Colville loves her Standardbred horse community. "Most generous people I know," she says.

So many of whom, like Colville, care for horses from birth to death, with every bit of heart, smarts, and lolly they have, and feel it's nothing less than a privilege and an honour.

A hooded sweatshirt available for purchase on the OSAS Facebook page has a message emblazoned within a heart on the front of it.

The message reads: "Yes. Standardbreds Aren't For Everyone. But The Best Never Is."

TERMINOLOGY

GLOSSARY OF STANDARDBRED AND HARNESS RACING TERMS
(Courtesy Standardbred Canada)

Backstretch: The straightaway on the far side of the racetrack. Also refers to the stable area.

Barren: A broodmare who has been bred at least once, but is not pregnant.

Blanket finish: A finish that finds several horses finishing very close together at the wire.

Boxed in: When a horse is racing along the pylons and cannot improve his position in a race because of the presence of other horses in front, behind, and beside him. Also called "locked in."

Break: When a horse breaks from its gait into a run or gallop.

Breeding season: The usual breeding season runs from February 15 to July 15.

Broodmare: A mare that has been bred at least once.

Card: Another term for a program of racing. For example, someone might say there are ten races on a "card," meaning there will be ten races contested that day.

Catch driver: A driver who doesn't train his/her horses and is hired by other trainers and owners to drive their horses.

Colours: The special colourful jacket worn by drivers in a race. Unlike Thoroughbred jockeys, drivers register their own colours and wear them every time they race.

Colt: A male horse three years of age or younger.

Conditioned race: A race where eligibility is based on age, sex, money won, or races won.

Conformation: The physical attributes of and bodily proportions of a horse.

Cover: A horse that races with another horse in front of him is said to race with cover, as the leading horse cuts the wind resistance.

Dam: The mother of a horse.

Dead heat: When the judges cannot separate two horses at the finish line even with the aid of the photo finish.

Distanced: When a horse finishes more than thirty-five lengths behind the winner.

Division: A race that has too many entries and must be split into two or more divisions.

Driver: The person holding a license or permit to drive harness horses. There are different types of licenses, which correspond to differing levels of experience.

Entry: Two or more horses starting in a race owned by the same person.

Favourite: The horse considered most likely to win based on the odds and past performance.

Filly: A female horse three years of age or younger.

First over: The first horse to make a move on the leader in a race, moving up on the outside.

Free-legged: A pacer that races without wearing hopples.

Foal: All baby horses are called foals.

Garden Spot: The second position on the rail during most of the race.

Gelding: An altered (neutered) male of any age.

Hand: A unit of measurement (four inches) by which a horse's height is measured. A horse that stands fifteen hands is five feet tall at its withers.

Handicapping: The first step in successfully picking a winner (or handicapping) is becoming familiar with reading the racing program. Each program has a section explaining the information format used at that track. Probably the best place to start when handicapping Standardbreds is time. Since over 99 percent of all harness races are conducted at the one-mile distance, valid comparisons can be made among the horses.

Harness: The gear used to attach the sulky to the horse, to carry the hopples, and to enable the driver to steer the horse.

Home stretch: The straight length of the track, nearest the spectators, where the finish line is situated.

Hopples: The straps that connect the front and rear legs on the same side of a horse. Most pacers wear hopples to help balance their stride and maintain a pacing gait. The length of hopples is adjustable and a trainer registers the length that best fits his/her horse. There are also trotting hopples that work through a pulley system to help trotters maintain their gait.

In foal: A pregnant mare.

Lame: The term used to describe a horse that is limping or has difficulty walking properly.

Leasing: As opposed to buying a harness horse, people have the option of leasing one. Just as some people lease a car instead of paying the money up front, leasing a horse gives people use of a horse without large capital outlay. An agreement or contract must be drawn up between the two parties and the lease must be registered with the relevant controlling body.

Length: Measure of distance based on average length of horse.

Maiden: A horse that has never won a race with a purse. (Also refers to a mare that has never had a foal.)

Mare: A female horse four years of age or older.

Objection: A claim of foul lodged by a driver, upheld or dismissed by the judges.

Parked out: When a horse cannot find a position along the rail in a race and is forced to race outside those on the inside. Is also called taking the overland route.

Photo finish: When two horses cross the finish too closely to identify a winner, officials call for a photograph of the race, taken exactly at the finish line, to help them determine the winner.

Pedigree: Refers to a horse's family tree, paternal and maternal ancestors. A horse's pedigree provides insight into its potential ability and value.

Post position: Generally, the closer a horse starts to the inside rail, or barrier of the track, especially on a smaller track, the better its chance of winning. At the start, horses must either "leave" (start quickly) to get a good position or else find a place on the rail to avoid racing on the outside of other horses. When racing on the outside the horse is said to be parked out and loses ground on every turn. A horse on the inside has a better chance to get to the rail or quickly get a good position.

Post time: The starting time of a race.

Qualifier: A race in which a horse must go a mile below an established time standard to prove itself capable of competing in parimutuel races.

Scratch: The removal of a horse from a race after its entry has been accepted.

Sire: The father of a horse.

Sires stakes: Stakes races designed to promote Standardbred breeding and racing within a jurisdiction. Eligibility to compete in the sires stakes events depends upon the rules of the jurisdiction.

Stakes race: A race where owners make a series of payments, starting well in advance, to keep a horse eligible. If an owner misses a payment, the horse is ineligible.

Stallion: A male horse four years of age or older.

Starter: The person responsible for starting a harness race. The starter controls the start of the race from the back of the mobile starting gate.

Sulky: Also known as the cart or racebike, the sulky is attached to the harness and carries the driver.

Time trial: An attempt to have a horse beat its own best time in a non-competitive event. A time trial is not a race. Galloping horses hitched to sulkies, called prompters, are used to push a horse to its best effort.

Tote board: An electronic board, usually in the infield of a racetrack, which posts the odds, amount of money bet, results of a race, and the wagering payoffs.

Yearling: Any horse between its first and second birthday.

GAITS

Pacer: Pacers move the legs on one side of their body in tandem—left front and rear, right front and rear. Pacers are also referred to as side-wheelers. Pacers account for approximately 80 percent of all harness horses and are aided in maintaining their gait through plastic loops called hopples. Some pacers perform without the aid of hopples and are called free-legged pacers. Pacers are generally faster than trotters due to the sureness of their action.

Trotter: Trotters move with a diagonal gait, the left front and right rear legs move in unison, as do the right front and left rear. Trotting is the more natural gait for the Standardbred, but it takes a great deal of skill to train and maintain a trotter.

CONDITION SYSTEM

Claiming race: A race in which each horse carries a price tag (claiming price) and may be purchased. Claiming races are established according to price, i.e., $25,000 claimers.

Conditioned race: A race in which eligibility is determined based on age, sex, money, or races won. Examples: Four-year-olds and younger; non-winners of $50,000 lifetime.

Early and late closing events: A race requiring payments starting closer to the actual date of the race compared to stakes events. Early and late refer to the time period involved.

Invitational (open or free for all): Usually a weekly race for the top horses at that racetrack.

Stakes race: See page 261.

Supplemental entry: Some stakes events allow you to make a supplemental payment days prior to the running of the stakes if your horse(s) is ineligible to the stakes.

BETTING TERMINOLOGY

Win: The horse you select must finish first in the official order.

Place: The horse you select must finish first or second in the official order.

Show: The horse you select must finish first, second, or third in the official order.

Understanding Odds
(Courtesy Ontario Racing)

The odds listed in a race program are the "morning line" odds. These are the odds placed on the horses by the track's handicapper when the race program is published, before the wagering starts. At the track, the odds will be posted on the tote board before the race; they change up until post time, depending on how customers are betting on each horse in the race.

The horse that customers have bet the most money on is called the "favourite." This horse will have the lowest odds.

"Longshots" have the least money wagered on them and therefore have the highest odds. The racetrack handles the money, keeps a percentage (called a "take-out"), and calculates the horses' odds based on the amount of money wagered on each horse. The remaining money is then paid back to the players who have winning tickets.

Win odds are based on $1 unless otherwise noted. A "3" displayed next to a horse's number on the tote board indicates that the horse is 3-1. An example of an exception to this general rule is when "5/2" is shown. The tote board does not show decimals, therefore, 5/2 odds means that the odds on a horse are 5 divided by 2, or 2.5-1. Win payoffs are calculated based on a $2 wager because at most tracks this is the minimum bet.

For example: A horse that wins at 5–1 will return $5 for every $1 wagered. If you had placed the minimum bet of $2 on that horse to win, your payoff will be $10 (5 x 1 x $2) plus your original bet of $2—for a total of $12.

ACKNOWLEDGEMENTS

FIRST OFF—I ACCEPT FULL RESPONSIBILITY FOR ANY MISTAKES that might appear in the story of Beach—a fact-and-number-filled tale, which had fifteen primary interviews, and many more secondary ones, some of which I sadly wasn't able to use, as there simply wasn't room (Harrisburg auctioneers, and traditional country harness racing tracks, next time!). Every attempt was made to present the story accurately and fully, from many points of view, for richest storytelling effect. I hope I succeeded in that.

Second—many people kindly shared their knowledge with me about Somebeachsomewhere and the Standardbred breed during the course of writing this book. I am indebted to you all. If I somehow manage to not acknowledge you fully here, or even, I regret to say, omit your name and exact contributions, please know that I am grateful for your help.

Sincere thanks to Nimbus Publishing for your initial and sustained enthusiasm about the book, and to my editors, Whitney Moran and Angela Mombourquette, for their hard work on the manuscript, polishing it up to its shiniest best. Thanks as well for understanding that this was a heart-book for me, and had to be the absolute best it could be.

Deepest thanks and gratitude go to the MacGrath family—Brent, Rhonda, and Josh—who always made time to help me.

Rhonda, your keen memory and sense of humour were so helpful. And bless you for the loan of your huge paper archive of newspapers and magazines, without which the book would have taken twice the time to research. I am also so grateful for the author photo and others, which you took at Truro Raceway, along with the video of the intrepid author driving a sulky for the first time!

Brent, thanks so much for answering countless questions and always being available to do that on the telephone, via text, and by email. Big thanks for making a dream come true with my first sulky drive.

Josh, your interview was one of my favourites in the book; thank you for your insights, honesty, and grand good humour. Without you all, there would be no book.

To the original members of Schooner Stables—Brent MacGrath, Garry Pye, Pam Dean, Reg Petitpas, Stu Rath, and Jamie Bagnell—thank you so very much for speaking to me about your experiences as the co-owners of Somebeachsomewhere. Without you I could not have told this story with as much immediacy and colour.

To Dr. Bridgette Jablonsky, executive vice-president, Hanover Shoe Farms—thank you for your time, expertise, deep caring, and your precise articulation about the racehorse Beach was, and the stallion he was, both under your care at Hanover, and from historical and future perspectives.

To Stephanie Smith-Rothaug, owner/operator at Rails Edge Farm, and Somebeachsomewhere's breeder—thank you for being all trusting and open heart, and for your tender and caring memories. Thank you for being a brilliant breeder of Standardbred horses. Your experience of "Beach" was singular—because it was in fact double. You not only loved the vocal and brash colt you helped to bring into the world, you loved his mama from the moment you saw her, and forever. Without that generous, slightly impulsive heart of yours, and your confidence in both magic and hard work, there would be no story of Somebeachsomewhere. I predict that another heart-horse is coming to your barn...soon.

To Paul MacDonell, gentleman, respected horseman, and Hall-of-Fame driver—thank you for your stories and for taking me, in my imagination, aboard your sulky as you raced Beach. You were lucky to have him during the course of your driving career—and he was wonderfully fortunate to have had you, with your soft reinsman's hands and resolute, winning ways.

To David James and Donna Egan, owner/operators of Empire Stables—thank you for taking me "Down Under" to beautiful Avenel, and for sharing your lives together at your extraordinary farm which, once upon a time, included Somebeachsomewhere in his own stallion paddock. Like the sulky rides alongside Paul MacDonell, visiting Australia happened only in my imagination. But I have Australia on my wish list, and you can depend on a visit in Avenel if I do make it there!

To Dave Briggs, sportswriter; editor at *Harness Racing Update* and *Canadian Thoroughbred Magazine*—thank you so much for our long interview, where we covered a lot of territory, and I learned so much. Beyond that, every article I read that had your byline I knew would be informative, fun, and accurate.

To all the sportswriters of the time, 2006 to 2018, Canadian and American, who covered Beach's career—thank you for your lively and fact-filled stories, all of which made my job easier. Thanks, as well, for making me feel I was right there at all of Beach's races, or in that big damp barn after the OSS Super Final at Woodbine, in Toronto, jam-packed with well-wishers from all over Canada, but especially with Maritimers, all of Schooner Stables, and Beach's caretaker and trainer, Jean Louis Arsenault.

Huge thanks to the sports photographers of the time, too, who again, and with such skill and visual beauty, brought me close to all of Beach's magnificent races and his life off-track, with his human family, fans, and caretakers. Huger thanks to those who have provided images for the book, and to Dave Landry, for the dramatic cover.

To the race announcers who called Beach's races, which I found on various sites online—you are among the world's seven wonders. I love your specialized, punchy language, and I particularly love your verbs, which rock the world! Thank you for your passion and knowledge, and thank you for allowing me to use your public-record words to spice up my retellings of the races.

Silver Donald Cameron and Marjorie Simmins on the first day of the Harrisburg Yearling Sale, November 2019. (AUTHOR PHOTO).

To Joanne Colville, Administrator Coordinator, Ontario Standardbred Adoption Society—thank you for your hard work for and commitment to the Standardbred breed. You are a superhero for these amazing, unflappable, and multi-gifted horses. After my own trip to the Harrisburg Yearling Sale in November 2019 with my late husband Don, I can tell you that the slender, bump-nosed Standardbreds I knew from my West Coast childhood are long gone. The Standardbred is a much-changed breed. Big! Bold! And they are gorgeous, head to toe, along with being smart, personable, and almost uniformly kind. (Every animal—every human—is a product of their particular genetics and early environment.)

To Barb Wilson at Member Services at *Standardbred Canada*: thanks so much for all the fun information about how to name a Standardbred.

To Carolyn Gibson, Transcriber Extraordinaire, from Truro, Nova Scotia—thank you for your accuracy and for your timely, excellent work. The confidence your interview transcriptions gave me was immeasurable. Thank you for all the top-notch work you've done for the Cameron/Simmins household over the years, on so many different books and writing projects.

To my first readers, Denise Saulnier, Brent MacGrath, Rhonda MacGrath, and Karen Allen, Program Administrator, Ontario Sires Stakes Marketing—thank you so much for your careful reading of first and subsequent drafts of the book. You all know how I wanted to tell the story accurately, and to honour Beach.

To Robert Samson of Petit-de-Grat, Nova Scotia —our "tech guy" and friend—who answered the phone at 8:00 A.M. on a Saturday to help me with a computer problem I couldn't solve, which then allowed me to finish the manuscript —thank you for this and so much else this past year.

Thank you to my cherished Simmins and Cameron families, and many friends and colleagues for their unwavering support and enthusiasm. In particular, I thank you all for the many kindnesses and love you've shown me in these past two tough years.

And finally, thank you to my late husband, Silver Donald Cameron, for all the miracles you were, and will always be. I will hold you in my heart forever.

ALSO BY MARJORIE SIMMINS

Coastal Lives: A Memoir
Year of the Horse: A Journey of Healing and Adventure
Memoir: Conversations and Craft